The Polity of

Thomas Paine and the Polity of the Blood

with an Appendix on the Bones

Michael Laccohee Bush

Published by Mot Juste, Canterbury, UK

Published by Mot Juste, Canterbury, UK
www.motjuste.co.uk

Copyright © 2023 Michael Laccohee Bush

All right reserved. No part of this book may be reproduced in any form or by any electronic or mechanical means, including information storage and retrieval systems, without written permission from the publisher, except by a reviewer who may quote passages in a review.

British Library Cataloguing in Publication Data.
A catalogue record for this book is available from the British Library

Includes bibliographical references and an index

ISBN 978-0-9569670-6-0

Book design by Peter Erftemeijer, Mot Juste
Printed in Bulgaria by Pulsio Print

Contents

Acknowledgments   1

Introduction   3

I Paine on Hereditary Right

    a Paine's Rejection of Hereditary Succession   11
    b Grounds for the Public's Rejection of Paine   16
    c Paine's Tolerance of the Hereditary Right to Private Property   23

II The Provenance of Paine's Political Ideology

    a The Essence of Paine's Republicanism   27
    b Origins   32
    c The Making of *Common Sense*   36
    d Paine versus Whiggery   47
    e Paine's Debt to the Radical Enlightenment   51
    f The Consistency of Paine's Political Thinking   60

III *Rights of Man:* its Sale and Suppression

    a Composition   65
    b Initial Sales   66
    c The Readership   69
    d Cheap Editions   70
    e The Censorship of Part II   75
    f Overall Distribution in Britain   77
    g Suppression and its Impact   80
    h Conclusion   84

IV Paine and the Tradition of Radical Reform

    a Richard Carlile's Promotion of Paine   87
    b Radical Reform's Antipathy to Paine   89
    c Radical Reform's Republican Moment   92
    d The NUWC and its Promotion of Paine   95

	e O'Brien Makes his Mark	107
	f The NUWC's Persistence with a National Convention	116
	g The Fiasco at Cold Bath Fields	120
	h Carlile's Last Stand	131
	i The Limitations of Paineite Republicanism Exposed	134
	j The Chartist Aversion to Paine	138
	k Democracy versus Democracy	146
V	**General Conclusion**	149

Appendix: The Tale of Tom Paine's Bones

a Flawed Versions of the Story	155
b Paine's Repatriation and its Problems	158
c A Public Funeral Denied	166

Select Bibliography   183

Reference Notes   199

Index   247

Acknowledgments

The idea of researching and writing this work arose, circuitously, from the chance acquisition of an old scrapbook that came to light a decade ago in Galway, Ireland. It had once belonged to Benjamin Tilly, a tailor by trade, a friend of William Cobbett and the official custodian of Thomas Paine's bones. Partly by hand, partly in print, it offers a unique insight into the Cobbett Club, a political society which met in the Fleet Street area during the late 1830s and early 1840s. The scrapbook's significance was first spotted by the journalist, historian and Middle East traveller Penny Young, whose helpful summary of its contents was published in 2014, as a special supplement to the present-day *Cobbett Society Magazine*. As the study developed, it came to owe much to encouragement, suggestions and criticism from Barry Arden, Chris Hooper, Chris Brant, Robert Forder and Louis Henry. It is also indebted to Richard Henry for photographing the house in Ford Square Stepney where, in the 1840s, Paine's skeleton was stored; and to Louis Henry for drawing the map of Cold Bath Fields.

Involved in the research project was a quest for Paine's bones, a trail ending in the Rosary Cemetery, a tolerant, non-denominational burial ground in Norwich. In the 1870s, the Reverend Alexander Gordon, the final keeper of Paine's bones and who was known to have planned a quiet interment for them (see Appendix), conducted burials there as minister of the Unitarian Octagon Chapel in Colegate. In this capacity he was provided with the opportunity to bury Paine discreetly and in a pleasant and appropriate spot. But where exactly? Hope of an answer was raised by a chance meeting in the cemetery with Mark Shopland, one of its Friends, who, shortly afterwards, sent me its burial records neatly contained on a small memory stick, with the warning, however, that it was not a complete tally. Unfortunately, these records made no mention of Paine, perhaps a consequence of his abiding contentiousness.

Composed during the Pandemic, when access to public libraries was difficult and even dangerous, the study became very much dependent upon my own collection of books, as well as upon a host of second-hand book dealers in the

USA, Canada, England, Scotland, Wales, Ireland, France, the Netherlands and Germany for supplying me with relevant monographs and early editions of pertinent texts, especially the very rare cheap editions of *Rights of Man*. To them I owe my gratitude and extend my thanks.

Michael Bush
Wanstead
London
January, 2023

Introduction

Why did Thomas Paine reject hereditary monarchy? His steadfast concern to expose the unnaturalness, illegality and absurdity of this form of government, and to advocate its abolition, runs as a dominant and constant thread throughout his political works and political activities. It was there in the 1770s as well as in the 1790s. His *Common Sense* (1776) specifically identified 'Of monarchy and hereditary succession' as a major complaint on the title page, and the first two, of its four, sections are devoted to its condemnation. His *Rights of Man* (1791-2) made the same objection, and did so at considerable length and with great force. Paine was equally and for the same reasons against hereditary nobility, his aversion obliging him to condemn several republics with electoral systems on the grounds that their electorates were confined to a hereditary order. His onslaught on the principle of hereditary government rendered him opposed to every political system of the time with two exceptions, both newly created and shaped by himself: the American Republic, as established by 1787, and the French Republic, as established in 1792.

This book proposes that Paine's rejection of hereditary rule was the most important feature of his political philosophy. In doing so, it expands on a point originally made by Gregory Claeys in *Thomas Paine: Social and Political Thought* and developed in recent years by Carine Lounissi in her essay 'Thomas Paine's democratic linguistic radicalism'. In taking this line, the book makes objection to Mark Philp's influential article 'English republicanism in the 1790s'.[1]

This book also proposes that Paine's rejection of hereditary rule was a very unusual stand to take, with most critics of the Crown objecting simply to royal absolutism, whereas Paine's approach was to oppose constitutional monarchy as well. As Paine expressed it in a letter to Condorcet and others of June 1791: 'Monarchy and hereditary succession are totally inconsistent with the very fundamental principles of constitutional government.' In other words, the constitutional monarchy as found in England was as repugnant to him as the royal absolutism found prior to the revolution in France.[2] The provenance of his thinking on this point is obscure but, rather than directly linked with the Commonwealth sentiment that had survived the Restoration and thrived in consequence of the Glorious Revolution, it probably derived from the egalitarian (as opposed to elitist) republicanism of the late seventeenth-century Dutch philosopher and lens-grinder, Baruch de Spinoza, and the influence his *Tractatus Theologico-politicus* (1670) exerted through the medium of the Radical Enlightenment (see ch. II *e*). Likewise, this study also departs from the standard account in explaining the nature of Paine's chosen method of creating a new constitution. His national convention is not seen as derived from the schemes proposed in the 1770s by James Burgh and John Cartwright (as Caroline Robbins originally suggested) but from the 'General Will' theory of Jean-Jacques Rousseau.[3] Paine's device differed significantly from the national convention designed to restore the constitution through petitioning parliament to reform itself (the procedure, for example, the Chartists followed). Instead, it aimed to transform the constitution completely by abolishing the hereditary element. The difference between the two was evident in the government's reaction: tolerant to the former and extremely hostile to the latter.

The study's basic theme is not just the unusual nature of Paine's republicanism but also the way society responded to it, notably in Britain. Initially, sales of *Rights of Man* were spectacular but after 1792 relatively few copies were sold (see ch. III *b*). Why did his type of republicanism receive a limited reception here, after enjoying so much success in North America and France? Partly responsible was a severe crackdown by the British government with Paine fleeing the country to escape trial for political sedition and booksellers and printers convicted of the same charge, the consequence of the hostility expressed to hereditary monarchy in *Rights of Man* part II (see ch. III *g*). Also working against Paine was the reputation he quickly gained as an enemy of the nation for his involvement in attempts by the French to invade England, as an enemy of religion following his publication of *The Age of Reason* in 1794, and as an enemy of the constitution because of his refusal in *Rights of Man* to believe in its self-balancing nature (see ch. I *b*).

Paine's rejection came not only from conservatives but also from radicals: the reception given to Paine's political ideas in Britain, particularly by the various organisations associated with Radical Reform (i.e., proponents of universal suffrage), provides further evidence of the problems Paine and his cause had to face (see ch. IV *b*). Three of these organisations were appreciative of Paine's republicanism: namely, the London Corresponding Society, its members stirred in the early 1790s by the recent publication of Paine's *Rights of Man*;

the republican following of Richard Carlile, active in the 1820s and early 1830s; and a political party called the National Union of the Working Classes and Others, led by Henry Hetherington and also active in the early 1830s (see ch. IV *a* and *d*). The supporters of Carlile and Hetherington busied themselves, if not in conjunction, to promote Paine's ideas by publishing his works and by organising metropolitan and provincial societies for their circulation and discussion. However, other Radical Reform movements, especially those with the largest memberships, kept their distance from Paine, principally through adhering to the reform plans originally created in the 1770s by Major John Cartwright. Such plans placed priority on reforming the House of Commons, principally by making it answerable to the nation through an electoral system based upon universal suffrage. This was the cause adopted, from the 1790s to the 1840s, by the supporters of Horne Tooke, John Cartwright, Henry Hunt and the Chartist leader, Feargus O'Connor, who could see no point in abolishing the Crown or the Lords and, as Christians, were alienated from Paine by the hostility expressed in his *The Age of Reason* (1794) towards their religious beliefs (see ch. IV *b* and *i*). The longevity and popularity of this monarchist strand of Radical Reform sprang from the demagogic leadership of Hunt and O'Connor, the effect of which was to cause large numbers of working men and women to steer clear of supporting a Paineite republic. Thereafter, the same strand of radicalism – represented in the 1860s by the Reform League, and later by the Liberal and Labour parties – continued in the traditional manner to advocate universal suffrage while, for fear of alienating support, shying away from Paine's solution to political reform.

As for the survival of Paineite republicanism, it was promoted in the 1790s by Daniel Eaton's *Politics for the People* (1794-5) and, in the 1820s and early 1830s, by popular weekly periodicals such as Carlile's *Republican*, *Prompter* and *Gauntlet* and by Hetherington's *Poor Man's Guardian* (see ch. IV *a*, *c* and *d*). Each of these strands of republicanism, however, came to nothing. In an alien world created by a long war with the French Republic, British republicanism in the 1790s was crushed by government action and the suppression of Paine's works. Regenerated between 1817 and 1820 by Sherwin and Carlile's republication of Paine's works, and Carlile's role in organising working-class clubs for the discussion of Paine's political and religious ideas, republicanism in the 1830s suffered a mortal blow following Carlile's sudden retirement from politics in 1835.[4] This was compounded by the impact upon working-class opinion of Bronterre O'Brien, editor of the *Poor Man's Guardian* (1832-5) and a string of newspapers in the late 1830s. O'Brien was not against getting rid of the monarchy and peerage, but much preferred the republicanism of Robespierre to that of Paine.[5] According to him, abolishing monarchy would not solve society's basic problems. Rather than the political revolution envisaged by Paine, a social revolution was needed, aimed at remedying the gross imbalance between capital and labour – an injustice Paine had simply overlooked – by ensuring that the workers fully enjoyed the fruits of their labour.

In 1853 Thomas Paine's bones – having lain in storage for over three decades after William Cobbett had returned them from the USA in 1819 – came up for auction, the result of the bankruptcy of their current keeper, Benjamin Tilly, a journeyman tailor (see Appendix). They were purchased by James Watson, a former follower of Carlile, a keen republican and atheist, and the chief publisher of Paine's works from the 1830s to the 1850s. Watson had plans to give the bones a proper burial, the one, in fact, that Cobbett had intended in 1819. Instrumental in his failure to do so was the dawning realisation in radical circles that Paine's political solutions were out of date and largely irrelevant to the pressing problems of the day. The republics that had emerged so far in the world had confounded Paine's naive expectation that, compared with monarchies, they would conduct themselves peaceably and free from corruption, thus wrecking the argument used by Paine to justify their creation (see ch. IV i).

Also working against Paine was the emergence of radical movements offering alternative and variant forms of republicanism. One such movement was essentially in support of a very limited monarchy. Paine would have dismissed it as bogus republicanism because it accepted the hereditary principle for both Crown and nobility. Originating in the late seventeenth century, and thriving in the eighteenth century as a backlash against oligarchic rule, it found expression in several guises throughout the nineteenth century: for example, in Sherwin's *Republican* (1817), the political writings associated with Benjamin Tilly and the posthumous Cobbett Club (1838-42) and in C.G. Harding's *Republican* (1848). It also found voice in Frederic Harrison's *Order and Progress* (1875), with a chapter headed 'All Free Government is Republican'.[6]

Another variant of republicanism emerged following the revolutions of 1848, in response to their suppression. The creation of W.J. Linton, W.E. Adams and others, it was purveyed in several journals, notably *The English Republic*, edited by Linton, and the *Northern Tribune*, edited by Adams. Its inspiration was the republicanism of Joseph Mazzini, who, in contradiction of Paine, stressed the importance of the 'Duties of Man' as opposed to the 'Rights of Man', on the grounds that the latter could do nothing to lift the bulk of the population out of poverty irrespective of the form that government took. In opposition to Paine, Mazzini's republicanism was deeply religious with a motto of 'God and the People' and the belief that, to solve the political and social problems of the time, men needed to follow the example of Christ. Also distinguishing Mazzini's republicanism from that of Paine was its focus on liberating nations from the imperialistic aggression of royal despots and its eventual willingness to tolerate monarchy on condition that, by ceasing to be absolutist, it adopted a constitutional form of government.[7]

Another type of republicanism alien to Paine's way of thinking had emerged by that time. It derived, in the 1830s and 1840s, from the socialist schemes of O'Brien and Robert Owen, whether it be land nationalisation (O'Brien) or the creation of communist communities or worker cooperatives (Owen). Both men had links with republicanism, but neither could be associated with Paine since for them social welfare was much more important than political reform.[8] Yet another type of republicanism was embodied in the National Republican League. Led by Charles Bradlaugh, it burst onto the political scene in the early 1870s, partially inspired by the establishment of the Third Republic in France. In the Carlile manner, it operated through a network of republican clubs, their activities registered in a weekly journal, the *National Reformer*. It lasted four years.[9] Deploring socialism, Bradlaugh's republicanism was in no danger of being side-tracked by that particular cause. But his adherence to secularism, coupled with his abhorrence of violence, and his preference to promote republicanism by emphasising the defective personalities of kings (rather than the superiority of republican, over hereditary, government) worked to the same effect in distinguishing his republicanism from Paine's. Bradlaugh remained true to Paine, but, for him, the message imparted by *Rights of Man* was supplanted by that of *The Age of Reason*: in other words, establishing a secularised society became more important than getting rid of the polity of the blood.

Another expression of republicanism emerged in the 1880s, featuring the Fabian Society, the Socialist League, and the Social Democratic Federation.[10] While prepared to profess republicanism, these parties followed in the footsteps of O'Brien rather than Paine, their reform efforts concentrated on the establishment of a system of state socialism. For each of them, capitalism was the enemy, and monarchy, a secondary concern. A final strand of British republicanism, the only one to achieve a republic, emerged in late nineteenth-century Ireland. Deeply religious, taking the form of an anti-colonial struggle and driven by a long history of peasant insurrection, as well as encouraged, directed and funded by Irish expatriates republicanised from living in the USA, it had nothing directly to do with Paine: that is, apart from a short period in the early 1790s when the recently published *Rights of Man* (1791-2) was all persuasive and before *The Age of Reason* (1794) had proclaimed his enmity to the Christian religion.[11] This book, however, is not about the prevalence of republicanism in Britain. Its principle subject is specifically the republicanism associated with Paine and centred on the abolition of hereditary rule.

Paine remained in the public consciousness of Britain throughout the twentieth century, both as hero and bogeyman, but his programme of political reform lost all meaning as a viable plan of action. Consequently, the ancient and primitive principle of succession in the blood, embodied in Crown and peerage, was able to remain a central part of British government. Upholding it, as one might expect, was a loyalism that stemmed partly, from the charity and honours dispensed by the Crown, along with the spectacular pageantry monarchy was capable of displaying; partly, from a primal fear of 'the swinish multitude' that rendered democracy suspect, thereby justifying the preservation of constitutional checks that, by virtue of birthright, were not answerable to the people; partly, from the survival of pre-democratic attitudes, such as social deference and respect for hierarchy; partly, from the smoke-screen allegation that, in reality, Britain was already a republic thanks to the limited powers of the Crown and the House of Lords; and partly, from the uniquely cohesive function the Crown exercised in relation to the British Empire, the Commonwealth, and the component nations of the United Kingdom.[12] Assisting in the maintenance of the hereditary principle was the tendency of critics of the establishment to vent their fury and contempt against royals and aristocrats but not to demand the abolition of the hereditary institutions: i.e. the monarchy and the House of Lords.[13] Finally, working to the same effect were changes in the character of republicanism, with the emergence of republican movements prepared to reach an accommodation with a monarchy of the constitutionalist kind, even though their political principles dictated otherwise.

A belief in Paineite republicanism of course had been, and continues to be, frequently advocated by private individuals. But since it was no longer organised, the call for abolishing hereditary rule could be ignored. Thus, Britain survived the wave of revolutions that, in the course of the late nineteenth and twentieth centuries, removed monarchy and nobility from much of the world. Yet at what cost? Paine would say at considerable cost, given the absurdity of rule by hereditary right, especially within a professed democracy.

The thesis of this study, then, is that Paineite republicanism became a potent force in Britain from the 1790s until the late 1830s. But sapping its effectiveness was not only an enduring loyalty to the Crown, one that ran throughout society, but also the willingness of the majority of the country's radicals to repudiate, or disparage, or overlook the central message of Paine's programme of political reform: namely, the necessity of terminating rule by right of birth. Why they should have done so is the basic question to which this study seeks an answer.

The Polity of the Blood

Chapter I
Paine on Hereditary Right

a | Paine's Rejection of Hereditary Succession

'Independence is my happiness', Paine declared in his *Rights of Man* (1792).[1] By this he meant, among other things, his independence of aristocratic connections, whether it be through kinship or clientage, and his independence of the web of patronage that centred upon the royal court. Thanks to this independence, he was able to liberate his thinking, more decisively than most other British political philosophers, from the concept of 'a polity of the blood'. No matter whether it inclined to limit or extend the authority of the executive, the political thought of the time had no problem in accepting a birthright to rule, if not for the Crown, then at least for the peerage, and usually for both; whereas Paine advocated its total extinction, the need for which he saw with mathematical clarity. 'There is not a problem in Euclid more mathematically true than that hereditary government has not a right to exist', he wrote in 1795.[2] His desire to abolish hereditary rule ran through all his major political works. It was to the fore in *Common Sense* (1776); it was the main concern of *Rights of Man* (1791-2); it was central to his *Dissertation on First Principles of Government* (1795).[3] For him it offered the political solution to society's main problems.

His complaint against hereditary monarchy covered several issues. He deplored it as a source of rule by persons incapable of the task; as a source of tyranny; as a source of internal disorder and wars abroad; as a source of foreign rule; as a source of illegitimate rule – in the absence of sanction by either nature or God – and as a source of costly government, with monarchs prone to profligacy on account of an ingrained lavishness of life-style and an irrepressible inclination to war.[4] Single-mindedly and repeatedly, he dwelt on the obvious absurdity of defining someone's suitability to rule in terms of a right of inheritance rather than in terms of experience, talent, maturity, virtue or public approval.[5] For him hereditary monarchy was not only absurd and ridiculous but also against nature and beyond the sanction of law, especially on the grounds that 'man has no authority over prosperity'.[6] A commitment of future generations to hereditary government breached their natural, free-born right of consent, subjecting them to a despotism that resembled 'a species of slavery'.[7] This belief led him to find fault with two revolutionary settlements: that of the Bill of

Rights of 1689, for conferring the Crown upon William and Mary and their heirs 'for ever'; and that of the French Constituent Assembly of 1789, for conferring the same perpetual privilege upon the line of Louis XVI.[8] If you sought a religious reason for hereditary rule, he argued, you might do so in terms of divine right, but that would go against Christianity in that the divine right of monarchs was unwarranted by Scripture.[9] And, he proceeded, if you sought a rational explanation for hereditary rule, all the evidence went against it.[10] And if you sought a legal justification, it could not be found. As he emphatically stated in his pamphlet *Dissertation on First Principles of Government*: 'We have only to examine whether there exists in a nation a right to set it (i.e. rule by hereditary succession) up...by what is called law, as has been done in England. I answer NO.'[11] Towards the end of his life in 1807 he re-emphasised the point to indicate his own originality in discovering it and its importance in achieving a republic: 'I know of no author' prior to the publication of *Common Sense* and *Rights of Man* 'that has exposed and attacked hereditary succession on the ground of illegality, which is the strongest of all grounds to attack it upon'.[12]

Consistently, Paine claimed, a political system could only be made just, rational, efficient and benign, especially in terms of upholding the public good, by obliterating the hereditary principle vested in the Crown and by substituting a purely representative system of government based upon popular election. For Paine hereditary monarchy was 'a nullity' in lacking legitimacy and usefulness, and in offering nothing of benefit to the nation.[13] In consequence, the claim made by kings to be benevolent rulers was a totally fraudulent one.[14] In addition, he thought the effect of hereditary monarchy was to debase human beings by treating them as if they were animals. On the one hand, subjects, as the inherited property of kings, were treated 'as if they were flocks and herds'. On the other, hereditary monarchs 'succeed each other not as rationals but as animals'. In acquiring their position and function simply by virtue of the blood, and with no human qualities taken into account in the process of selection, they were not only far from divine but also far from human. In fact, they were simply a species of animal cultivated by a process of special breeding but with no assured gain: the hoped-for lion frequently turning out to be an ass; the expected Solomon often turning out to be a fool.[15]

Paine's grievance was not simply against hereditary kings. Hereditary nobles were equally at fault, with the same vices: ignorance, selfishness, incompetence and absurdity.[16] He took Edmund Burke to task for suggesting that hereditary government is 'a contrivance of human wisdom': something disproved, Paine remarked, by the scarcity of Solomons not only in the line of kings but also in the House of Lords.[17] Linking the two again, he wrote: 'monarchy and aristocracy were frauds and impositions on mankind'.[18] Both had originated as plundering brigands and had developed the hereditary principle to conceal their coarse beginnings. This was achieved by making 'their race sacred' through the falsification of genealogical tables and 'the knavery of priests'.[19] As for what they could offer society, nobles, like monarchs, had nothing to give since they were naturally inclined to act only in their own self-interest and therefore as parasites.[20] In this respect, the House of Lords was just as unreasonable as, say, a house of brewers or a house of bakers; and hereditary legislators were as ridiculous as hereditary mathematicians or a hereditary poet laureate.[21] Paine dismissed parliament's upper chamber as 'an excrescence growing out of corruption', 'an ulcerated wen' on the body politic, and, quintessentially, 'an association for the protection of' stolen property.[22] Moved by the same resentment, he was strongly opposed to the introduction of a second legislative chamber to the American constitution, and remained dedicated to the idea of a single chamber legislature when engaged in creating a constitution for the French republic in late 1792.[23]

He was just as scathing about hereditary noble status and its titles. Inspired by the abolition of nobility in France, he launched into a bitter onslaught on its existence elsewhere. In contrast to the title of 'judge' or 'general', Paine claimed, hereditary nobility had no connection with 'office and character'. Meaning 'nothing', nobility was 'a chimerical nondescript', a non-functional 'folly', 'a sort of foppery' which, what with the wearing of ribbons and garters, feminised the holder and turned him into a child; yet, bizarrely, a child expected to exercise political authority over adults. According to Paine, by recently banning noble rank and titles, France had suddenly 'outgrown the baby-clothes of count and duke and breeched itself in manhood'. Rather than debasing society by a process of levelling down, the effect of removing the noble order had done just the opposite, since 'it had put down the dwarf to set up the man'.[24] Now was the time, he urged, either through the abolition of nobility or, at least, by making it a figure of ridicule, to redefine the criteria of social rank so that they rested not on inherited degree but on character, achievement and service.[25]

Switching to the nobility's landownership, Paine added parasitism to the theme of selfishness, arguing that landed nobles 'are not the farmers who work the land and raise the produce but are the mere consumers of the rent', existing 'only for lazy enjoyment'.[26] Moreover, in spite of their great riches and small numbers, they tended to be maintained at public expense – thanks to the receipt of pensions and sinecures from church and state funds – at a cost to the nation of almost as much as what was spent on the support of the poor.[27] Promoting their dependence on public funds, Paine believed, was the impact of the law of primogeniture, which 'disowns', in each noble family, all but the eldest son, rendering the remainder of the offspring 'cast, like orphans on a parish, to be provided for by the public, but at a greater charge' since 'unnecessary offices and places in governments and courts are created at the expense of the public to maintain them'. For Paine this was a monstrous state of affairs.[28]

Paine had nothing to say in extenuation of nobility.[29] Whig historiography had accorded it a protective function, as a defence against royal tyranny; but Paine failed to recognise this role as anything special: rather than oaks shading a commonwealth, he saw the noble order as principally a servitor of the monarch and of itself, with both bent on plundering the communities of the realm through a regressive tax system.[30] Helped by the fiscal knowledge acquired as a former excise officer, Paine identified in late eighteenth-century Britain an 'inequality of taxation' caused by the government's growing reliance upon excises levied on articles of consumption coupled with a reduced dependence upon the land tax. Once upon a time, Paine indicated, the revenues from the two taxes were almost equal in amount. However, under Hanoverian rule, the land tax had fallen from £2.5 million to £2 million p.a., in spite of a doubling of rented income from land, whereas the yield from the Excise had soared from £2 to £13 million p.a. Paine attributed this profound change to the nobility's use of the House of Lords – presented as a 'combination' [i.e. union] devoted to protecting the landed interest – 'to ward off taxes from itself'. The outcome of this selfishness was 'a constant increase in the number and wretchedness of the poor', with 'a great mass of the community thrown into poverty and discontent' and therefore placed 'constantly on the brink of commotion'. All this demonstrated that the blame for popular disorder lay with the government's fiscal policies and the manner in which they had been directed, by the nobility's control of legislation, to fall disproportionately on the people.[31] A salutary contrast was provided by the new American republic where 'the poor are not oppressed, the rich are not privileged' and where taxation is not onerous 'because their government is just'. With 'nothing to render them (i.e. the poor) wretched, there is nothing to engender riots and tumults'.[32]

Paine's antipathy to hereditary nobility led him to make objection to a number of so-called republics – Holland, Genoa, Venice, Berne and Poland – where, he believed, the executive was selected not by popular election but merely by the noble order.[33] Since true republican government is based on an 'equality of rights', he reasoned, it cannot incorporate a nobility, the existence of which inevitably presumes 'an inequality of rights'.[34] For him, in March 1792, the USA was the only 'real republic' since it had rejected 'everything hereditary' in the sphere of government.[35] Before the end of the year France was admitted to the same honour, the abolition of nobility by June 1790 having been complemented in September 1792 with the termination of monarchy.[36]

Britain came in for a double rebuttal: on account of the political authority exercised hereditarily not only by the Crown but also by the peerage. Paine was convinced that, whether termed a monarchy or a republic, a mixture of the hereditary and the representative did not constitute a commendable political system.[37] Such a mixed system had long operated in Britain but was only able to function, Paine believed, not because, as was conventionally thought, the hereditary and representative elements were 'reciprocally checking each other', and so finely balanced, but because cementing them together was the prevalence of political corruption.[38] Responsible for the latter was the Crown as 'the giver of places and pensions'.[39] In this manner, the Crown had, in effect, 'engrossed the [House of] Commons', thereby blotting out the representative element. Thanks to the Civil List, 'the splendour of the throne is no other than the corruption of the state'.[40] But also responsible for the extent of corruption within the political system was the hereditary principle of primogeniture, as practised not only by the Crown but also by the nobility, which left its younger sons and daughters, in spite of family wealth, sycophantically dependent on public funds.[41] For Paine, the very presence of hereditary monarchs and hereditary nobles was a fatal flaw in the body politic. It represented 'the caterpillar principle' whereby, in the guise of courtiers, numerous pests fed relentlessly on the public good.[42] As 'the most base and humiliating idea that ever degraded the human species', Paine thought, hereditary succession deserved, 'for the honour of humanity', to be 'destroyed for ever'.[43]

b | Grounds for the Public's Rejection of Paine

Weakening Paine's case against the polity of the blood was, arguably, the charge that he had got things out of proportion, especially with regards to Britain, since, by the late eighteenth century, the constitutional powers of the Crown appeared far from despotic and already very limited. What was the point of creating a republic if its establishment would change so little? It could even be claimed that, in practice, Britain was already a republic.[44] Yet such an argument did not destroy Paine's case since, quite apart from the political authority and influence it had managed to retain, the Crown remained a major source of unnecessary expenditure and corruption and, thanks to the principle of hereditary succession and the absence of the nation's consent, it could be regarded as despotic, no matter how restricted its powers, on the grounds that future generations were saddled with the same dynasty irrespective of its proven congenital incapacity to rule.[45] Moreover, because of the same hereditary principle, the nobility, through the House of Lords as well by virtue of their landed estates, and the influence they exercised in the House of Commons, continued to hold considerable legislative, judicial and political authority throughout the nineteenth century. Obvious gains, then, could conceivably be made by disposing of both Crown and peerage, thereby converting the country into a complete, rather than a semi-, democracy.

Also working against a ready acceptance of Paine's common-sensical dismissal of rule by birthright was the extreme, extensive and shocking nature of Paine's radicalism: that is, when measured against the conventions of the time. Standing alongside his rejection of the polity of the blood was his repudiation of Christianity. Especially objectionable to Paine was Christianity's fraudulence and hypocrisy: i.e. a religion of the sword preaching 'love thy enemies'; an alleged aid to salvation used as an instrument of political control and priestly greed.[46] Rather than the word of God, and therefore true, Paine dismissed the holy scriptures as a compound of fables.[47] Christianity's ecclesiastical organisation he condemned as an agency of the state and principally devoted to persuading the people to accept their inferior lot.[48] His case against Christianity was made fully and explicitly in *The Age of Reason* (1794), but his hostility was already evident in *Common Sense* (1776) where he obscurely remarks that hereditary succession 'hath no parallel in or out of Scripture but the doctrine of original sin' (in the sense that both were equally absurd).[49] In the same work, it is true, he employed scriptural evidence to disprove that kings ruled by divine right.[50] Yet, in all likelihood, this was no more than a tactical ploy, an appeal made by a Deist to the Christian beliefs of American colonists, not a genuine statement of faith in scriptural authority.[51] His hostility to Christianity was also evident in *Rights of Man* (1791-2), notably in his brash declaration: 'my religion is to do good'.[52]

Adding to the offensiveness of Paine's political philosophy was his willingness to accept popular revolution, and its implicit violence, as a viable means of political reform. In fact, his political reform programme could easily appear predicated on an overthrow of the old regime by popular revolt. In 1791 he declared: 'revolutions may be considered the order of the day'.[53] And not any old revolution: 'the revolutions which formerly took place in the world', he considered, were little more than a change of persons and measures, and, since they did not involve a change of principle, they 'had nothing in them that interested the bulk of mankind'.[54] Now, however, the revolutionary aim was profoundly different and far more appealing. It was to establish a political system resting on the sovereignty of the nation, rather than the sovereignty of the Crown. Its primary purpose was to benefit all, rather than just the monarch, the nobles and their minions. Its means of reform was to create a social system based on an equality of rights rather than differential privilege, and to found a government determined by elected representation, rather than hereditary succession: in other words, to apply new principles rather than simply to achieve a change of government personnel and policy.[55] According to Paine, this departure from tradition was the result of recent examples of revolution that characteristically featured an underlying and permanent popular outrage against monarchs for overtaxing their subjects in order to maximise their own patronage and increase their military might. Such outrage was especially explosive, Paine claimed, when the bulk of the population was unable to make peaceful complaint through a system of representation.[56]

While not insisting that revolutions against government had to be violent – let us 'produce revolutions by reason and accommodation' rather than by 'convulsions', he wrote[57] – Paine was inclined to demonstrate their nature with reference to the American and French Revolutions, both of them a physical struggle to overthrow the old regime in which the willingness of the people to take up arms and spill blood was clearly evident, of vital importance and necessary.[58] As part of this revolutionary scenario, Paine was ready to exonerate popular insurrections since, he felt, they were not the fault of the people but a defensive response to the oppressiveness of government, especially in the form of an inequitable tax system that regressively fell heavily upon the poor and lightly upon the rich.[59] He was also prepared to declare that, by a natural right of sovereignty, 'a nation has at all times an inherent, indefeasible right to abolish any form of government it finds inconvenient and establish such as accords with its interests, disposition and happiness'.[60] Putting the matters in a nutshell, he asserted: 'It is possible to exclude men from the right of voting, but it is impossible to exclude them from the right of rebelling against that exclusion, and when all other rights are taken away, the right of rebellion is made perfect.'[61] Having proposed in 1786 that, within a system of hereditary rule, the only 'modes of redress' available to the people were petition or insurrection, by 1792 he had ruled out petitioning as an effective means of political reform, because a corrupt government could hardly be expected to reform itself. By this time he had also dismissed a reformed House of Commons as an inadequate means for achieving the same goal.[62] Instead, he was recommending a national convention to formulate a new constitution, while suggesting that this procedure was only likely to work in a revolutionary situation created by the revolt of the people against their exclusion from the political system.[63]

In mitigation of relying on reform by revolutionary insurrection, Paine professed to have great faith in the natural cohesiveness of society. As a result, he could claim that government was, at least for a time, unnecessary, so much so that its abrupt abolition – say, in the early stages of an old regime's destruction – would not lead to the social chaos predicted by Hobbes but to greater unity. As he put it in the first chapter of *Rights of Man* part II: 'The instant formal government is abolished, society begins to act. A general association takes place, and common interest produces common security.' In other words, the commonly held belief that a removal of government inevitably leads to social disintegration is untrue. Rather, it was a ruse invented by the old order to prevent its own revolutionary rejection.[64]

His approval of 'popular revolution' was coupled with his dismissive scorn for the normally recognised achievements of 'aristocratic revolution': that is, 'British liberty' and its revered constitutional pillars, Magna Carta (1215), and the Bill of Rights (1689).[65] According to Paine, in England no such thing as a constitution existed. This was because, thanks to the Norman invasion of 1066, the English system of government 'arose of conquest and not out of society'.[66] Nor should one trust antiquity or historical precedent to provide the authority to justify rights and liberties.[67] In Paine's opinion, 'government by precedent…is one of the vilest systems that can be set up' since reliance on it was just a conservative trick 'to deaden [man's] faculties' and distract him 'from the scene of revolutions'.[68]

Innovation on the basis of principles worked out by reason was Paine's recommended means of political reform.[69] By proceeding, then, from first principles rather than precedent, by using, in other words, a philosophical rather than an historical set of criteria, he was clearly following in the footsteps of John Locke.[70] On the other hand, the role he expected government to fulfil was very different. Contrary to Locke's prime concern for the sanctity of property, and the privileged position he was therefore prepared to award proprietorship, Paine felt that to make the ownership of property an exclusive right of political representation would mean 'a total departure from every moral principle of liberty'. Instead, although not denying the need to safeguard the individual ownership of property – the second of his proposed principles in *Rights of Man* included its protection – for him the primary aim of civil society was to preserve the equality of rights enjoyed by mankind when living in a state of nature.[71] Paine's programme of reform, then, was to regain an equalisation of the rights of man. This was to be achieved by getting rid of crown and nobility and replacing the polity of the blood with a system of representative government, 'the true and only true basis' of which is 'an equality of rights' that confers on 'every man...a right to one vote, and no more, in the choice of representatives'.[72]

In elevating personality over property as the qualification for the right to vote, Paine had one serious forerunner: Major John Cartwright whose seminal work *Take your Choice* was first published in 1776, the same year as Paine's *Common Sense*.[73] But the criterion the two of them offered for a system of one-man-one-vote was quite different. In the late eighteenth and early nineteenth centuries, and largely under Cartwright's influence, political reformers regarded the Anglo-Saxon constitution as the original embodiment of British liberty. They therefore argued for reform by a process of restoration, not innovation. Essentially, they saw themselves as acting within the law and as patriots. This led them to advocate a representative system dependent on universal suffrage, annual parliaments and the secret ballot, but not to propose the abolition of hereditary rule. In contrast, the only restoration Paine was prepared to countenance was the equality of rights that had existed in a prehistoric state of nature. Otherwise, for him it was a matter of building a system from scratch, based upon a blueprint of principles worked out by reason.[74] Moreover, Cartwright's method of reform was emphatically not by force of arms but by peaceable persuasion. The historical provenance of his reform programme led his supporters directly to a criticism of Paine. Take, for example, John Baxter's *A New and Impartial History of England*, published in 1796 by a member of the London Corresponding Society, to which it was dedicated. In the preface Baxter declared 'our constitution is derived from our Saxon ancestors' and then proceeded to say: 'Much as we respect the opinions of Thomas Paine in many particulars, we cannot agree with him that we have no constitution.'[75] In contrast, Paine stuck to a reform programme centred on the production of a written constitution and based on first principles that might well need to be implemented by force. Moreover, the Civil War and Glorious Revolution, the aristocratic revolts of the seventeenth century, along with the baronial rebellions of the Middle Ages, were all seen by Paine not as confirmations of constitutional liberty but as extensions of aristocratic power at the expense of both Crown and commons. Royal absolutism and complete anarchy may have been avoided by such acts of resistance, but this was at the cost of an entrenchment of aristocratic control and a further subjugation of the people.[76] The perceived offensiveness of Paine's doubts about British liberty resulted in his trial and conviction for political sedition in 1792, the charges specifically focused on his having libelled the Glorious Revolution and the attendant Bill of Rights in the second part of *Rights of Man*.[77]

Equally offensive was Paine's universalism, evident in the presentation of himself as 'a citizen of the world', and in his claim that 'my country is the world'.[78] This conceit rendered it even more difficult for fellow reformers to regard him as a patriot, in spite of the precautions he took to defend his patriotism: first, by accusing the devotees of hereditary monarchy of unpatriotic conduct for having, within the last hundred years, yielded possession of the British throne to Dutch and German ruling dynasties; and second, by conceding that events from the country's past could inspire faith in the correctness of first principles.[79] In his opinion, an awareness of history could serve to 'refresh our patriotism'.[80] To emphasise the point, a long footnote in *Rights of Man* offered the worthy example of Wat Tyler's revolt against oppressive taxation in 1381, for which, Paine proposed, Tyler deserved a monument in Smithfield.[81] On the other hand, undermining Paine's reputation for patriotism was not only his contempt for the ancient constitution but also his willingness to participate in a military invasion of the country led by none other than Napoleon.[82]

Providing a final source of alienation was the deliberately pitched popular appeal of Paine's writings. Previously and exclusively, dangerous sentiments had tended to be published anonymously and in expensive works. Shrouded in recondite argument and esoteric language, and often written in Latin, the books and pamphlets in which they appeared had tended to lie squirrelled away in gentlemen's libraries, along with titillating prints and novels of an intimate nature. In contrast, Paine – under his own name and in cheap editions[83] – had openly, succinctly, wittily and pointedly broadcast his political and religious views in clear, provocative, hopeful, sententious and memorable prose, the aim of which was not only to reach the working population of artisans, traders and labourers but also to incite them to political action by showing how remedy lay in their hands and that an obligation to humanity fell upon them to bring it about. Increasing his popular appeal, and his dangerousness, was the approachable image imparted in his writings, thanks to details recorded there from his own life of an engaged polemicist with highly relevant grievances to share, rather than an aloof philosopher intent, from the safety of a book-lined sanctuary, on searching for a profound truth.[84]

His knack of offending the major shibboleths of the time rendered Paine's programme of reform generally repugnant in Britain, an attitude shared, throughout and beyond the nineteenth century not only by all of loyalist persuasion but also by many professed radicals. While bitterly opposed over the issue of parliamentary reform, both groups tended to share an ingrained respect towards the orders of the blood, a reverence for Christianity (which permitted an acceptance of monarchy and nobility as divinely appointed through the mechanism of hereditary right) and grave doubts about achieving political reform through innovation or by force of arms. For these reasons, Paine's philosophy of political reform tended to be regarded as too visionary to command much respect, even in progressive circles. Its general objectionableness might therefore be seen as upholding in practice belief in the polity of the blood.

Finally, working against the acceptance of Paine as an oracle of plain truth and a beacon of common sense was the way history, as it unfolded, tended to prove him wrong. His hatred of hereditary systems of government led him, in counteraction, to make the idyllic claim that a purely representative system was the perfect form of government.[85] Yet it soon became evident that so-called true republics were no different from monarchies in their proclivity to despotic rule, their tolerance of social inequality and their proneness to war. The point was trenchantly made by Paine's great champion, the American Moncure Conway, who, in 1872, warned against looking to the USA for guidance on how best to run a republic arguing that, in view of the conduct of Ulysses Grant, an American president could be just as corrupt and wilful as any European monarch.[86] In time, the large claims Paine made for the answerability of republican governments to their citizens, and their natural willingness to follow policies of peace rather than war, were exposed as simplistic and naive. Moreover, Paine placed great stress on the nation in his plan for a new order but appeared to be totally unaware of the disruptive force of nationalism. In addition, he also wrongly assumed that nations under a republic preferred peace to war and believed that, once government policies had been wrested from the war-mongering grip of kings and their noble ministers, peace would settle on the world.[87] Furthermore, in accounting for the wretchedness of society, he blamed it exclusively on the nature of government and the willingness of kings to plunder their subjects through regressive systems of taxation.[88] Transformed into republics, he thought, states would be less costly to run and therefore have less need to impose heavy taxes.[89] As a result, the citizens of a republic would become much more prosperous than the subjects of a monarchy.[90] All this proved to be wrong. Other forms of exploitation, economic rather than political in nature, tended to be ignored by Paine. Another world, arising from the consequences of mass production, of world trade and of European powers competing to gain or retain empires in the Americas, Africa and India, created a set of problems to which Paine offered no answer. In Paine's works, capitalism was above censure, class was not considered as a cause of social oppression, and even colonialism was tolerated, in spite of the fact that the revolt of the American colonies had provided Paine with the first opportunity to announce his republican sentiments to the world.[91]

Such blatant omissions and false hopes were bound to create, in the course of time, serious cracks in the credibility of his political philosophy, cracks that were not so evident in the late eighteenth century when, in the dawn flush of revolution, the spotlight of blame fell exclusively upon the intrinsic defectiveness of governments run by nobles and kings. However, such cracks had become clearly exposed by the late nineteenth century when, politically if not religiously, Paine's reputation as a relevant reformer had ossified, turning him into little more than a mythical hero, his writings on politics regarded as dated in style and content, his solutions seen as no longer applicable to the pressing problems of the present.

c | Paine's Tolerance of the Hereditary Right to Private Property

A distinctive peculiarity of Paine's antipathy to hereditary right was its confinement to matters of government and degree. Surprisingly, it did not extend to honestly-acquired landownership, even though several of the arguments he deployed against hereditary rule or rank were applicable to hereditary property as well. Paine certainly had misgivings about the individual ownership of property – especially in the form of great estates – on the grounds that much of it had been originally taken by force or deviously acquired, and also because control of the legislature by the landed interest went against the principle of an equality of right, inevitably resulting in the under-taxation of the rich.[92] He firmly opposed the landowners' monopoly of electoral rights and parliamentary membership, and sincerely believed that, within the political system, the protection of personal rights should have priority over property rights.[93] Furthermore, as we have seen, for him the law of primogeniture, a device to preserve the integrity of aristocratic estates, was a major source of political corruption.[94] In other words, he had grave reservations about the system of landownership and its means of operation. Yet none of these reservations caused him to question its hereditary character. Even though the heir of an estate might prove as incapable as the heir to the throne, that for Paine was unobjectionable. His reverence for property allowed him to list it as one of 'the natural and imprescriptible rights of man' that 'all political associations' were obliged to preserve – along with 'liberty', 'security' and 'resistance of (i.e. from) oppression'.[95] In consequence, he rejected, as a means of reforming society, both compulsory redistribution of the land (i.e. by Agrarian Law) and compulsory nationalisation of the land (i.e. by Agrarian Monopoly).

In 1797 he published a pamphlet called *Agrarian Justice* which ruled out such extreme remedies.[96] Following John Locke's *Two Treatises of Government* (bk II, ch. 5), Paine's pamphlet proposed that all land was originally held in common but only fell, initially and inevitably, into private hands as a natural consequence of its cultivation.[97] In the process, it became hereditary because of an 'inability to separate the improvement made by cultivation from the land upon which the improvement had been made'.[98] Its engrossment in aristocratic hands, he claimed, came of the latter's greed and power.[99] In spite of this, Paine repudiated the idea of a return to common ownership: declaring 'I equally defend the right of the possessor to the part that is his.'[100] Yet, he was not prepared to forget that the land was once held in common, and that therefore in a state of nature 'every person would have been born to property'.[101] This led him to argue that compensation was required for what 'the introduction of the system of landed property' had taken away, namely 'the loss of his or her natural inheritance'. The compensation he proposed was a 10 per cent duty liable for payment, upon every landowner's death, by his heir. Placed in a so-called National Fund, the revenue from this death duty would be distributed to the rest of society as follows: a lump sum of £15 to every person, male and female, on reaching the age of 21, and £10 annually to every person, male and female, on reaching the age of 50.[102] These generous proposals, however, failed in the eyes of society to exonerate Paine either for his republicanism or for his opposition to Christianity. In addition, they placed him at odds with an important strand of radical reform that sought to reintroduce the common ownership of land in place of its individual ownership.

This agrarian movement first found expression with the Spenceans, as Thomas Spence criticised Paine along these very lines, arguing that Paine's focus on the greed and lavishness of the government overlooked the fact that also at fault for creating poverty and misery were the landlords who, having swept away the customary rights of the manorial tenantry, through the introduction of short-term, rack-rented leases, and through enclosure of the commons, were just as responsible for the social ills of the time.[103] The Spencean solution required the rents levied on property, now conceived as commonly held and acknowledged as 'the people's farm', to pass to the former tenantry rather than to the former proprietors. This solution for the ending of private landownership persisted throughout the first forty years of the nineteenth century, even being taken up in the 1830s by the National Union of the Working Classes, initially a Paineite party. But then it was replaced by an agrarian reform programme created by Bronterre O'Brien that involved placing the land in the ownership of the state, an idea which from the 1880s established itself in Britain as a concern of state socialism, thanks to the advocacy of H.M. Hyndman, backed by the Social Democratic Federation, and of A.R. Wallace through the Land Nationalisation Society and the support of the Independent Labour Party.[104] Paine's tolerance of hereditary property thus became another means of rendering his programme of reform out of date, even though, ironically, it provided the prototype of the old-age pension, and even though, in Britain, land nationalisation was never achieved. It also created a major problem for his programme of political reform. If the latter had succeeded in removing the monarchy and the House of Lords, a republic would have come into existence, but left intact, at least for a time, would have been the aristocratic presence of the great estate.

The Polity of the Blood

Chapter II

The Provenance of Paine's Political Ideology

a | The Essence of Paine's Republicanism

In *Rights of Man* Paine identified two basic modes of government: first, a government exclusively by election and representation that was 'known by the name of a republic'; and second, government by hereditary succession that was 'known by the name of monarchy and aristocracy'. He saw the first as driven by reason and the second by ignorance. He also identified a third mode, a mixture of the two, typically found in Britain and rendered operational by the practice of corruption.[1]

Personally, Paine liked to distinguish what he termed 'real' or 'true' republics from putative republics, the distinction quintessentially lying in whether monarchy and nobility were included in, or excluded from, the political system.[2] In Paine's eyes, the American colonies became a 'real' republic not only through declaring themselves independent of the British monarchy in 1776 but also through denying kingship or nobility a role in the new government. This was achieved by 'rejecting everything hereditary, and establishing government on the system of representation only'.[3] Moreover, according to Paine, France did not become a proper republic when it replaced absolute by constitutional monarchy in 1789 or when it abolished nobility in June 1790, but only when it had abolished kingship. So not before September 1792.[4]

And yet some present-day historians doubt the authenticity of Paine's republicanism. Refusing to take his claims and reputation at face value, they incline to see him as a crypto-monarchist, or, at most, no more than a half-hearted republican. At the same time, they are prepared to admit to the republican camp certain political systems featuring a hereditary royal or aristocratic presence. The uncertainty created by such revisionism, arguably, has muddied the waters, at the expense of failing to grasp the simple truth about Paine's political philosophy and its impact on the development of republicanism in eighteenth- and nineteenth-century Britain. The historian Frank Prochaska reveals how he underwent a 'eureka' moment upon coming across the following remark in Paine's *Rights of Man*: 'What is called a Republic is not any particular form of government.'[5] His response was to conclude that for Paine the only indispensable feature of a republic was a government that could be said to operate in the public interest. He went on to argue that 'even Paine did not rule out the possibility of a republic with a king, at least in theory'. Having made this discovery, he proceeded to write a book provocatively entitled *The Republic of Britain 1760-2000*, which dubiously rested on the assumption that, judged on its record of dispensing public good, the limited monarchy of the United Kingdom might well be regarded as a republic. Given the British government's laissez-faire attitude in the nineteenth century towards the welfare of most of the population, and the extent of poverty that consequently persisted, in spite of the enormous wealth generated by industrialisation, this seems a totally implausible claim to make.

Prochaska was not alone in regarding Paine as capable of appreciating monarchy. Mark Philp, a historian of political thought, reached a similar conclusion in a collection of essays focused on the period 1789-1815 and entitled *Reforming Ideas in Britain*. He regards Paine's commitment to republicanism as evolving over several years. Initially, Paine is seen as moved by political beliefs developed in reaction against Stuart despotism and associated with the temporary abolition of the House of Lords and the monarchy in 1649, the establishment of the Commonwealth in the early 1650s, and the achievements of the Glorious Revolution of 1688-9. The effect of these beliefs was to generate the view that a mixed government, a combination of monarchy, nobility and commons, was, in Philp's words, 'not just a form of, but the best form of, republican government'. This, according to Philp, allowed Paine and Burke to agree in the 1780s on what constituted the most satisfactory system of government, so much so that they could breakfast together and go about as friends.[6]

Thus, on the eve of the French Revolution, Philp seems to think, Paine regarded republicanism as some form of representative government but not one entirely stripped of monarchy and nobility.[7] Offering apparent support for this view was a report Paine made to George Washington in March 1790, on a speech recently given by Louis XVI, suggesting, probably with a hint of sarcasm, that the French king 'prides himself on being head of the revolution'.[8] Later in the same year Paine appeared to show further sympathy for this monarch, again with a suggestion of irony, by declaring in *Rights of Man* that Louis XVI was very different from the usual run of kings in his willingness to promote the revolution by not using his royal veto to oppose the revolutionary changes of August 1789.[9] Moved by the compliancy of Louis XVI, and the prospect it opened for a peaceful disposal of the old regime, it would seem that, for about a year, Paine was prepared, in spite of his republican principles and strictly for a pragmatic purpose, to tolerate Louis' retention of the crown: that is, on condition that he accepted his constitutional position as servant of the nation rather than sovereign of the state.[10] Paine's actual attitude to monarchy was clarified in June 1791 after his trust in the king had been shattered for good by the latter's attempt to flee the realm.[11] The following month Paine presented himself unequivocally as 'the avowed, open and intrepid enemy of what is called monarchy'; and, bearing in mind 'the exactions, the wars and the massacres with which monarchy has crushed mankind', he declared his resolve, as a 'good republican' , to wage war against 'all the hell of monarchy'.[12]

Philp's account of Paine's progress as a political thinker overlooks the fact that the republican philosophy made explicit in *Rights of Man* (1791-2) had been clearly outlined by 1776 in the pages of his *Common Sense*, an anonymous pamphlet hastily written and rushed into print to aid the American colonies in their revolt against the British government but, nonetheless, a brilliantly written tour de force against kingship. Its title was originally the Quakerish-sounding 'Plain Truth' but altered to the unQuakerish 'Common Sense' on the suggestion of a Philadelphian friend, Benjamin Rush. Since in the work there was very little reference to 'common sense', the title under which it was published was a misnomer, its content difficult to connect with the tradition of argument identified by Sophia Rosenfeld in her book *Common Sense, a Political History* (2011).Paine's aim in composing *Common Sense* was clarified in his *American Crisis Paper* of December 1776 when he promised to 'bring reason to your ears and, in language as plain as ABC, [to] hold up truth to your eyes'. In this respect 'Plain Truth' would appear to be the more apposite title.[13] Rather than to man's common sense, justification for the views held is attributed to nature and to reason.[14]

The purpose of *Common Sense* was to persuade the American colonists to abandon all reconciliation with British rule and to establish an independent and completely representative system of government. Royal rule, as currently found in Britain (and therefore in the thirteen colonies), was scathingly described as 'the remains of monarchical tyranny' and the peerage, as 'the remains of aristocratical tyranny'.[15] And for the following reason: since both were hereditary, they were independent of the rest of the nation and therefore 'in a constitutional sense...contribute nothing towards the freedom of state'. Paine claimed to have written *Common Sense* not only to support American independence but also because he had come to realise that, rather than a necessity, 'monarchy and aristocracy were frauds and impositions on mankind'.[16] In addition, *Common Sense* rejected as 'farcical' the mixed system, with its three components (i.e., crown, peers and commons) 'reciprocally checking each other'.[17] Having cited Sir William Meredith's designation of the British political system as 'a republic', Paine then repudiated it as 'unworthy of the name' since the Crown, thanks to the corrupting power of its position and patronage, had 'effectively swallowed up the power of the House of Commons', thus denying the latter any chance of exercising properly its representative function. As a result, he claimed, the British government had been rendered 'nearly as monarchical' as the royal absolutisms found in France and Spain. Paine's damning verdict was as follows: 'when the republican virtue fails', the result of the Crown taking possession of the representative element, 'slavery ensues' and so does a proclivity to war.[18]

Common Sense mapped out a new constitution for the former American colonies. By means of it, Paine defined precisely the sort of republic he favoured at that time. It would be, exclusively, a representative system, with each of the thirteen colonies having its own elected assembly, all of them united by an elected Congress and an elected President. Further unity would be provided by 'a Continental Conference' whose task was to frame a 'Continental Charter'.[19] But 'where is the King of America' in this new scheme of things, Paine abruptly asked his reader, offering this answer: he comes in two forms, the one reigning in Heaven (i.e. God); the other ruling on earth, not as a person but in the law. For Paine, the tables had to be turned. Instead of the king being the law, 'the law is king'. In *Rights of Man* the same point is made, less wittily but more clearly: in place of 'monarchical sovereignty', there should be 'the sovereignty of the nation'.[20] Generalising on the point, he added: 'in free countries...there ought to be no other'.[21] To ensure that this was so, he reasoned, in America's case 'the articles of government should be formed first' and a government then established in keeping with them.[22] This procedure, he noted, would be in sharp contrast to what had happened in England where, in 1066, a foreign ruler had simply annexed the country by an act of military conquest, and had then stamped his law upon it. In this manner, Paine was proposing that the English constitution was not of Anglo-Saxon provenance but simply founded by the Norman Conquest and then subjected to subsequent modifications.[23] In doing so, he was distinguishing himself from the strand of representational reform, exemplified by John Cartwright, that justified the adoption of universal suffrage in terms of an ancient constitution reaching back to Alfred the Great.

Universal suffrage was not specifically proposed for the new American state, but *Common Sense*, nonetheless, did call for a 'large and equal form of representation'.[24] To emphasise its importance, Paine claimed 'there is no political matter which more deserves our attention'. What he proposed for America in 1776, therefore, was a system of representational (rather than direct) democracy and a total elimination of the practice of hereditary rule, a prominent and typical feature of governments, whether monarchies or republics, since ancient times. *Common Sense* was intimately connected with the American Revolution, but by 1791 Paine had made it clear that the type of government it recommended for the New World was also applicable to the old. In *Rights of Man* part I he designated the time as 'an age of revolutions, in which everything may be looked for', predicting: 'hereditary governments are verging to their decline and that revolutions, on the broad basis of national sovereignty and government by representation, are making their way in Europe'.[25] *Rights of Man* part II clarified his meaning: 'I do not believe that monarchy and aristocracy will continue seven years longer in any of the enlightened countries in Europe', where revolution 'may be considered as the order of the day'.[26] Not only did Paine condemn the mixed system prevailing in Britain as ripe for rejection, but he also issued a clarion call for the republican polity, newly fashioned in America, to be adopted by the whole of the western world.[27] Government founded, he wrote, on 'a moral theory, a system of universal peace, on the indefeasible hereditary rights of man is now revolving from west to east by a stronger impulse than the government of the sword revolving from east to west'.[28] The dedication to Washington of the first part of *Rights of Man* underlined the same sentiment in praying that 'the rights of man may become as universal of society as your benevolence can wish' and that 'you may enjoy the happiness of seeing the New World regenerate the Old'. In this respect, the republican government, as advocated by his *Rights of Man* in 1791-2, a system of representation with no role for hereditary authority, had been first proposed fifteen years earlier in *Common Sense*.[29]

b | Origins

The origin of Paine's belief in this type of republic remains somewhat of a mystery, and necessarily speculative, on account of the scarcity of surviving evidence, although his father's Quakerism must have played its part, especially in causing Paine to prefer a republic to a monarchy because he thought it more inclined to preserve peace and develop trade.[30] Likewise, his Quaker upbringing must have influenced his political outlook by causing him to disparage the Classical World and to reject as model republics the examples associated with Ancient Greece and Rome. Thus, in 1778 he told the American people that 'Greece and Rome are frequently held up as objects of excellence and imitation. Mankind have lived to very little purpose if...they must go two or three thousand years back for lessons and examples. We do great injustice to ourselves by placing them in such a superior line'.[31] In omitting to justify his political beliefs by making reference to the Roman Republic, he set himself apart from a tradition of republican thought that, inspired by Machiavelli's discourses on Livy's history of Ancient Rome, found expression, following the revolution of 1649, in the works of James Harrington, Algernon Sidney and Henry Neville.[32] On the other hand, Paine did make several references to Athenian democracy. However, this was for the purpose of dismissing it as a usable model. While showing some appreciation for the Athenian republic, he characterised it as a system of direct, rather than representational, democracy, with the citizens participating personally in government rather than through the medium of elected representation. Direct democracy, he thought, might well be suited to a very small state, but not to one of any size; and therefore, was not to be recommended. To avoid confusion, he shied away from using the term 'democracy', reserving it for the Athenian system.[33] For the type of democracy that he preferred and made the bedrock of his chosen polity – one that operated entirely through election – he employed the term 'representative system'.[34]

Paine's Quaker upbringing made it easier for him to turn against the idea of being 'a subject', and therefore against kingship, as well as against the concept of 'degree', and therefore against nobility and priesthood. Another childhood development, the result of a Quaker-induced reaction against pomp, panoplied self-indulgence and cruelty, was to acquire 'an aversion from monarchy' for being 'too debasing to the dignity of man'.[35] Regarding the Bible as a historical record rather than the word of God must have come easily to him because of his Quaker background; as did the concept of 'original equality'; and as did a disbelief in original sin.[36] Finally, some reactive connection may have existed for Paine between the recently introduced (in 1737, the year of his birth) Quaker belief in membership by birthright to the Society of Friends – thus rendering him automatically a Quaker simply by virtue of being his father's son – and his belief in the injustice of hereditary rule, the central pillar of his political philosophy. For him birthright had conferred no privilege, only attachment to a religion incapable of appreciating the joy of nature and which he sought to escape by becoming a Deist; whereas for monarchs and nobles, birthright conferred inevitable privilege. But the outcome of both would suggest that birthright was an unjustifiable bond that deserved abolition.[37]

In *Common Sense* he cited the closing paragraph of the Quaker Robert Barclay's address to Charles II which required the king to obey the light of Christ within himself. Paine added it to an appendix that called upon the Pennsylvanian Quakers to terminate their loyalism and censure George III.[38] Barclay's *Apology for the True Christian Divinity* (1678) was as prominent in Quaker literature as Penn's *No Cross, No Crown* or George Fox's *Journal*. Its systematic thoroughness left no stone unturned and no question unanswered.[39] Essentially, it studied Quakerism from within, laying down rules for the Friends to follow rather than apply to the rest of society. But, when compared with Protestantism or Catholicism, it set out a challenging range of radicalism, proposing that the Bible was not the word of God and spiritual truth was imparted instead by 'immediate revelation'; that the doctrine of original sin, as presented in the Bible, had undergone adulteration to make it perpetual whereas, originally, it and the guilt attached was confined to Adam; that a clerical order was otiose since originally there was no distinction between laity and clergy; that the practices of worship used by the orthodox Christian churches – such as the recitation of prayers, the congregational singing of hymns, the clerical delivery of sermons, the ministration of the sacraments and the taking of vows – were all dispensable.[40] Moreover, in civil society, Barclay proposed that formal practices respectful of degree and wealth were open to denial, as were the formal customs in recognition of social superiority: such as doffing the hat, bowing the head and bending the knee. Monarchy and nobility were tolerated but regarded as superfluous.[41] A connection between Barclay's work and Paine's thinking in *Common Sense*, *Rights of Man* and *The Age of Reason* is palpable. Likewise, the dismissal of something as 'absurd' was common to Barclay as well as to Paine. If not encountered through his father, Paine must surely have come across Barclay's work in Philadelphia, capital of the Quaker colony of Pennsylvania, to which he emigrated in the mid-1770s.[42] On the other hand, Paine was no pacifist, nor was he, in the Quaker manner, unwilling to meddle in politics. However, he was close enough to the Quakers to request to be buried in a Friends grave yard, a request denied.[43]

Paine confessed to the personal and family origins of his political beliefs in a passage of remarkable intellectual autobiography. It is to be found in his *The Age of Reason* part I (1794). There he made the point that he had no interest in everyday politics which he characterised as 'jockeyship': that is, an unprincipled race for power. His motives for political engagement related rather to the need to discover for himself the most satisfactory system of government, especially one 'that accorded with the moral and philosophical principles in which I had been educated'. Awakened by 'the affairs of America', and moved by 'these motives…I published…*Common Sense*'.[44] But the process of discovery that produced *Common Sense* was also one of 'immediate revelation'. Paine confessed as much in *Common Sense* itself when he declares that, until April 1775, he had strongly supported the idea of reconciliation with Britain and, as a Quaker, was against taking up the musket to settle the matter. However, 'the Massacre at Lexington', as Paine termed it, occurred on 19 April, when, watched by a large crowd, a group of American militiamen, clad in leather-skins and broad-brimmed hats, came face to face with a line of red-coats on Lexington Green, whereupon the latter opened fire, killing eight and wounding ten of the militiamen. Its effect upon Paine was to bring about a sudden and profound conversion, instilling in him the belief that freedom from colonial rule was the only answer coupled with the conviction that, as George III was evidently not 'father of the people' but a 'hardened sullen-tempered pharaoh', the new government should dispense with kingship altogether.[45] Vouching for this conversion was not only Paine but also his friend Benjamin Rush.[46] Nonetheless, even at this late stage, Paine's republicanism, as typified by an objection to the principle of hereditary succession, had still some way to go before achieving completion since, in May 1775, he was able to publish an article condemning titles which overlooked to mention the absurdity of inherited honours.[47]

Of late, a speculative case has been made that Paine's beliefs owed something to his mother's Anglican side of the family, notably the fact that her father served as Town Clerk of Thetford Corporation and that, thanks to this connection, Paine as a boy was able to familiarise himself with the charters of the town and consequently to realise the importance of having the rights and duties of its inhabitants down in writing. This is seen as explaining his attachment in later life to the necessity of having a national constitution in writing, therefore rendering him fit to be called 'the Charter Man'.[48] The problem with this purely hypothetical notion is not only the lack of supportive evidence but also Paine's stated opposition to town charters for being sources of injustice, inequality and exclusiveness.[49] Since he held the same dismissive view of other documents revered as sacred constitutional texts, namely, Magna Carta and the Declaration of Rights of 1689, it would be more appropriate to call him 'the Anti-Charter Man'. For him a nation's constitution needed to be all-inclusive, founded on principle rather than precedent, and sanctioned by the authority of the people.[50] To put such a constitution in writing, and thus to give it a formal existence, was a natural corollary of its rejection of precedent, its reliance upon reason and Paine's conviction that the argument in favour of an unwritten constitution, as conventionally made by Burke and his contemporaries, was backward and absurd in comparison with the written constitutions associated with revolutionary America and revolutionary France. 'Government by precedent, without any regard to the principles of the precedent, is one of the vilest systems that can be set': one, in fact, that allows it to assume 'what power it pleases', Paine declared. The British government therefore was in 'want of a constitution' rather than functioning within the restraining limits of one. For him, then, the lack of a written constitution licensed tyranny rather than liberty.[51]

The influence of his mother's side of the family upon his intellectual development more likely stemmed from her Anglican religion, in which he was baptised and confirmed, and the part played by her sister, Paine's maiden aunt, Mistress Cocke. She helped to arrange that her nephew receive confirmation from the Bishop of Norwich. She also paid the school fees when he attended Thetford Grammar School. In all likelihood, she was the person who read to him a sermon about original sin, a momentous occasion occurring at the age of seven or eight. Afterwards, as he stood on the steps leading to the garden (this was recalled fifty years later), he objected to the idea that redemption should be intimately connected with the willingness of God to permit the execution of his own son.[52] Enabling him to make this objection were the differences evident between the Anglican and Quaker view of original sin.

Shaping his life was also a reaction against parental control: signified by his rejection of the stay-making trade, to which he had been apprenticed under his father, the insult he offered Quakerism by serving on a man-of-war in the English Channel, and his repudiation of the Christian religion into which he had been inducted by his mother and aunt. Shaping his thoughts was a theological clash between Anglicanism and Quakerism. This stemmed from the mixed religion of his family background, a conflict that opened the way to his substitution of 'original equality' for original sin.

Two traditions of republican thought prevailed at the time: one drawn from Ancient Greece and Rome; the other, from the struggle against Stuart despotism and Hanoverian oligarchy. While taking a little from both, Paine adhered to neither. In a manner redolent of Rousseau, he claimed that, in writing *Common Sense*, 'I followed exactly what my heart dictated. I neither read books, nor studied other people's opinions...I thought for myself'.[53] This cannot be true. As well as newspapers, he did read books, if not all that many; and, while he inclined to keep aloof from political parties, he did join intellectual circles, clubs and societies and, by doing so, subjected his thinking to a process of osmosis, his mind assimilating the ideas that such gatherings generated.

c | The Making of *Common Sense*

Paine's intellectual gregariousness first became evident during several short stays he spent in London prior to his leaving for America in 1774. These visits to the capital raise the question of whether the contacts he made there contributed significantly to the content of *Common Sense*. His first stay occurred in 1757-8 when he followed a course of full-time study over several months financed by the money earned from his employment on board a privateer operating against French shipping in the English Channel. 'The natural bent of my mind was to science', he admitted. He attended lectures on astronomy given by Benjamin Martin and James Ferguson, fans of Joseph Priestley.[54] His second stay was in 1766-8, when he again met up with Ferguson who introduced him to Benjamin Franklin. On this visit he underwent, it would seem, a process of political radicalisation as well as continuing with his scientific studies. In this time he taught English at an academy run by a man of Huguenot descent, Daniel Noble, who had been educated by Caleb Rotheram, a friend of Joseph Priestley. The latter in 1768 published *An Essay on the First Principles of Government* which advocated a system of egalitarian republicanism as ideally the best, if not the most practical, form of government.[55] Noble owned a library stocked with Dissenting and libertarian books to which Paine must have had access.[56] It may well have included not only Priestley's essay but also Edmund Burke's *Vindication of Natural Society*, a short tract written as a parody on the work of Lord Bolingbroke and published anonymously in the mid-1750s to achieve a third edition in 1766. It was subtitled *A View of the Miseries and Evils Arising to*

Mankind from Every Species of Artificial Society. By 'artificial society' it meant, in effect, every form of government known to man. Monarchy, aristocracy and democracy came in for severe criticism, as did the normally favoured mixed system of government. All were presented as intrinsically flawed, its condemnation of monarchy, aristocracy and the mixed system chiming with what Paine came to advocate. There is no certainty that Paine read it, but, if he had done so, it would mean that, whereas *Rights of Man* was written in reaction against Burke's *Reflections on the French Revolution*, his *Common Sense* was composed in support of Burke's tongue-in-cheek *Vindication*.[57] The greater likelihood, however, is that Paine acquired what Burke had proposed from reading a similar parody composed by Jonathan Swift. It was to be found in the fourth voyage made by Lemuel Gulliver: to an island with a society ruled by 'a government of reason' which, minimalist in character, relied upon the philosophical reasonableness of its equine inhabitants and which probably also came to be reflected in Paine's work on religion, *The Age of Reason* (1794) and in his own conceit as 'a man of reason'.[58] Paine admitted to being influenced by Swift, but this appeared to be through reading another of his works which regarded monarchy as totally unnecessary because of its extortionate cost.[59] Thus in *Rights of Man* part II he declared that, according to Swift, 'Government is a plain thing and fitted to the capacity of many heads.' Not calling for extraordinary skill, it therefore 'cannot merit very extraordinary recompense', whereas the outcome of monarchy was gross government spending and extensive corruption.[60] Swift was cited by William Godwin as having first turned him against monarchy by convincing him that it was 'a species of government unavoidably corrupt'.[61] The implication of Godwin's and Paine's debt to Swift, was that the best form of government had to be minimal and cheap, a requirement that ruled out monarchy. Paine first proposed this point in *Common Sense* where the complexity of the British system is deplored as costly and detrimental to freedom and internal security.[62]

Paine's third and final stay in London, prior to leaving for America, occurred in 1772-3 when, representing the officers of the excise, one of whom he had become, he lobbied politicians for a change in the law to enable the officers to be better paid and thus less prone to corruption.[63] Quite possibly during this stay he met the radical politician, John Horne Tooke from whom, Paine claimed years' later, he learned about John Locke's famous *Two Treatises of Government*.[64]

Between his second and third stays in London (i.e. from 1768 to 1774), Paine resided in the Sussex town of Lewes. During this period his political thinking was influenced by local politics: a struggle between the Society of Twelve (of whom he was a member) – a once banned and recently revived radical body of supporters of 'the Good Old Cause' who celebrated the execution of Charles I and the expulsion of James II – and the town's Court Leet, a loyalist assembly under the suzerainty of the Pelham-Holles family, Lords of the Manor of Lewes. Helping to shape and sharpen his political beliefs was his membership of the town's Headstrong Club, and his impressive performances in its political debates, as well as his radically-inclined friendships with Henry Verral, Samuel Ollive and William Lee, the proprietor of the *Sussex Weekly Advertiser*, all of them inhabitants of Lewes.[65]

Although Paine arrived in America at the end of 1774 on a stretcher, unable to walk and racked with typhoid fever, a quick recovery of his health allowed him to make use of certain facilities, situated in the city of Philadelphia, for improving his education, notably its public library and the bookshop run by Robert Aitken whose *Philadelphia Magazine* Paine edited and, in a few months, had turned into a spectacular success. He also enjoyed the company of men philosophically engaged in seeking an alternative to colonial rule. By browsing in the library and shop, and by entering the circle of a group of radical thinkers resident in the city, the political philosophy underpinning *Common Sense* was formed.[66] The circle included the physician Thomas Young who had taken up residence in Philadelphia shortly before Paine. He was already a committed enemy of monarchy, aristocracy and the church, thanks to ideas drawn from Baruch de Spinoza, notably the latter's advocacy of egalitarian republicanism as most in accord with the natural rights of man.[67] Another member of the group was Benjamin Rush, the man who persuaded Paine to replace the title of 'Plain Truth' for that of 'Common Sense'. In the late 1760s Rush, already a republican according to Caroline Robbins, had spent time in Europe conversing with philosophers and *philosophes*.[68] Then there was Benjamin Franklin whom Paine had first encountered in London, in 1768 and again in 1774, and who had played a major part in encouraging him to go to America. Indicative of their closeness, Franklin could refer to Paine as his 'adopted political son'.[69] In their company Paine became familiar with works and concerns relevant to the current issue of American independence. It was Franklin whom he cited in October 1792, when addressing the French Convention on the necessity to abolish monarchy, by stating that Franklin had claimed 'royalism', to be 'a crime as bad as poisoning', a sentiment reflected in *Common Sense* where the English constitution was presented as 'sickly' because 'monarchy hath poisoned the republic'(by which he meant that the Crown had taken control of the House of Commons).[70] Another indication of Franklin's influence upon Paine was his dismissal of the inherited legislative powers of the peerage as equal in absurdity to the idea of having hereditary professors of mathematics, an analogy used by Paine in his *Rights of Man*.[71]

Unless Paine had already come across them when living in London or Lewes, the works introduced to him at this time included, in all probability, Franklin's 'Poor Richard' writings, his 'Causes of the American Discontents before 1768' (*London Chronicle* for 1768 and 1774), plus other journalistic pieces that Franklin had published in the *Philadelphia Public Advertiser* for 1773, notably 'An Edict by the King of Prussia' and 'Rules by which a Great Empire May be Reduced to a Small One'. In all likelihood, Paine's preparatory reading on the eve of composing *Common Sense* (1776) also included Major John Cartwright's *American Independence: the Glory and Interest of Great Britain* (1774) and, as already suggested, Joseph Priestley's *An Essay on the First Principles of Government* (1768), the title of which was later reflected in Paine's *Dissertation on First Principles of Government* (1795).[72] Besides sharing Paine's preference for egalitarian republicanism and his reservations about hereditary rule, Priestley's essay, nonetheless, departed from Paine in proposing that kings and peers had political value as 'standing deputies' of the people – as opposed to the 'temporary deputies' represented by members of the House of Commons. Priestley therefore was not prepared to advocate their abolition.[73] Moreover, Paine's preparatory reading for *Common Sense* may well have included Algernon Sidney's *Discourses Concerning Government*, a popular text among the rebel colonists, with Paine and Sidney alike in their use of the term 'nation', in stating objections to hereditary rule, in defining slavery as subjection to the tyranny of one man, and in believing in the popular origins of political authority and the people's right of revolt against tyranny. Paine, however, was less inclined to use the term 'democracy' and could not possibly have shared Sidney's appreciation of mixed monarchy as the best form of government.[74]

If not already encountered in the library of Daniel Noble, or from the discussions of the Headstrong Club in Lewes, the same Philadelphian associates may well have introduced Paine to John Milton's ideas on the right of the people to resist and overthrow a king, as found in his *Tenure of Kings and Magistrates* (1649) and his *Defence of the People of England* (first published in Latin in 1651 and in English 1692). The role of both works was to justify the execution of

Charles I: an idea which clashed with Paine's disapproval of tyrannicide. Paine mentioned Milton but once in *Common Sense* and never again in his writings. Moreover, the citation did not directly relate to republicanism. It read: 'As Milton wisely expresses, 'never can true reconcilement grow where wounds of deadly hate hath pierced so deep'.[75] The quotation comes from his long poem *Paradise Lost* and forms part of Satan's exhortation to his followers to continue their resistance to God. But also in *Common Sense* is a separate and significant section that, on Paine's admission, is indebted to the poet. Entitled 'Of Monarchy and Hereditary Succession', it follows closely ch. 2 of Milton's *Defence of the People of England*. Both make the point at some length that, according to the Old Testament and its account of the relationship between the Jews and God, there is no such thing as the divine right of monarchy, only divine right republicanism. Paine discussed the biblical connection made in *Common Sense* with John Adams who mocked him for placing so much reliance on the Old Testament. In response Paine laughingly said that he did not believe in the Old Testament but had 'taken his ideas in part from Milton'. This suggests that Paine used Milton as a ploy to appeal to the biblical fundamentalism of the American colonists, in the bid to make *Common Sense* more acceptable to them.[76] And the tone of *Common Sense*, with its folksiness and preference for the practical and the popular, has to be seen as determined by the need to establish with them a common ground. At the same time, *Common Sense* must have been a response not only to the peculiar bottom-up and grassroots vigour of American Christianity but also to the special demands of American politics generated before 1774 by the years of resistance to British rule, and evident in a process of politicisation that, coming from below, had conflicted with the deferential, top-down patterns of political behaviour contracted from the old world. In this respect, *Common Sense* may have been a response to impressions picked up from the American press which, in the early 1770s, was capable of purveying the idea that a republic free of hereditary rule was the natural solution to the political problems raised by the question of independence.[77]

From the same Philadelphian circle, if not the groups he had joined earlier in London or Lewes, Paine acquired some knowledge of other anti-monarchical works that, like Milton's, had been provoked by the religious discord of the late sixteenth and early seventeenth centuries. Two deserve attention. Both were discussed by A. Owen Aldridge in his *Thomas Paine's American Ideology* (1984), but, arguably, with too much scepticism. In 1579 George Buchanan published *De Jure Regni Apud Scotos*. A century later, in 1680, it appeared in English as *A Dialogue on the Law of Kingship among the Scots*. Recognition of

The Provenance of Paine's Political Ideology

the book's dangerousness led to its incineration by Oxford University in 1683. It was cited in Barclay's *Apology*, raising the possibility that this was the source by which Paine had come across it.[78] Essentially, it proposed that the political authority of the Crown was not conferred from above but came from below. Rather than God-given, it rested on the consent of the people and therefore was retractable when royalty behaved in a tyrannical manner. Paine revealed his knowledge of the work, and his appreciation of it. First, he made the point that, prior to John Locke, several writers had commented on the absurdity of hereditary succession, 'but there they stopped' (i.e. they had offered no remedy). In contrast, Buchanan had not only criticised the eleventh-century king, Malcolm II, for establishing in Scotland the principle of hereditary rule – thereby opening the prospect of weak government through allowing a minor or a fool to occupy the throne – but had also proposed a reversion to previous practice whereby 'the Scots used to make choice of that prince of the royal family that was best qualified to govern and protect his people'. This was clearly not disposing of hereditary monarchy, only the rule of primogeniture. Paine suggested that *Common Sense* had gone further than Buchanan or any previous writer in denouncing hereditary succession, not only for its disastrous political consequences but also for being intrinsically illegal, and therefore for having no right to exist.[79]

The other opponent of monarchy to be associated with Paine in the composition of *Common Sense* was the Commonwealth writer John Hall. He had published in 1650 a short tract entitled *The Grounds and Reasons of Monarchy Considered*.[80] Like Buchanan's work its focus was upon Scotland, the rest of the title reading *Exemplified Out of Scottish History*. Besides generalising on the drawbacks of monarchical government, it provides a succession chronology of the Scottish monarchs. Simply by showing how many had turned out to be bad governors, it offered a convincing indictment of hereditary rule. Yet Paine never admitted to reading the work; and the only direct evidence of his familiarity with it lies in an accusation made by Charles Inglis, an Anglican clergyman of New York. In a pamphlet attacking *Common Sense*, Inglis alleged that the section devoted to condemning hereditary succession was mostly taken from Hall.[81] Aldridge dismissed this claim on the grounds that, because of its extreme rarity, Hall's work would not have been available to Paine. But this overlooks the fact that Hall's tract was included in Toland's edition of the works of James Harrington and therefore published frequently in the eighteenth century.[82] Hall may well have been one of 'several writers' (along with Buchanan) whom Paine many years later claimed to have 'remarked on the absurdity of hereditary succession'.[83] Hall actually declared the arguments made in favour of hereditary monarchy to be not only in error but also absurd and illegal.[84] Another intimation that Paine had read Hall lies in the way both describe the subjects of hereditary monarchs as being akin to domestic animals and therefore the property of their owner. In *Rights of Man* part II Paine wrote; 'To inherit a government is to inherit the people, as if they were flocks and herds.' This reflected Hall's remark that it was better for the people to be 'disposed of by a number of persons...than to be numbered as the herd and inheritance of one'.[85]

Paine's republicanism, at the stage of composing *Common Sense*, clearly owed a debt to what his precursors had written on the subject. Nonetheless, his conception of it possessed a certain distinction. It was therefore more than a mere borrowing. Whereas previous critics of monarchy had been largely content to provide a safeguard against tyrannical rule by developing theories of justifiable resistance, or through disproving claims that monarchs ruled by divine or patriarchal right by presenting them as answerable to the people, Paine's approach was very different. For him, the required remedy went well beyond overthrowing, or killing, or imposing constitutional restraints upon, a despotic king. Instead, the institution had to be totally abolished.[86] That Paine continued to hold such a view was made vividly evident in the stand he took in the debate conducted on the dethronement and execution of Louis XVI in late 1792. While claiming that Louis' deposition was fully justified, Paine argued that 'we do not effect much if we merely dethrone an idol'. Instead 'we must also break to pieces the pedestal upon which it rested'. This was because 'it is the office of royalty rather than the holder of the office that is fatal in its consequences'. With monarchy abolished, he reasoned, nothing was to be gained by killing the ex-king.[87]

Paine joined a fourth intellectual circle, this time by invitation. It happened long after the publication of *Common Sense* and shortly before composing *Rights of Man*. Situated in Paris, the group comprised a political salon hosted by the marquis of Condorcet and attended by radical thinkers such as Jacques-Pierre Brissot, Étienne Clavière and Abbé Sieyès, as well as revolutionary leaders such as Lafayette and Mirabeau.[88] Its concern was to ensure that the recent abolition of the French nobility was properly implemented and to reconsider the present polity in France which remained a monarchy but with a king bereft of the right of sovereignty. Following the attempted flight of Louis XVI in mid-1791, the group, centred upon Condorcet and inspired by the recent publication of *Rights* *of Ma*n, turned into a *Société des Républicaines* that pressed for the abolition of the French Crown, eventually with success in late 1792.[89] The intellectual historian Richard Whatman claims that Paine's association with this group distinctively influenced Paine's republicanism, especially in persuading him to call for the abolition of nobility as well as of monarchy, thus enhancing the French, at the expense of the American, impact upon Paine's attitude towards the polity of the blood.[90] However, the republicanism evident in *Rights of Man* seems substantially similar to that of *Common Sense*, with the difference that in the former, and probably thanks to Paine's association with the Parisian circle, there is more emphasis on the evils of aristocracy. Otherwise, the message remained unchanged: whether held by kings or nobles, hereditary rank and its privileges had to be expunged in order to achieve a true republic.

Shaping Paine's political thought, with regard to writing *Common Sense*, was not only his entry to a succession of intellectual circles but also his encounter with certain key thinkers, the result of reading and assimilating their works. But did this include John Locke? Very late in life, Paine claimed, in rebutting a charge of plagiarism made by his enemy, James Cheetham: 'I never read Locke (he meant his *Two Treatises of Government*), nor ever had the work in my hand.' He then appeared to contradict himself by stating: 'It is a speculative, not a practical work, and the style of it is heavy and tedious, as all Locke's writings are.' At the same time, he admitted that his knowledge of Locke had derived from discussions with the radical politician, John Horne Tooke. Aldridge dated these discussions to the period between 1787 and 1791.[91] The problem with such dating is that Paine's acquaintance with Locke's works might well have preceded his writing of *Common Sense*: that is, prior to 1775. Suggesting that this was so lies in a marked resemblance between a passage in *Common Sense* about hereditary succession – arguing that it is undeniably illegitimate because, among freemen, a contract cannot be made binding in perpetuity – and a passage making the identical point towards the close of Locke's *Two Treatises*.[92] The same point was also made in *Rights of Man* part I (1791) and again in *Rights of Man* part II (1792), and yet again in *Dissertation on First Principles of Government* (1795).[93] What the point meant to Paine was made clear two years before his death when he stressed its importance in justifying the abolition of hereditary monarchy.[94] This same conclusion was not reached by Locke, whose keenness to refute Filmer's argument that men are born in patriarchal subjection to their prince, and 'therefore under the perpetual tie of subjection', allowed him unwittingly to undermine the principle of hereditary succession while continuing to stick by it.[95]

The only alternative to attaching this line of thought to Locke is attributing it to Joseph Priestley. For in his *An Essay on the First Principles of Government* (which Paine seems to have read prior to composing *Common Sense*) Priestley touched on the same contractual point: 'Though it may be supposed that a body of people may be bound by a voluntary resignation of all their interests to a single person, or to a few', Priestley wrote, 'it can never be supposed that the resignation is obligatory on their posterity because it is manifestly contrary to the good of the whole that it should be so'.[96] Priestley could have taken the idea from Locke, but if we accept that Paine had borrowed it directly from Priestley, the surviving evidence falls more satisfactorily into place, with Paine's account of his dealings with Locke rendered largely true.[97]

In spite of major differences, there were several ideas that Locke and Paine shared: notably the need for religious toleration, the importance attached to private property, the preference for principles rather than precedents, and the concept of 'original equality'. But rather than taken directly from Locke, these ideas may have been drawn from a pool of ideas in which political radicals at the time tended to fish. A much stronger case for the specific source of the radicalism evident in *Common Sense* could be made, arguably, by looking to Priestley rather than Locke. For instance, central to Paine's political beliefs was his faith in the direction provided by principles rather than by precedent. This was very much in accord with Locke, but it was also to be found in Priestley's *Essay* which bluntly claimed that, rather than justifying the continuation of long-established forms of government, precedent supplies 'the strongest argument for their abolition'. To achieve progressive reform, Priestley went on to say: 'The necessity of the thing, in the changing course of human affairs, obliges all governments to alter their general rules.' He then asked: 'And why may not a proportionably greater necessity plead as strongly for the alteration of the most general rules…affecting the most fundamental principles of any government, and the distribution of power among its several members?'[98]

Also aligning him with Paine, Priestley approved of a system of egalitarian republicanism which distinguished him sharply from Locke, who chose to ignore such a polity. Both Paine and Priestley agree that the best form of government was a representative democracy freed from the checks of monarchy or nobility, on the grounds that it would be most in keeping with the natural rights of man.[99] Both, moreover, accepted that the main object of a political system was to induce and preserve a state of general happiness. This proto-utilitarian principle was asserted at the start of *Common Sense* where society is presented as promoting man's happiness positively 'by uniting our affections', and government was regarded as promoting it negatively by 'restraining our vices'.[100] *Rights of Man* elaborated on the point: 'Whatever the form, a constitution of government...ought to have no other object than the general happiness.' Another passage showed how this might be brought about: the object of government being to provide for the 'good of all' by allowing 'everyman to pursue his occupation, and to enjoy the fruits of his labour and the produce of his property in peace and safety, and with the least possible expense'.[101] The general import of Paine's thinking was that representative republics were more likely to attain this goal because kings were more prone, for dynastic reasons, to engage in war, either to ward off usurpers to the throne or to attack other kings, and did so without taking into account the misery resulting from the pillage and carnage caused, or from the weight of taxation imposed, by their military endeavours.[102] Such sentiments reflect those of Priestley who argued that one should consider what form of government 'is most conducive to the happiness of mankind at present, and most favourable to the increase of this happiness in futurity' and to bear in mind that 'the good and happiness of [the majority] of the members of any state is the great standard' whereby the quality of a political system should be measured and that this consideration is 'the only true and proper foundation of all the governments subsisting in the world'.[103] It would seem that Paine, along with Bentham, shared the belief that political systems revealed their quality in the happiness of the majority rather than in the splendour of the few, a belief derived from Priestley.[104]

Paine failed to mention Priestley in any of his writings, but two authors were recognised in *Common Sense* as having influenced its content. One was Giacinto Dragonetti, a Neapolitan nobleman, whose *Treatise on Virtues and Rewards* was translated into English in 1769. Clearly impressed, Paine described him as 'that wise observer on governments'. He chose to quote from it not only in *Common Sense* but also in *A Letter Addressed to the Addressers on the Late Proclamation*, a work published sixteen years later in 1792.[105] On the latter occasion, Paine claimed that in Dragonetti's treatise was 'a paragraph (i.e., XII) worthy of being recorded in every country in the world'. In doing so, he revealed that he knew it was unusually divided into long paragraphs rather than chapters, and therefore showed that he had read it rather than simply lifting the passage from some other source.

Dragonetti held no grievance against hereditary monarchy and was even prepared to explain the happiness of the people in terms of the benevolence of the prince.[106] In contrast, as we have just seen, Paine saw happiness as residing in society and as threatened by government.[107] Dragonetti also held the view, which Paine could not possibly share, that in England 'the people wallow in wealth'.[108] Dragonetti was, moreover, keen to stress the importance of public duty as a source of virtue, something that Paine was inclined to overlook.[109] Nonetheless, they shared a dislike of hereditary nobility.[110] They were also inclined to regard the happiness of the citizenry as the goal of government and to think that the less spent on government the better since it lightened the burden of taxation. In *Common Sense* Paine commended Dragonetti for proposing that the politician should be engaged 'in fixing the true point of happiness and freedom'. He then quoted Dragonetti on the need to discover 'a mode of government that contained the greatest sum of individual happiness with the least national expense'.[111] Thus, Paine's concern with the issue of popular happiness, may have owed something not only to Priestley but also to Dragonetti, even though Paine saw it as impeded by, and Dragonetti saw it as promoted by, princely government. A remarkable similarity exists between *Common Sense* and *Virtues and Rewards* with regard to composition, suggesting, stylistically, that Paine was inspired by Dragonetti: since both works are brief and heavily reliant upon a succession of aphorisms to hammer the point home.

The other work explicitly acknowledged in *Common Sense* is James Burgh's *Political Disquisitions* (1774). It is not mentioned in the text but only in a footnote with the comment: 'Those who would fully understand of what great consequence a large and equal representation is to a state, should read Burgh's *Political Disquisitions*.' In the text it was attached to an incident in which Mr Cornwall, a member of the British government, had dismissed a petition from the Assembly of New York on the grounds that the latter was not sufficiently representative to be taken seriously. For Paine this reflected an admission of the British House of Commons' inadequacy to represent the nation; and, sarcastically, he offered thanks to Cornwall 'for his involuntary honesty'.[112] Burgh's work was a three-volume exposure of the shortcomings of the Commons, and a powerful call for electoral reform. Knowledge of it must have affected Paine's view of the limited and unfair extent of the British franchise, as well as serving as a step towards his realisation that, to establish a republic, it was not sufficient simply to get rid of hereditary succession.[113] Burgh's work was also critical of the Glorious Revolution on the grounds that 'it was so imperfectly established at that time', a point of view which chimed with Paine's hostility towards it while going counter to the sentiment of most radicals who felt that the political problems they faced sprang rather from what had followed the Glorious Revolution rather than from the revolution itself.[114] A connection between Burgh and Paine might also be found in Burgh's advocacy of 'a grand national association', echoed perhaps in Paine's 'national convention'. However, the purpose of Burgh's association was 'for restoring the constitution' whereas Paine's convention was meant to create a completely new constitution.[115] The one might have suggested the other but not with much likelihood.

Paine rarely referred in his writings to the works of other political thinkers. It is therefore quite possible that the gist of *Common Sense* was, as he claimed, thought out by himself.[116] In *The Age of Reason* (1794), Paine declared that thoughts came to him in two ways: those that follow a process of reflection and cogitation, and those 'that bolt into the mind of their own accord'. The first presumes prior assimilation, the second, a flash of lightening that comes from nowhere. As for the latter type of thought, which he described as 'voluntary visitors' – meaning spontaneous occurrences or 'immediate revelations' – he claimed to treat them with 'civility' (i.e. respect), 'taking care to examine... if they were worth entertaining'. As a result, 'it is from them [that] I have acquired almost all the knowledge that I have'.[117] Bearing this in mind, it is quite possible that many of Paine's ideas, including his appreciation of egalitarian republicanism in 1775, were eruptions of originality, resembling, perhaps, the biblical revelations (miracles or prophecies) that he was prone to ridicule, or eureka moments known to scientists, or, more likely, a switching on of 'the inner light' (i. e. immediate revelation) derived from his Quaker upbringing. If so, the role of his reading was not to implant new ideas in his mind but to provide confirmation of what he had already thought out.

d | Paine versus Whiggery

Whiggery in its various guises must have influenced Paine's republicanism, thanks to a culture of political thinking created not only by the liberty-defending ideas of Milton, Sidney, Locke, Molesworth, Hoadly, Burgh, Price, Priestley and Cartwright but also by the 'liberty' polemics of Gordon, Trenchard and Wilkes.[118] Nonetheless, as we have seen, at work in Paine was a counter-suggestibility, a paradoxical bent, that renders him in some respects original, as well as awkward to categorise.[119] For Whigs, the settlement enacted by the Bill of Rights of 1689, following the expulsion of James II in 1688, was, apart from the signing of Magna Carta, the most celebratory political event in British history; but for Paine it was to be deplored for conferring upon William and Mary and their heirs a perpetual right to occupy the British throne.[120]

In Paine's eyes, the hereditary succession that the Bill of Rights sanctioned was treating future generations of freemen as though they were slaves. Rather than the guardian of British liberty, the Glorious Revolution was presented as a form of enslavement.[121] Contrary to the natural rights of man, the legislation upon which it rested could only be regarded as unlawful. Through publicising this accusation in *Rights of Man*, Paine was successfully convicted of libelling the Glorious Revolution in December 1792. Moreover, he was against imposing limits on monarchy, as well as against expressing hostility to individual monarchs, since he much preferred its complete abolition.[122] Regicide was not a weapon in his arsenal; and purifying monarchy by rooting out corruption was pointless and impossible. Furthermore, because of his antipathy to nobility, he was unable to appreciate its part in resisting royal absolutism, regarding Magna Carta and the Bill of Rights ('Bill of Wrongs') as spurious documents designed to uphold the power of aristocracy against the interest of the people.[123] In Paine's works problems are seen as arising not from infringements of the constitution, as the Whigs alleged, but from the lack of a constitution. For this reason, his solution to the problem of a system intrinsically riddled with bribery, fraud and greed lay not in respecting precedent and tradition, or in restoring the balance between the hereditary and representational elements. Instead, it lay in founding a new constitution distinguished by the absence of succession.[124]

Such views separated him from British radicals who, in the early eighteenth century, operated in a 'Good Old Cause' or Commonwealth tradition founded by resistance to the political ambitions of Charles I and James II, and who, in the late eighteenth century, acted through the medium of the Society for Constitutional Information and the London Revolution Society, and, comprising a mixture of Whigs and Rational Dissenters, revered the Glorious Revolution and demonstrated their appreciation of the French Revolution by holding Bastille dinners to celebrate the end of French despotism.[125] Having much in common with Paine, so much so that they promoted the sale of Paine's *Rights of Man* and shared its repugnance for Burke's *Reflections on the French Revolution*, he and they, nonetheless, remained poles apart on the issue of hereditary rule, with Paine's clear commitment to its abolition providing a total contradiction to their abiding faith in mixed monarchy.[126] Paine had little

The Provenance of Paine's Political Ideology

to learn from them, and *Rights of Man* was written largely either independent of their direct influence or, at most, in reaction to their beliefs. Rather than ideas, it was a much needed popularity that he gained from their promotion of *Rights of Man*, plus the opportunity to recruit support for his republican cause from among their membership.

Setting Paine apart from the Whig tradition of republican sentiment was the emphasis he placed upon the evil of hereditary succession, whether it applied to monarchs or nobles. For him tyranny sprang not simply from royal or noble attempts to override liberty but from the way in which the privileges of monarchy or nobility could be acquired simply by right of inheritance. A benign king (Louis XVI briefly excepted) or a charitable noble was anathema to him: both were objectionable because hereditary right had left them unanswerable to the nation. The polity of the blood did not figure as a major objection in the Whig tradition, no matter what Locke had said about the inevitable way the hereditary principle placed an unconsenting bond on future generations. Typical of its attitude to civil government was Dr Richard Price, a leading member of the London Revolution Society, to whose defence Paine came in *Rights of Man* part I, after Edmund Burke had sought to condemn Price as a populist intent on overthrowing the old regime because he had interpreted the Glorious Revolution (1688-9) as bearing a strong resemblance to the French Revolution of 1789. Paine's point was that Burke had grossly misrepresented Price by assuming he had stated that in England, by virtue of the Glorious Revolution, the government was answerable to the people when, in reality, Price had meant the nation.[127] Paine had certainly read Price's work and had used it in composing *Rights of Man*.[128] But basic differences separated their points of view, notably on the subject of what required reform: with Price approving the revolutionary settlement of 1689, and with Paine rejecting as illegal its conservation of an hereditary monarchy and peerage.

Within the Whig tradition, however, objection was, on rare occasions, explicitly expressed against the principle of hereditary government. It was made in John Lilburne's *Regal Tyranny Discovered* (1647). As we have seen, it was also made in a tract by John Hall entitled 'The Grounds and Reasons of Monarchy Considered'. First published in 1650, this tract was reprinted several times in the eighteenth century, thanks to its inclusion in John Toland's edition of the works of James Harrington. In 1701 and 1706 Daniel Defoe cast telling aspersions on the hereditary principle in his best-selling poems *The Trueborn Englishman and Jure Divino*. Then, there was the critical essay 'Inquiry

The Polity of the Blood

into the Doctrine of Hereditary Right', written by either Thomas Gordon or John Trenchard and included in *Cato's Letters*, no. 132 (1723), which also went through several editions (e.g. 1724, 1734, 1748, 1755).[129] In addition, there were the reservations about hereditary kingship made by Algernon Sidney in ch. I, sections 18-20 of his *Discourses Concerning Government* (1698 and many subsequent editions). Furthermore, Locke, in his *Two Treatises*, book II, paras 90 and 107, made the point that hereditary monarchy could lead to royal absolutism. Richard Price agreed in 1777 when he claimed that royal or aristocratic tyranny sprang from polities in which 'the power of government... descend from father to son'. Joseph Priestley expressed similar objections.[130] But such criticism produced no commitment to the cause of abolition. As true for Locke's commitment to mixed monarchy was that of Trenchard and Sidney, with one of *Cato's Letters* declaring that Sidney was 'agreeable to our own constitution, which is the best republic in the world, with a prince at the head of it'.[131] The Whig tradition, as typified by Philp, tended to favour an elitist republicanism that allowed for inherited degree.[132] This was in sharp contrast to Paineite republicanism which was quintessentially egalitarian and based on the belief that 'men always continue free and equal in respect of the rights of man' and that 'civil distinction' should not be conferred in the blood but only by public service.[133]

Finally, Paine departed from the Whig tradition in his attitude towards political representation. Paine had no difficulty in accepting the importance of private property and in making its protection a prime duty of government. But he was faced at the time with the problem of a legislature totally controlled by the landed interest. For him this problem was to be solved partly by abolishing the privileges of peerage and partly by making the House of Commons representative of the nation. In this latter respect, he and Cartwright were at one; as they were, along with Burgh, in advocating the removal of the landed property qualification from MPs to render the Commons truly answerable to the needs of the people, the majority of whom were property-less.[134]

For Paine there was only one solution to the problems associated with hereditary monarchy: to replace it completely by a system of representation. Yet this solution did not admit elective monarchy, an antipathy to which he shared with Joseph Priestley.[135] He made this clear in discussions that followed the flight of Louis XVI in mid-1791, notably with Abbé Sieyès, and which found expression in *Rights of Man* part II. Sieyès recommended keeping the French monarchy but not the principle of hereditary succession. Paine found his arguments for doing so preposterous. If elective monarchy was superior to hereditary monarchy (and Poland appeared to prove so), it did not overcome the objection (which Sieyès shared) that both were intrinsically bad. That one was less bad than the other was no argument for retaining monarchy in one form or another, and even less so now there was available, as evident in America, a purely representative system in which sovereignty lay with the people.[136]

e | Paine's Debt to the Radical Enlightenment

Paine's antipathy to monarchy, then, stemmed not from objection to the tyranny specifically associated with royal absolutism, but from the very rank and rule of royalty itself. In this sense, he stood apart not only from the Whig tradition but also from one major strand of the European Enlightenment – represented by Voltaire and Montesquieu – that was prepared to support constitutional monarchy and the noble order. Nonetheless, Paine's radicalism was closely aligned with another strand. Currently termed the Radical Enlightenment, as opposed to the Moderate Enlightenment, it had begun a century earlier with Spinoza and then underwent a resurgence in the eighteenth century thanks to Spinoza's influence on English Deism and Dissent, through the writings of Charles Blount, John Toland, Anthony Collins and Joseph Priestley, and on the French salon of Baron d'Holbach, which included Denis Diderot.[137] The question remains, however: although Paine clearly belonged to the Radical Enlightenment, did he actually derive his ideas from that source? After all, restricting his direct access was the fact that much of it was written in languages about which Paine had little knowledge, notably Latin, Dutch and French.[138] Furthermore, at the time that Paine was formulating his political beliefs (i.e., in 1775-6), only a very small proportion of this literature was translated into English. For instance, four of the key texts, all in French and as yet untranslated – d'Holbach's *Essai sur les Prejuges* (1770), his *Système de la Nature* (1770), his *Système Sociale* (1773) and his *La Politique Naturelle* (1773) – would have been beyond his direct comprehension.[139] On the other hand, a work, originally composed by Nicolas Antoine Boulanger, but edited and prepared for publication by d'Holbach under the title *Recherches sur l'Origine du Despotisme Oriental* (1761), was translated into English in 1764 by none other than John Wilkes; so in time for Paine to study prior to composing *Common Sense*.[140] However, while using the term 'despotism' and applying it, like Boulanger, to Africa, Asia and Europe, Paine did not follow Boulanger in attributing it to theocracy, other than to condemn the priesthood for their part in upholding the old regime. Much more important for him as a source of despotism was hereditary monarchy which Boulanger supported as a beneficial system, so long as it operated constitutionally within the law, while condemning republicanism as a source of anarchy.[141] The two men, it would seem, had little in common.

A second work associated with the Radical Enlightenment and accessible to Paine through translation, was the *Histoire Philosophique et Politique des Établissemens et du commerce des Européens dans les Deux Indes* (1770), a massive study which, by 1780, having gone through three editions in a decade, comprised nineteen books in six volumes. Although published under the name of the Abbé Raynal, it was a collaborative and frequently revised venture, in which, rather like Diderot's *Encyclopédie*, members of the d'Holbach circle had clandestinely participated, with Diderot serving as the major contributor.[142] It expressed certain basic ideas characteristic of Paine's *Common Sense*, notably a call for the abolition of hereditary rule but not of hereditary property, a call for an equalisation of rights but not an equalisation of wealth, and a condemnation of international war, for which it held kings culpable, but not of civil wars bent on overthrowing monarchy.[143] In addition, it touched upon certain points redolent of Paine: such as the way hereditary rule turned the people into 'so many beasts', and how hereditary succession was both an absurd means of selecting rulers as well as a source of tyranny.[144] There was also an affinity between the two in deeming the republic a superior political system to monarchy and in assuming the English constitution originated not with the Anglo-Saxons but with the Norman Conquest.[145] Yet several profound differences distinguished *Common Sense* from Raynal's *Philosophical and Political History*. Like Boulanger, Raynal held in high esteem the system of mixed monarchy as practised in Britain. 'The mixed government of the English', Raynal claimed – by 'combining the advantages of [monarchy, aristocracy and democracy] which mutually observe, moderate, assist and check each other' forms 'an equilibrium from which liberty arises', therefore serving the national good by virtue of the principles upon which it is based. For Raynal, 'this constitution...ought to serve as a model to all people' and was likely to endure for a long time because it had 'originated as the work of reason and experience'. The same system had been condemned by Paine as a form of tyranny in both *Common Sense* and *Rights of Man*.[146] This differing attitude to the English constitution led to a differing regard for the Glorious Revolution, which Raynal regarded highly because it re-established a bulwark of liberty for the people by ruling out arbitrary taxation, and which Paine condemned as an instrument of tyranny because of its reaffirmation of the hereditary principle.[147] A further difference between Paine and Raynal lay in the former's belief in

The Provenance of Paine's Political Ideology

the original equality of man and the latter's substitution of this belief with one of natural inequality.[148] In view of these differences, it seems more likely that Paine's political philosophy, distinguished by its rejection of all types of monarchy, emerged in reaction to Raynal's work rather than in accordance with it.

But did Paine ever read the portions of Raynal (mostly contained in book XIX) that discussed systems of government in general terms? The first English translation of Raynal's *Histoire Philosophique et Historique* appeared in 1774, opening up the possibility that it influenced the composition of *Common Sense*.[149] But there is no evidence to suggest that Paine ever read it. What is certain is that he was able to borrow a copy of Raynal's *The Revolution of America* in late 1781, soon after its publication in an English translation.[150] This had been extracted from the full work: essentially, book XVIII. That Paine had read it was made clear in a letter from him to Raynal published in 1782, the purpose of which was to correct certain errors concerning the American Revolution. They centred on Raynal's conception of it as a revolt to restore lost rights, not a revolution bent on innovation. [151] In *Rights of Man* Paine credited Raynal as an inspirational writer 'in favour of liberty' but criticised him, on grounds of impracticability, for failing to reveal the means to achieve it.[152] At the same time, it included him in a list of authors whom Paine regarded as instrumental in undermining the ancien regime.[153] In Raynal's case, as with Rousseau, it was because of his 'animation'. All this renders it possible that Paine acquainted himself with book XIX (printed along with book XVIII in volume VI, the final volume of the work) prior to writing *Rights of Man* in 1791-2, but, given the earliest publication date of the first English translation (i.e. 1780), not before writing *Common Sense* in 1775.

A third 'Radical Enlightenment' influence upon *Rights of Man* was probably Comte de Mirabeau's *Considerations on the Order of Cincinnatus*, a pamphlet translated from the French by Sir Samuel Romilly and published in 1785 in both Philadelphia and London. Employing sentiments that Paine could easily share, it expressed fierce opposition to what appeared to be a plan to establish an order of hereditary nobility in the USA. In doing so, it condemned generally the principle of a noble order, arguing that nobility and democracy could not mix, since, by virtue of its hereditary nature, nobility was alien to the representative system and counter to the principle of equality.[154] A distinctive difference between Paine's *Common Sense* of 1776 and his *Rights of Man* of 1791-2 stemmed from extending the complaint against the hereditary principle to focus upon nobility as well as monarchy. This difference may have reflected upon Paine's familiarity with Mirabeau's work or the debate of which it was a part. It certainly reflected upon a major event in the very early stages of the French revolution, the abolition of the noble order in 1790 and the accompanying reasons given for carrying it out: an occurrence in which Mirabeau, as a leading member of the National Assembly, had a major part to play.[155]

Paine in 1792 declared that, at the outbreak of the American Revolution, he realised that 'monarchy and aristocracy (i.e. nobility) were frauds and impositions upon mankind', and 'on these principles I published the pamphlet *Common Sense*'.[156] But in *Common Sense* there is little about nobility: in fact, no more than a brief criticism of it in association with Paine's rejection of the claim that British liberty rested on a self-checking balance between crown, peerage and commons. This balance could not work, Paine reasoned, because 'by being hereditary, [the crown and the peerage] are independent of the people', rendering them the remains of 'two ancient tyrannies' and creating an imbalance that went totally against the purpose of a mixed government.[157] In contrast, *Rights of Man* part I waged an extensive onslaught on nobility, offering reasons for its abolition.[158] No longer was it criticised just for being an integral part of the English mixed system of government (spurned by Paine as 'an imperfect everything' held together by corruption), but was now condemned, in its own right, for being self-serving, useless, ignorant, greedy, a cause of poverty and absurd.[159] 'This is the general character of aristocracy', Paine claimed in the first part of *Rights of Man*,'or what are called Nobles or Nobility, or rather No-ability, in all countries'.[160] Inspiration for such remarks came from France which had recently abolished its noble order. Another possible source was his association with Benjamin Franklin.[161] *Rights of Man* part II continued the attack, especially by focusing on the House of Lords, predicting that the noble order, along with monarchy, would soon be abolished throughout much of Europe.[162]

Another likely source for Paine's political radicalism was, as already suggested, Spinoza's *Tractatus Theologico-politicus* (1670)[163]. First published in Latin, a French version had appeared in 1678 and English versions in 1689, 1720 and 1737. Spinoza's treatise stands as the key text for the Radical Enlightenment, generating republican and anti-christian beliefs in England and France.[164] Spinoza's direct connection with Paine is less obvious, although Paine certainly knew of him, regarded him as 'of great learning', and was even prepared to cite one of his works: a treatise published but once (in 1678) and only in French.

Entitled *Traitté des Ceremonies Superstitieuses des Juifs*, this work was used by Paine to cast doubt on Moses' authorship of the Pentateuch and also upon the Jewishness of Job. Unmentioned by Paine, and possibly overlooked by him, was the fact that this work was none other than a translation of Spinoza's key work *Tractatus Theologico-politicus*.

Paine's earliest reference to the work appeared in *The Age of Reason* part II, indicating that he had come across it just after the publication of *The Age of Reason* part I and therefore in 1794 or 1795. A second mention occurred in Paine's response to an apology for the Bible, published by the Bishop of Llandaff in 1796.[165] Paine's religious position, however, lay far apart from that of Spinoza and his followers. Though the two were equally dismissive of Christianity, the divinity of Scripture, and the need for a priesthood, they differed profoundly, in that Paine continued to believe in the soul, the afterlife and an external God, whereas Spinoza chose to regard the world as consisting of one substance and nothing but nature.[166] Totally rejecting the supernatural, Spinoza's system of belief was, at bottom, a materialistic one that depended on motion but not spiritual direction. In contrast, Paine and Spinoza's political ideals boiled down to much the same thing: for what was declared in Paine's *Common Sense* and *Rights of Man* (i.e., a system of egalitarian republicanism based upon natural right, with democratic representation determining the nature of government and its laws, with no place for either nobility or monarchy, and with a general happiness, promoted by the generation of trade as its goal) was set out in Spinozas's *Tractatus Theologico-politicus* and less obviously in his unfinished *Tractatus Politicus*.[167]

How did this replication come about? There is no evidence to show that Paine read either of these works prior to formulating his political philosophy, whether it be in *Common Sense* (1776) or in *Rights of Man* (1791-2). Yet a strong possibility exists for his making indirect contact with Spinoza's political philosophy exactly at the time of composing *Common Sense* (i.e. 1775). This was through discussions with Thomas Young, a disciple of Charles Blount who was the first translator of Spinoza's work into English, and also through the agency of Joseph Priestley, whose *An Essay on the First Principles of Government* (1768, 1771) strongly reflects Spinoza's 'On the foundations of the state, on the natural and civil right of each person, and on the authority of sovereign powers', published as chapter 16 of his *Tractatus Theologico-politicus*.[168] Priestley's *Essay* does so by proposing that the best of all political systems is a democratic republic since it approximates most closely to man's natural right of equality and the liberty associated with that right. As Priestley put it: 'where every member of the society enjoys an equal power of arriving at the supreme offices [and therefore of 'directing...the whole community'] there is a state of the most perfect political liberty' because it allows every man to retain 'the only right... of relieving himself from all oppression': that is, through his right of consent, 'the only true and proper foundation of all governments subsisting in the world'.[169] In making this claim Priestley echoed Spinoza who, in establishing 'the foundations of the state', awards priority to 'a democratic republic' because it seems to be 'the most natural' form of government in that it 'approaches most closely to the freedom nature bestows on every person'. Spinoza elaborated: in such a system 'no one transfers their natural rights to another' and consequently 'in this way all remain equal as they had been previously in the state of nature'.[170] Both Priestley and Spinoza agreed, then, that a democratic (i.e. egalitarian) republic is superior to any other polity because it more closely complied with the essential nature of man. In this respect, their political preference resonated with that of Paine and his desire to safeguard man's 'original equality' against the state's unnatural encroachment upon his liberty through the establishment of hierarchy and degree. The same could be said of the approach all three favoured: philosophical, not historical, with a reliance upon reason and a compliance with nature to found first principles, rather than to employ tradition and precedent to provide the principles upon which a polity should stand.[171] It is known that in 1775 Paine was deeply interested in Priestley as a chemist, an interest that extended back to the late 1750s when, resident in London, he attended lectures given on the natural sciences by two of Priestley's devotees, the astronomers Benjamin Martin and James Ferguson.[172] It is unlikely that Paine would have ignored Priestley's essay on government when composing *Common Sense* in 1775, given his long-term fascination with Priestley and his own particular concern with political theory at that time.[173] As a result, it is likely that he became attached to Spinoza's reverence for egalitarian republicanism, no matter the extent to which it contradicted a constitutional tradition established by history in which precedent was founded upon custom and law. Where Paine differed from Spinoza, and also from Priestley, was in his fierce desire to end the succession rights of kings and nobles. The priority he awarded this aim, as the best practical means of political reform, owed everything to himself.

Besides Spinoza and Priestley, Paine's programme of political reform reflected something of Jean-Jacques Rousseau, whose *Du Contrat Social* was translated into English in 1764 as *Social Compact*, and therefore became accessible to

Paine prior to composing *Common Sense*. Like Spinoza, Rousseau was raised in a republic, the former in the Netherlands, the latter in Switzerland. Neither republic, however, was acceptable to Paine since both featured a hereditary nobility, and therefore remained, even though free of monarchy, subjected to the principle of hereditary rule.[174] Paine made no mention of Rousseau in *Common Sense*, but there is, in its opening pages, a strong suggestion that by then he had read *Social Compact*. This appears in an idyllic description of an early form of government where every adult male in the community would meet as equals under the spreading branches of an ancient tree to determine its rules and regulations. Rousseau made the very same point towards the close of *Social Compact*. Certain similarities characterised the two visions, notably the image of a primitive society which, although without hierarchy or individual rulership, was far removed from the savagery predicted by Hobbes and well capable of functioning peacefully and efficiently as a direct democracy.[175] And both were 'promeneurs solitaires', noted for communing with nature and fashioning provocative thoughts on long solitary walks. In Paine's case, one such walk in early spring inspired him to compose the closing reflection in *Rights of Man* part II, in which he mused that, having plucked a twig and noticed that on it 'a single bud...had begun to swell', it would be irrational to suppose that 'this was the only bud in England' but more natural to conclude that the same was happening everywhere and that 'all will be in leaf in the summer, except those which are rotten'.[176]

On the other hand, there were basic differences between the two works. One was Paine's preference for representational democracy and his rejection of direct democracy for all states, irrespective of size. Another was Rousseau's tolerance of monarchy and aristocracy, if circumstances required. In *Rights of Man* Paine had linked Rousseau with Raynal, claiming to find in their writings 'a loveliness of sentiment in favour of liberty that excites respect and elevates the human faculties'. However, restricting the usefulness of both, he thought, was a lack of application: for 'having raised this animation, they do not direct its operations'. Consequently, they 'leave the mind in love with an object without describing the means of possessing it'.[177] For Paine, Rousseau's approach was an academic one in the sense that it pointed out weaknesses and strengths but proposed no actual reforms. It was as if he were simply bent on provoking debate. In contrast, Paine saw himself as man of action: intent, as he put in the subtitle of *Rights of Man* part II, upon 'Combining Principle and Practice'. For him the essential means of achieving reform was to persuade men that monarchy and nobility, on account of their hereditary character, were unnatural and unlawful.[178] On this issue *Common Sense* was emphatic, whereas Rousseau's *Social Compact* had next to nothing to say.

Following upon *Common Sense*, an explicit connection with Rousseau was made in an address Paine delivered to the French Convention in October 1792, when, celebrating its achievement in France, he associated republicanism with Rousseau's exposure of the defects of kings and nobles, in book three of his *Social Compact*.[179] Furthermore, tell-tale signs of an affinity between the two men lie in *Rights of Man* where reference is made, for the first time in Paine's works, to 'the general will of the nation'.[180] In the same year, it recurs in Paine's *Letter Addressed to the Addressers on the Late Proclamation*.[181] On each occasion, the phrase is used in connection with the idea of holding a national convention, partly to enable an expression of the general will on the matter of political reform, and partly in reaction to the idea of allowing expressions of political reform to be left to parliament which, rather than representing the nation, only represented vested interests, or to individual groups making protests through petitions to the government and, in response to the proclamation of 15 May 1792, through addresses in defence of the constitution. This notion of giving the whole nation a means of expression, rather relying exclusively on vested interests to do so, was very close to Rousseau's appreciation of the General Will as the best means of identifying 'the general good'.[182]

Also resonant of Rousseau were other remarks made in *Rights of Man* part II, notably that 'government is nothing more than a national association acting on the principles of society' and that, in producing a new government, first in Pennsylvania and then for the United States of America, there was 'no such thing as the idea of a compact between the people on the one side and the government on the other' (i.e. as Locke proposes). Rather 'the compact was that of the people with each other'.[183] This would indicate that, when compared with the Whig tradition, and, in all likelihood, under Rousseau's influence, Paine had acquired an unusual way of looking at the relationship between society and government.[184] But it needs to be added that this difference of viewpoint was already evident in the opening chapter of *Common Sense* and then became substantiated in chapters one and two of the second part of *Rights of Man*. In *Common Sense* society was presented as naturally 'a blessing' while government was reckoned 'but a necessary evil'. Society was seen as a source of happiness and basically cohesive, cooperative, self-sufficient and peaceful. Some form of government was needed only to secure 'freedom and property for all' and to offer protection from external attack.[185] However, driven by the greed of kings and nobles, government had become a predator whose fiscal exactions left society impoverished and disorderly; so much so that, as Paine colourfully put it, 'the palaces of kings are built on the ruins of the bowers of paradise'.[186] *Common Sense* had thus provided, as early as 1775, a distinctive take on the relationship between government and society: one that had departed from the Whig tradition with its tendency to see society as prone to anarchy, if left to its own devices, and therefore to require, as necessary correctives, two infringements of man's natural right of equality: i.e. a limited parliamentary franchise and a society stiffened by degree.

A second work of Rousseau's may well have influenced Paine: a short tract entitled *Jugement sur le Projet pour la Paix Perpetuelle de l'Abbé de Saint Pierre*. It first appeared in English in 1761 under the title *A Project for a Perpetual Peace*. Paine revealed, shortly after the publication of *Common Sense*, that he had read it.[187] Its proposals are reflected in two of Paine's works: first, in *Common Sense* where Paine thinks in terms of a congress as a means of uniting the thirteen American colonies in one independent but interdependent state; and second, in *Rights of Man* part II where an aspiration appears for a 'universal peace', so far ruled out by the natural bellicosity of monarchs but something a cooperation of republics might well achieve.[188] More than ideas could have been imparted to Paine from a reading of Rousseau. As he had with Dragonetti, Paine might well have fallen under the spell of Rousseau's style since the language of *Social Compact* and *Common Sense*, declamatory, provocative, counter-suggestive and passionately rhetorical, is remarkably alike.[189]

Nonetheless, one should not forget that running through Paine's work was an independent and paradoxical current. As we have seen, he did not seek justification in classical example or the interpretations placed by others on historical events or legal precedents. Essentially, he was a self-educated polemicist, who, coming from a humble background, had left school at the age of twelve, after being placed, on his father's orders – thanks to a Quaker repudiation of the Ancient World as a necessary component of education – in the class that received no instruction in Latin. For much of his life he had no knowledge of languages other than English. His interests were those of a mechanical engineer rather than a scholar. Nor did he seek to please, or to rely upon, royal or noble patrons, although he did have a number of aristocratic friends, such as Charles James Fox, Condorcet, Lafayette and Lord Edward Fitzgerald.[190] In this outsider manner, he may have acquired, by default, an originality that, arguably, makes a search for philosophical connections, or a rumination upon the derivative nature of his thoughts, of secondary importance.[191] In this respect, as already suggested, the role of reading was to confirm what he had already discovered. Arguably, of greater importance is to identify the very originality and offensiveness of his reform plans, and to explore their impact upon the public's reception of his political philosophy.

ƒ | The Consistency of Paine's Political Thinking

In an article entitled 'From liberalism to radicalism: Tom Paine's *Rights of Man*', and first published in 1989, Gary Kates provocatively proposed that Paine, having declared himself a republican in *Common Sense* (1776) switched to supporting monarchy in *Rights of Man* part I and then reverted to requiring its abolition in *Rights of Man* part II.[192] Others have followed suit in stressing the protean nature of Paine's basic beliefs. Thus, in a recent study entitled *Chartism, Commemoration and the Cult of the Radical Hero* (London, 2019), the historian Matthew Roberts attributes Paine's popular appeal to the fluidity and adaptability of his republicanism. This was evident, Roberts thought, in the ambiguity of Paine's position 'on the clear-cut issue of monarchy versus republic', and the fact that it could 'shift according to the context' and evolve in the course of time.[193] In connecting Paine's republicanism with the Chartist movement, Roberts cites a speech delivered in May 1839 by the Chartist leader Feargus O'Connor. In it O'Connor declared a preference for hereditary monarchy over an elected monarchy while professing, nonetheless, to be a republican 'in the real sense of the word'. Roberts comments that such a view 'is perfectly compatible with Paine'.[194] This, however, is tantamount to saying that Darwin was, to some extent, a creationist. What is striking about Paine's republicanism is its lack of ambivalence and its remarkable consistency. From his first commitment in print on the subject in 1776, to the more refined statements published in 1791-2, Paine believed that government should be founded on 'the indefeasible, hereditary rights of man', not on the succession rights of monarchs or nobles.[195] This he coupled with a fierce loathing of hereditary rule, whether it be in the form of monarchy or nobility.[196] Paine's objection covered the whole gamut of kingship. For him, to substitute constitutional monarchy for absolute monarchy, or even replace hereditary with elected monarchy, was totally ruled out. Moreover, his proposed reforms of parliament allowed no scope for hereditary membership. The polity of the blood therefore had to yield to a system of government completely determined by representation.

The Provenance of Paine's Political Ideology

Despite its single-minded hostility to hereditary succession, however, Paine's political philosophy was far from static. This allowed it to undergo certain significant changes as time went by. One concerned what he termed the 'representative system of government'. In *Common Sense* mention was made of the need for a 'large' franchise. Its context suggests that universal suffrage would not have been inappropriate for what he wanted, but it made no specific mention of the term. By then, as he admits in *Common Sense*, he had consulted Burgh's *Political Disquisitions*, a work which exposed the limitations of the British parliamentary system and suggested that the larger the electorate the better, and that, if parliamentary seats were more equally distributed in relation to the spread of the population, the system of representation would be much improved.[197] Paine pursued the franchise issue in association with the question of sovereignty, notably in his pamphlet *Dissertations on Government, the Affairs of the Bank and Paper Money* (1786). There, he declared that common to all governments was the principle of sovereign power. In despotic monarchies, he claimed, this is 'lodged in a single person', whereas, in republics modelled on the USA, it lies 'where nature placed it in the people'.[198] In the former, he proceeded, freedom is confined to the monarch while, in the latter, the people retain the sovereignty and enjoy the freedom that goes with it.[199] Central to his case was the presumption that in a republic people would exercise their sovereignty through the right to elect legislative representatives, along with the implication that, subject to the normal restrictions (excluding females, minors and the insane), the suffrage should extend to the whole indigenous population. In 1792 *Rights of Man* pursued the matter further by condemning the system of incorporated towns. It was a major source of injustice, he argued, partly because only a fraction of the inhabitants of corporations had voting rights and partly because in many large towns, such as Manchester, Birmingham and Sheffield, there was no parliamentary representation at all. As a result, the House of Commons was rendered almost as exclusive as the House of Lords. Having been brought up in Thetford which, thanks to its charter of incorporation, possessed two MPs but only thirty electors, and was, in practice, a borough in the pocket of the dukes of Grafton, and therefore hardly representative of the town, Paine's objection, then, sprang from personal experience as well as from the moral indignation aroused by his reading of Burgh. For him what was required was not only the abolition of monarchy and the Lords but also a thorough reform of the Commons, with a suffrage widened sufficiently to remedy the injustice present in the old representative system. The issue was: how wide did the suffrage need to be, bearing in mind that many parliamentary reformers were keen to exclude the unpropertied? Implying universal suffrage, *Rights of Man* part II stated: 'I presume that, though all the people of England pay taxes', a consequence of the government's reliance upon indirect taxation, 'not a hundredth part of them are electors'.[200] The imposition of excises and customs upon basic consumables, and therefore upon everyone, gave trenchant meaning to the slogan 'no taxation without representation'. That he had come to believe in universal suffrage was first made indisputably evident in his *Letter Addressed to the Addressers on the Late Proclamation* (1792), which recommended a system of one-man-one-vote as a natural corollary of his belief in the equality of the rights of man.[201] But not until 1795 did he provide an unequivocal confirmation of his belief in universal suffrage. That was expressed in his *Dissertation on First Principles of Government*: since 'the true and only true basis of representative government is equality of rights', it asserted, 'every man has a right to one vote, and no more, in the choice of representatives'.[202]

The second change to affect Paine's attitude towards republicanism concerned 'the public good'. Initially, he had expected the latter to be achieved by reducing the expensiveness of government through the abolition of monarchy and nobility, by introducing religious toleration, by rooting out political corruption, by making government answerable to the nation, by remedying the iniquities of the tax system. Such measures, he thought, would create a state of happiness and freedom for all to enjoy.[203] But by 1792, and towards the end of *Rights of Man* part II, the idea had surfaced of using a portion of the country's tax revenues to provide welfare for the poorer elements of society. It came of his being struck by the gross injustice of a system that gave so much of government funds to the rich – by means of the grant of pensions, stipends and dividends – and next to nothing to the poor. Observing that the poor (and this came from personal experience) were especially burdened by the cost of raising children and of caring for the elderly, he proposed giving them an annual allowance for every child under fourteen and an annual pension for men and women over fifty, plus one-off payments for births and marriages.[204] The idea underwent a further elaboration in his *Agrarian Justice* (1796) when a similar scheme was proposed, this time funded not out of general taxation but from a death duty imposed on landowners and, in order to denote that it was a right of man and not a charity dispensed to the poor,[205] applied to the whole of society.

What failed to emerge in Paine's conception of a genuine republic was the obligation of 'public duty', a typical requirement of citizenship in the history of republics and one usually fulfilled through the virtues of public

The Provenance of Paine's Political Ideology

service and patriotic spirit. This was something eventually impressed on British republicanism by the Italian patriot, Joseph Mazzini. In contrast, Paine's emphasis remained focused on the rights of citizenship, not the citizen's obligations to the state. According to Paine, man learns his duties automatically: that is, essentially by understanding his rights 'for, when the rights of man are equal, everyman must finally see the necessity of protecting the rights of others as the most effective security of his own'.[206] The distinctive absence of 'public duty' from Paine's ideal polity would suggest, yet again, that his concept of the 'real' republic owed more to his own untutored originality than to a weight of learning drawn from the scholarship and opinions of others. Essentially, its emphasis was upon procuring a political organisation that had no place for rule by birth. In this respect, he was proposing a radical departure from a universal tradition that had exclusively favoured the polity of the blood. By doing so, he was expressing a consistency of vision that dominated his conception of a republic from at least 1775 until his death in 1809.

Central to the maintenance of monarchy was (and still is), a theory of divine right. It rested on the belief, propagated by the Anglican priesthood and supposedly revealed in the Scriptures, that monarchy was a calling from God, and that reigning monarchs were actually appointed by the hand of God, exercised through the principle of hereditary succession. Doubts were expressed about the principle by leading philosophers, such as Hobbes, Locke and Hume, by Deists – a freethinking movement, to which Paine belonged from the mid-1770s, that was intent on exposing priestcraft and on dispensing with the worship, organisation and rituals of the Anglican church – and by Dissenting critics such as Daniel Defoe.[207] Further scepticism followed the deposition of the divinely appointed Stuart dynasty. Within the established church there even developed a denial of rule by divine right, led by Bishop Benjamin Hoadly's attack on 'the patriarchal scheme of government' (which sought to trace a royal descent from Adam).[208] In response to such dissent, the Church of England stuck grimly to a belief in the holiness appertaining to royalty by descent. And, thanks to the power and influence exercised by its bishops in the House of Lords, to its special, symbiotic relationship with the Crown, to enforceable laws of blasphemy, to an exclusiveness over the tenure of office created by the terms of the thirty-nine articles, and to the sermonising weight of parochial clergy, it was well-equipped to hold its own.

As an opponent of monarchy, it was in Paine's interest to debunk the mystery of divine right. Eventually, he did so openly by repudiating Christianity in his book *The Age of Reason*(1794). But prior to the 1790s he had employed another approach. This was made evident in *Common Sense* where, perhaps tongue-in-cheek, or perhaps as a tactic to appeal to evangelical colonists, he rested his argument against monarchy on a foundation of scriptural proof. The Old Testament revealed, according to Paine, that rather than in favour of monarchy, God was its enemy. Monarchy could therefore be interpreted as a punishment for sin rather than as God's blessing on man.[209]

In sharp contrast to *Common Sense*, *Rights of Man* made the case against monarchy without resort to scriptural authority.[210] Paine's message remained the same, nonetheless: i.e. the polity of the blood was an undeserved curse upon mankind. It therefore should be replaced by a political system in which birth right imparted equality not degree, and government matters were determined by a process of election. In such a formulation of democracy, Paine had, unusually, prioritised exclusion of the birth right to rule before the extension of representation; for, as noticed above, despite its centrality to his belief in the equality of rights, he did not declare the specific necessity of universal suffrage until 1795.[211]

Chapter III
Rights of Man:
its Sale and Suppression

a | Composition

Thomas Paine's *Rights of Man*, quintessentially a persuasive polemic against hereditary rule, originally appeared in two separately published parts, the first in March 1791, the second in February 1792.[1] The title of the first part was self-explanatory: 'Rights of Man, being an Examination of Mr Burke's Attack on the French Revolution.' Initially, however, it was not called 'part I' since the idea of a 'part II' had yet to materialise. Moreover, it did not originate as an objection to Burke's attack on the French Revolution for it was first intended as a 'brochure' aimed to inform President George Washington of the events that over the last three years had led to the overthrow of royal absolutism in France. This latter piece was started around January 1790 but never completed.[2] Yet it survived in two substantial passages of *Rights of Man*, both uninspired narratives, amounting to 11,000 words – or roughly a quarter of the work.[3] Another relic of the brochure was the dedication of part I to George Washington.

Rights of Man directly resulted from the publication in November 1790 of Burke's *Reflections on the Revolution in France*, itself an elaboration on a speech Burke had delivered in the Commons the previous February. Burke's work was not simply an attack on the French Revolution but also upon British reformers for expressing their appreciation of it. This was declared in the subtitle 'on the Proceedings in Certain Societies in London Relative to that Event', a reference to the London Revolution Society and the London Constitutional Society. This secondary concern of Burke's book played an important part in extending the appeal of *Rights of Man* and its circulation through sparking off a lively debate on the nature of government that generated a plethora of printed responses. It also attracted much support from the membership of the two societies concerned.[4]

Rights of Man part II sported the provocative subtitle 'Combining Principle and Practice': in other words, it was not just playing with ideas in the manner of a philosopher; it was also, in the manner of a politician, proposing a means of implementation. Whereas the first part focused on Burke and, in doing so, advocated the destruction of the present political order (which Paine rejected because it was prescriptively founded on the past and intrinsically absurd for being predicated on hereditary succession), the second part largely ignored him. Instead it proposed the construction of a new political order, egalitarian rather than elitist, that rested not upon precedent but upon principles, reason and nature. Of all the printed attacks levelled against Burke's *Reflections*, the first part of Paine's work was of exceptional quality, excelling contributions to the same debate from such luminaries as Catherine Macaulay, Mary Wollstonecraft, Joseph Priestley and James Mackintosh. Yet part II was far superior to part I, both in analysis and argument. It is more of a book, with chapter headings and a table of contents; whereas part I is more of a pamphlet, without separate chapters other than a section called 'Miscellaneous Chapter' clumsily tacked on at the end.

Given the historical importance of *Rights of Man*, much has been written, understandably and deservedly, on its composition, meaning and impact. Yet several significant matters still require exploration, especially the work's circulation at the time and the light this sheds on its availability to, and influence upon, the British public. To make analytical sense of a complicated and ill-documented story, more than the usual overview is required to obtain a clearer picture.[5] Instead, it helps to distinguish the publication of the first part from that of the second. Then the expensive and the cheap editions need to be examined separately. Finally, the differences evident between the various editions call for some analysis, especially on the distinction between the ones subjected to censorship and those that remained true to the original text.

b | Initial Sales

Documentary evidence for the circulation of *Rights of Man* part I lies first in a letter from Paine to President George Washington dated 21 July 1791. It accompanied a gift of 50 copies, a bid by Paine to get the work known in the USA.[6] The letter revealed that, during the four months since the original publication in March, 16,000 copies had been printed in London, of which 12,000 had been sold.[7] At three shillings a copy and a high print-run of 1,600 copies per edition (calculated on the fact that ten editions were published between March and July), this was an impressive sale, if not a complete sell-out.[8] In addition to this expensive version, Paine's letter indicated that a cheaper edition had been printed in Ireland with spectacular results. He cited a letter of 10 May 1791 from Dublin which showed that, in two months, the work had gone through four editions, the second of which had a print-run of 10,000.[9] Surviving copies reveal that, with a much smaller/closer print and on poor quality paper, the Dublin version must have sold for much less than three shillings. Optimistically assuming that the print run was the same for each edition, Paine concluded that in Ireland 40,000 copies had been sold.[10] Impressed by these sales figures, he told Washington that 'the work has had a run beyond anything that has been published in this country on the subject of government'. What is more, he was convinced that, with such sales and the demand still continuing, he had 'got the ear of the country'.[11]

In November 1791 Paine provided a further report on the work's circulation. It was made in a letter to John Hall, a fellow enthusiast on the construction of bridges.[12] By this time according to Paine, of the expensive English edition, the 3-4,000 copies remaining unsold in July had 'gone off', its sale now amounting to almost 16,000. As for the cheap Dublin edition, Paine did not have additional information to what he had known in May and therefore told Hall that the sale was 'above 40,000'. Paine's letter to Hall also revealed the existence of a Scottish edition, accounting for 1,000 copies 'printed cheap'. According to Paine, having been printed in England, copies of this edition were sent to Scotland in response to a request from some of his friends there.[13]

In February 1792 Paine provided a third and final estimation of how well part I had sold. It appeared in the preface to *Rights of Man Part the Second*. Putting part I sales at between 40,000-50,000 copies, Paine indicated that the estimate applied to England, Ireland and Scotland, thereby revealing that it included copies in the cheap as well as the expensive format.[14] Paine's estimate, then, was not implausible. Bearing in mind that, over a longer period, Burke's best-selling *Reflections* had not sold more than 18,000 copies under its original copyright, such a sale of Paine's first part, occurring within less than a year, was a remarkable achievement for a work of political philosophy, especially one that had not as yet featured cheap editions for the English market.[15] Paine's jubilation over the sale – expressed in his letters to Washington and Hall – was therefore understandable. And his boast to Hall that, within the span of 1791 alone, '*Rights of Man* has had the greatest run of anything ever published in this country, at least of late years' was not an idle one.[16]

The sale of *Rights of Man* part II occurred in somewhat different circumstances, thanks to the appearance in 1792 of cheap English editions, along with a repressive movement of public protest against seditious publications that was aroused by a royal proclamation inciting the nation to treat seditious writers (Paine was the unnamed target) as the enemy from within. In response, loyalist petitions (addresses) were produced, signed and published, and loyalist groups were formed, as mobs or associations, to take action against writers, publishers or booksellers engaged in libelling the constitution.[17]

Publication of the original edition of part II (in February, 1792), made in the same expensive format as part I, was soon followed by a succession of cheap London editions. These cheap editions priced at sixpence per copy, were not only one sixth of the price of the expensive edition but also had been censured by Paine and so were less likely to suffer prosecution and more likely to sell.[18] But this development could not have impinged on the circulation of the expensive editions since the latter had been a complete sell-out prior to its occurrence.

The prosecution that Paine had feared in 1791 eventually happened in May and June 1792. Curiously, it only applied to part II which, at the price of three shillings, had by then passed through ten editions, each a run of 5,000 copies.[19] In other words, between February and May 1792, as many as 50,000 copies of the expensive version came up for sale. This means that together the distribution of the two parts, published by J.S. Jordan at three shillings each, could well have amounted to 66,000 copies, all printed between March 1791 and May 1792, the run suddenly terminated when Jordan, to escape trial and punishment, admitted guilt to the charge of seditious libel, specifically for publishing *Rights of Man* part II, and was subsequently constrained, by his plea of guilty, to desist from future publication of the work.[20] That the 66,000 copies were all sold is suggested by Paine's gift in July 1792 to the London Society for Constitutional Information (SCI) of £1,000 which he described as 'royalties so far generated on the book' (i.e. *Rights of Man*). As he was keen not to make profit on cheap editions of the work, in order to minimise the price of each copy, these royalties could only have derived from the expensive editions published by Jordan. With royalties at ten per cent, a sale of 66,000 copies would have realised close on £1,000.[21]

c | The Readership

Without a doubt, the enthusiastic reception given *Rights of Man* in 1791-2 owed much to support from the Society for Constitutional Information (SCI), a parliamentary reform club that had been suddenly revitalised by the outbreak of the French Revolution and by the public debate provoked by Burke's denunciation not only of the revolution but also of the SCI for offering it sympathy and support.[22] *Rights of Man* was appreciated by the SCI as a robust defence against Burke's attack. The Society's membership contained a strong element of Dissenters, including merchants, manufacturers, ministers, doctors, lawyers and affluent tradesmen, all excluded, by virtue of refusing to accept the thirty-nine articles, from a university education, public office and a system of ecclesiastic and political patronage reserved for members of the church of England. Incensed by Burke's specific attack on its membership for being friends of the French Revolution as well as by Paine's exposure of issues such as political corruption and non-representation, the SCI enthusiastically promoted *Rights of Man* from the very start of its publication in March 1791: by funding newspaper advertisements and by distributing copies to its members. Such support, however, entailed overlooking prominent features of Paine's work, notably its rejection of monarchy and aristocracy, its belief that the country had never had a constitution, and its thesis that the Glorious Revolution was a source of tyranny rather than liberty.[23]

For Paine, the value of this support stemmed from the warm appreciation of *Rights of Man* not only by the SCI in London but also by its provincial branches, located in highly populated industrial townships such as Manchester, Sheffield, Birmingham and Norwich.[24] Paine latched onto the SCI, attending its London meetings, offering thanks for its 'honourable patronage', and giving it money (£300 in 1791, £1,000 in 1792) for the purpose of purchasing copies of the work to sell on, or distribute freely, to the society's provincial membership.[25] Eventually the relationship foundered, the result of the French Revolution lurching into republicanism and mob rule in August 1792, thus justifying Burke's forebodings and branding *Rights of Man* as a recipe for political chaos. Until then, members of the SCI had regarded the French Revolution as an attempt to replace French royal absolutism with the British system of constitutional monarchy. From August 1792 this was ruled out. Nonetheless, by then the SCI had served its purpose, enabling Paine to achieve an astounding circulation for a work whose extreme radicalism should have guaranteed immediate suppression.

d | Cheap Editions

To what extent was the overall circulation of *Rights of Man* affected by the production and distribution of cheap copies? A remarkable feature of its publication history was the slowness with which Paine permitted the printing of cheap London editions of part I. Also remarkable was Paine's unwillingness to allow provincial printings, as well as his lack of enthusiasm for the printing of abridgements. Only two of the latter came into existence.[26] Moreover, when Thomas Cooper, a member of the Manchester Constitutional Society and a keen Paineite republican offered to produce one, his letter requesting Paine's approval went unanswered.[27] And yet Paine was reputed to have adopted a very liberal attitude towards the work's publication. This was thought to have boosted its circulation, especially through the distribution of very cheap and free copies.[28] Thus, in May 1791 it was reported that Paine had relinquished the copyright on *Rights of Man*, selling it to the SCI whose aim was to distribute at least 80,000 free copies after meeting the printing costs by public subscription.[29] But this was no more than wild rumour: Paine retained the copyright for both parts. His hostility towards giving it up was revealed on the eve of publishing part II when its printer, Thomas Chapman, offered to buy from Paine the copyright of both parts for £1,000. Paine curtly rejected the offer with the revealing rebuke that he 'would never put it in the power of any printer or publisher to suppress or alter a work of his by making him master of the copy'; especially a work 'which I intended should operate as a [matter of] principle [rather than profit]'.[30]

According to William Sherwin, one of Paine's earliest biographers, Paine decided, in a bid to increase distribution, to 'give up the copyright in favour of the public [good]', and did so 'about two months after the appearance of the second part'.[31] But, there is nothing to substantiate this claim. In all likelihood, Sherwin had confused the issue of releasing the copyright with Paine's declared plan to reduce the price of the cheap edition by taking no profit for himself. In 1802 Paine recalled, in a published letter to the citizens of the USA, that his method in selling *Rights of Man* was the same as with *Common Sense*: 'I relinquished to the people of England, as I had done to those of America, all profits for the work.'[32] This chimes with what he had told George Washington, shortly after publishing the first part.[33] It had nothing to do with a release of copyright. Paine kept a tight proprietorial rein on the work and its distribution in order to prevent others from making harmful alterations to the text.

Paine claimed that, in publishing *Rights of Man*, his preference was to bring it out first as a cheap edition, but that several persons with more knowledge of publishing than himself (i.e., Joseph Johnson, the original publisher, and Paine's close friends, Thomas Holcroft, William Godwin and Thomas Brand Hollis) had persuaded him that the 'proper method' was initially to publish the work at 'the same price which books of that size commonly are [published]'.[34] Hence its first appearance as a handsome edition priced at three shillings. Following publication in March 1791, the matter of a cheap edition remained his concern, as he made clear in his letter to Washington of July. Moved by an awareness that, at three shillings a copy, the work was beyond the reach of 'the generality of the public'; and that the sale of the Dublin edition had been truly spectacular because of its cheapness; and recalling the swift and massive circulation of *Common Sense* in 1776, he informed Washington of a plan to print a cheap edition, once the expensive edition had sold out. Following his practice in publishing *Common Sense*, he intended to reduce the price per copy to a minimum by setting it at no more than the cost of production.[35]

But, for the rest of 1791, no further step was taken. In November, with the expensive edition of part I virtually sold out, he should have proceeded, according to what he had told Washington, to print an English cheap edition. But by then he had undergone a change of mind, thanks to his preoccupation with completing 'Rights of Man, Part the Second'. His new plan was to produce a cheap edition – he reckoned on 100,000 copies for each part – but only after part II had been published in the expensive form. By this time he was receiving provincial requests for cheap editions, notably from Birmingham which asked permission to print its own edition of 10,000 copies.[36] However, his determination to publish '*Rights of Man*' part II in the three shilling form, before allowing the publication of cheap English editions of either part, held firm.[37] He had two reasons for proceeding in this manner. One was his wish to match Burke's *Reflections* in fineness of production (i.e. leather-bound, in large print and on quality paper), thus rendering the two parts of *Rights of Man* fit to be bound together and to stand alongside, or even bound up with, Burke's book on the shelves of gentlemen's libraries.[38] The other reason was his feeling that the expensive edition was more likely to be tolerated by the government since, in that refined form, it was less likely to infect the multitude.[39]

A threat of suppression had hung over *Rights of Man* from the very start, dramatically affecting the original publication of part I as well as part II. For fear of prosecution both Joseph Johnson, the original publisher of part I, and

Thomas Chapman, the original printer of part II, had withdrawn from the assignment at the last moment.[40] Moreover, Paine's apprehension that the government were more likely to take action if provoked by the publication of a cheap edition, proved to be justified. This became clear at Paine's trial in December 1792, when the prosecution rested its case not simply on the sedition evident in part II but its outrageous appearance as a sixpenny tract.[41]

There were several ways to produce a cheap edition. One was to cut costs by using cheap paper and by employing very small and close print to reduce the number of pages per copy. Another device was to combine this approach with a continuous pagination which turned the two parts into one work, thus halving the overall price. A third device was to abbreviate the text by abridgement or digest. Paine had no desire to use the latter, which would have allowed copies to be sold at twopence or threepence but at the possible expense of a mangled text. His preference was for a complete text in very small print on cheap paper with a separate pagination and title page for each part, enabling each part to be sold separately at sixpence a copy. The earliest editions produced in this format were all printed in London and dated 1792 on the title page. There were four in number, each a publication of both parts. An edition produced by J.S. Jordan, the publisher of the three shilling version, was followed by an edition published by Paine himself, another by H.D. Symonds and yet another by Joseph Parsons. These sixpenny editions can be roughly dated, principally by relating them to the indictments brought against publisher and author in late May and early June of 1792.

The only sixpenny edition to precede the May/June indictments was published by Jordan. This can be deduced from the fact that, faced by an indictment for seditious libel in mid-May, Jordan pleaded guilty in order to avoid trial.[42] By doing so, he brought his relationship with Paine to an abrupt halt. Paine pressed him to make a stand in court, offering to pay his legal fees, but to no effect. What is more, the plea of guilty completely severed Jordan's connection with *Rights of Man*. Although the legal proceedings taken against the work had focused exclusively on part II, Jordan's response was to cease from publishing the first part as well.

Little is known about Jordan's cheap edition. It was not specifically mentioned in Paine's correspondence or in his other writings; and very few copies have survived. The title page of each part, however, gives a clue. Indicating the existence of a variant of the first part is the mention of 'part I' on the title page of some copies and its absence on the title page of others, suggesting that some copies were issued before the publication of the original edition of part II (i.e. mid-February). This variant may well have been the cheap edition Paine had sent into Scotland in late 1791.[43] As for the copies with part I on the title page, they were published in April 1792, along with Jordan's cheap edition of part II. Paine revealed as much when he declared, later in the year, that 'the cheap edition of the first part was begun about the middle of last April'. Moreover, in a letter to Thomas Walker of Manchester, dated 30 April 1792, he wrote: 'The first and second parts of *Rights of Man* are printed complete and not in extract.'[44] This appeared to be making a dismissive reference to a recent publication from a certain 'Free Born Englishman' entitled *Paine's Political and Moral Maxims, Selected from the Fifth Edition of Rights of Man, Parts I and II*: a digest composed by someone who justified the work on the grounds that no cheap edition was available (and had not been for months) and who claimed it was published to meet the needs of those who could not afford the original edition of both parts (which together were priced at six shillings).[45] Paine added in his letter to Walker: 'As we have now got the stone to roll [thanks to the spectacular sales of the original, expensive editions of the first and second parts] it must be kept going by cheap publications.' He thought such a move would, more likely than anything else, 'embarrass the Court gentry [i.e. those in government circles] because it is a ground they are not used to'.

As for the second part of Jordan's cheap edition, every surviving copy is distinctive in two respects: one is the title page which describes it as 'the sixth edition', raising the suspicion of a ruse to create the impression that more copies had been printed than was actually the case. If so, it might well have backfired through provoking the government to take legal action. Secondly, this version of part II is unique among the cheap editions of 1792 in being unexpurgated: a clear indication that its publication had preceded Jordan's admission of guilt in mid-May.

With the removal of Jordan, Paine resorted to another means of publishing *Rights of Man* in cheap format. Rather than employing another publisher, he decided to publish it himself. His aim, he said, was to produce a cheap London edition 'under my own direction'.[46] The outcome was an edition of both parts, each identifiable on the title page as printed in London 'for the booksellers'.[47] Also printed on each title page was the price of sixpence, although in some surviving copies this is scratched out, suggesting an attempt to sell at a higher price, perhaps ninepence. The intention of this edition, as with the aborted sixpenny Jordan edition, was to meet a demand from the provinces for copies that people could afford. This demand had taken the form of requests from towns such as Rotheram, Leicester, Sheffield, Chester and Birmingham, to publish editions of their own. Paine was initially sympathetic on grounds that 'the original edition of the first and second part having been expensively printed...the high price precluded the generality of people from purchasing'. Consequently, 'many applications were made to me from various parts of the country to print the work in a cheaper manner'. But, with the exception of Sheffield, Paine withheld his permission. As he put it, 'the people of Sheffield requested leave to print two thousand copies for themselves, with which request I immediately complied'.[48] The outcome was *An Illustration of the Rights of Man* by J. Crome of Sheffield in 1792. It appertained only to part I and, published in January, appeared before the publication of part II.[49] As for the other provincial requests, Paine choked them off on the grounds that, by resorting to 'a very numerous edition in London', he could ensure a 'more perfect' printing and at a lower price than was achievable by 'printing small editions in the country of only a few thousand' each.[50]

The first part of his own edition appeared in June 1792, the second part in July.[51] Paine threw light on what he intended in a couple of letters, one dated 18 May and sent to Major John Cartwright, chairman of the SCI; the other sent to the same society on 4 July. These letters are best understood against a background provided in his *Letter Addressed to the Addressers on the Late Proclamation*, a pamphlet published in October 1792 and sometimes called 'Rights of Man, Part III'.[52] The first letter offered information on the production of a cheap London edition.[53] It was written to thank the SCI for 'repeatedly' supporting the publication of *Rights of Man*. In complying with requests contained in 'a great number of letters from various parts of the country' for printing the two parts in a cheaper format, Paine claimed to have taken 'the proper means': presumably, by allowing the publication of the sixpenny Jordan edition. He also revealed that, since meeting the need for a cheap edition of both parts, he had learnt that the government 'intends bringing a prosecution' against him. This made it even more necessary that the nation as a whole (i.e. the poor as well as the rich) should be familiarised with the work so that it could judge if the prosecution was justified and whether it infringed the freedom of the press.[54] Hence his decision to self-publish a cheap edition of both parts, the unstated purpose of which was to replace the cheap edition forfeited by Jordan's guilty plea.

The prospect of prosecution was clearly revealed when a royal proclamation of 21 May 1792 called upon the king's subjects as well as his officers to take action against seditious publications. It named neither Paine nor *Rights of Man* but its target became clear when it defined 'wicked' writings as those seeking to bring into contempt 'the wise and wholesome provisions made at the time of the Glorious Revolution'.[55] On the very same day, a summons to appear in court to answer a charge of seditious libel was left at his lodgings.[56] Shortly afterwards, on 8 June, Paine was indicted for seditious libel, the charge stating that *Rights of Man Part the Second* was a seditious libel on the Glorious Revolution. It specified several passages from the work to prove the point.[57]

Paine's letter of 4 July to the SCI, completed the picture outlined in his letter to Cartwright of 18 May.[58] Part II of his own cheap edition was not yet published but, nonetheless, at the printers and therefore imminent, while part I of the same edition had been published a month earlier (and therefore at the time of his indictment), and was apparently selling very well. Paine remarked on its popularity: thanks to its price of sixpence, it was 'circulating for the benefit and information of the poor'. He sensed that the 'very great demand' for it had been 'exceedingly increased' by the May proclamation. He later reckoned that within one month 32,000 copies of the two parts were sold.[59] His letter of 4 July concluded: 'I have now done by the people of England as I did by those of America [i.e. by publishing *Common Sense* in a cheap format] and I sincerely wish them the same happiness [i.e. the benefits attendant upon a republic].'[60] In the same letter, he offered the SCI £1,000, the accrument, as we have seen, of royalties from the sale of the three shilling editions of both parts. The aim was to promote further the circulation of the cheap edition by purchasing copies to give away. Signalling a vital change in its relationship with Paine, the society turned the gift down.[61]

e | The Censorship of Part II

In contrast to Jordan, who had admitted his guilt to avoid prosecution, Paine stood firm, denying the indictment on 8 June 1792. His trial was fixed for the following December. During that critical interval, he published, as we have seen, his own cheap edition of *Rights of Man* to replace the one lost by Jordan's defection. However, this edition offered an important concession to the government since, removed from it, were the very same passages cited as seditious in the indictment. Given Paine's claim that the prosecution of *Rights of Man* would infringe press liberty and represent a despotic act worthy of the

Russian Tsar or the Turkish Sultan, his submission to such censorship was surprising, especially as it entailed extensive alterations, all of them confined to part II.[62] Yet, they undoubtedly carried his consent: Paine admitted as much by replacing two of the deleted passages with lengthy explanatory footnotes addressed to the reader from himself.[63] Enforcing his consent was not only the impending trial but also pressure from his printers who were insisting on alterations to the text in the bid to avoid their own prosecution. Paine was therefore complying with these alterations to ensure the work's continued publication, as well as to circumnavigate an attempted suspension on future sales that the government appeared to be informally imposing by delaying the trial until December.[64]

The passages removed, eight in all, were the same as those declared libellous in the indictment.[65] The outcome was the deletion of 180 lines, a considerable alteration to the text. Removed were highly provocative statements about the non-existence of a constitution, the absurdity of hereditary monarchy, the despotic conduct of individual kings, the selfishness of the House of Lords, the uselessness of the House of Commons as representative of the nation's interest, and the spuriousness of the claim that the Glorious Revolution had provided a defence of British liberty on the grounds that by illicitly granting William and Mary and their heirs the right to hold the Crown in perpetuity, the Bill of Rights (1689) had snatched it away.[66] Such deletions, must have found approval among many radical reformers of the time. It is therefore possible that, by making them, Paine was seeking not only to avoid prosecution and to continue sales but also to restore his relationship with the SCI. As well as to deletions, the text was also subjected to certain additions, mostly explanations for the passages removed.[67] However, much remained in the text to support Paine's hostility to the polity of the blood, not only in part I which was left untouched but even in the heavily censored part II.

What was removed did not offer protection against prosecution, as Paine discovered when he was pronounced guilty in December 1792, and as Daniel Eaton found when brought to trial on the same charge in February 1793.[68] So many passages suggestive of seditious libel remained couched within the text. Furthermore, the fact that uncensored copies, both cheap and expensive, continued in circulation meant the government did not have far to look to find material evidence for pressing the original charge.

Rights of Man: its Sale and Suppression

Paine's lead in publishing an expurgated *Rights of Man* was followed by two publishers from Paternoster Row, H.D. Symonds and Joseph Parsons. In all likelihood, as well as receiving permission from Paine to publish, they were financed out of the £1,000 royalties that Paine had initially offered the SCI: a move made by Paine perhaps to make up for the poor sales suffered by his own cheap edition following the SCI's withdrawal of support.[69] Both publishers produced sixpenny editions in late 1792, with the same passages removed.[70] A distinctive feature of this censorship, then, was its confinement to part II, even though the first part was, arguably, open to the same seditious charge in calling for the abolition of monarchy and aristocracy in an edition which, at sixpence a copy, could no longer be excused (as with the three-shilling edition) for being closed to the masses by virtue of its price.

By the start of 1793, then, the publication of *Rights of Man* comprised expensive and cheap editions of the two parts, all published by J.S. Jordan of 166 Fleet Street, as well as cheap editions of the two parts published by Byrne in Dublin and by Paine, Symonds and Parsons in London. No J.S. Jordan or Byrne edition suffered censorship while, as we have seen, the second part of the Paine, Symonds and Parsons editions all underwent substantial alteration.

In addition, there had entered the British market a semi-expensive *Works of Thomas Paine, Esq.*, published late in 1792 by the mysterious and possibly piratical D. Jordan of Piccadilly. He appeared to have no connection with his namesake, J.S. Jordan. It contained, with their own title page and discrete pagination, Paine's major writings but minus his *Letter Addressed to the Addressers on the Late Proclamation*, thus suggesting that the collection was first published prior to October 1792. Several items in the D. Jordan edition were termed 'the ninth edition', but this can only be regarded as fictitious since no earlier editions of the work appear to exist. Moreover, in spite of being designated 'the ninth edition', the D. Jordan version of *Rights of Man* bears no relationship in format, pagination or lay-out to the ninth edition of *Rights of Man* as published by J.S. Jordan in 1791 for part I and in 1792 for part II, although it is likewise unexpurgated.

f | Overall Distribution in Britain

Otherwise, for sale by the close of 1792 were the cheap editions published by Paine himself, by Symonds and by Parsons. How many copies were sold is beyond precise calculation. However, common sense suggests that, together, the cheap, sixpenny editions would have circulated more copies than those priced at three shillings: i.e. more than 66,000. J.S. Jordan's cheap edition of the second part (uncensored and therefore published prior to Jordan's plea of guilty in May 1792) apparently went through at least six editions, but this claim is also likely to be fictitious since every surviving copy claims to belong to the sixth imprint. Paine had originally envisaged, as he told his friend John Hall in November 1791, a run of 100,000 cheap copies for each part, but there is no good reason to believe that this was ever attained.[71]

Estimating sales of *Rights of Man* in Britain, from a broad-sample study of today's survival of the various British editions published in 1791-2, makes this much evident. With one exception, the cheap 1792 editions appear to have had a surprisingly limited sale. Paine's self-published edition is extremely rare (24 copies or 4.6% of survivals), even though at the time Paine claimed that 32,000 copies had sold within a month of its publication.[72] Also rare are the surviving sixpenny editions published by Jordan and Parsons: 33 and 18 copies respectively, or 6.3% and 3.4 % of survivals. This might be attributed to their intrinsic fragility and a reduced chance, compared with the expensive editions, of finding protection in a sturdy binding or refuge in a gentleman's library. However, the same could not be claimed for Symonds' equally fragile sixpenny edition which has survived in relative profusion (127 copies or 24.4 % of survivals), if not in numbers equal to J.S. Jordan's three shilling edition (271 copies or 52.6% of survivals).[73] Judged on this evidence, it is possible that the Symonds edition might have achieved a total distribution of 100,000 (perhaps through the auspices of the newly formed London Corresponding Society and its provincial connections).[74] Working against this possibility is the fact that, at this time, the work was under threat from Paine's impending trial, with booksellers vulnerable to attack from the John Reeves' Association for the Protection of Property against Republicans and Levellers, and with Paine supporters fearful of mobs bent on burning their hero in effigy or, following the incineration of Priestley's house, laboratory and library in July 1791, of having their property deliberately destroyed.[75]

In contrast to the cheap editions, the sales and profitability of J.S. Jordan's expensive *Rights of Man* can be worked out, as we have seen, thanks to knowing the retail price per copy (three shillings), the print-run for each part (1,600 copies for the first, 5000 for the second), and the number of editions (10 for each part). At most, then, 66,000 copies were sold realising, on the assumption of ten per cent royalties, a profit to the author of £240 for the first part and £750 for the second part, all within the short time-span of thirteen months. When measured against book sales in general at that time and, even more so, when compared with sales for books on political philosophy in the late eighteenth century, this was a spectacular publishing achievement.[76] Finally, for the sale of the semi-expensive edition of *Rights of Man* published by D. Jordan, the sales figures, in the absence of contemporary evidence, are totally dependent on today's survival rate (i.e. 26 copies or 4.9% of all copies registered in the sample).

All these editions were published in London. Left for consideration is the sale of editions published in the English provinces, Ireland and Scotland. The English provincial editions were few and far between, despite a large number of requests by individual townships to print editions of their own. As we have seen, Paine was prepared to grant only one of these requests: that is, to the people of Sheffield who were permitted to print 2,000 copies of part I, but only for members of the town's Constitutional Society, not for general circulation. 1,400 subscribers in and around Sheffield raised the capital to print 1,600 copies, selling at sixpence each.[77] To meet the other provincial requests, Paine decided to print 'a very numerous edition in London'.[78] But his first two attempts at meeting the provincial demand were not a great success. It looks as if the sixpenny edition published by J.S. Jordan had to be withdrawn when he pleaded guilty to the charge of seditious libel for producing part II. This was quickly replaced by Paine's own sixpenny edition whose disappointing sale is reflected in its rarity today.[79]

When calculating the distribution that the first part of *Rights of Man* had achieved by February 1792, Paine referred to sales in Scotland and Ireland as well as in England.[80] These sales undoubtedly included copies of the expensive edition published by J.S. Jordan. However, both Scotland and Ireland produced editions of their own, mostly in the form of cheap publications. Writing of the time in early 1792, when requests were reaching him for permission to produce a cheap edition, Paine revealed that some had come from several towns in Scotland, admitting that 'I had already sent a cheap edition to Scotland': probably the sixpenny edition published in London by J.S. Jordan.[81] Later, in 1792, however, an Edinburgh edition appeared in the form of a short twenty-three page abridgement of both parts, composed and printed by John Thomson, probably without Paine's permission. Its limited sale is evident in its limited survival today, with just one copy known to exist.

As for Ireland, the very first of the cheap editions, the only one, in fact, dated 1791, was published in Dublin. Commissioned by over thirty Irish booksellers, it was printed by Patrick Byrne. By the time it had reached its fourth edition (May 1791) Paine reckoned 40,000 copies had been sold. In the same year, another cheap edition was published in Londonderry, 'printed at the desire of a society of gentlemen'. In the following year appeared three-shilling and sixpenny versions of *Rights of Man, Part the Second*, both published by Byrne of Grafton Street, Dublin. Byrne's cheap edition, according to title-page claims, had undergone thirteen imprints of part I and three imprints of part II by the end of 1792. Paine stressed the strong reception given to *Rights of Man* in Ireland.[82] Relative to Scotland this assessment is certainly correct. Encouraging a high circulation were political organisations such as the Whig Club of Ireland and the Society of United Irishmen, along with the active presence of affluent Dissenters and disaffected gentry, who through subscription raised the capital to publish very cheap editions of *Rights of Man*. By doing so, they replicated in Ireland the SCI's promotion of the sale of Paine's work in England.[83] Nonetheless, the survival data base registers only 17 copies printed in Dublin and 10 copies printed in Londonderry (i.e. 5.1% of copies sold in the UK in 1791-2).

g | Suppression and its Impact

In calculating the circulation of *Rights of Man* in Britain during the 1790s, one is struck by the fact that the publication of both parts, no matter whether in the cheap or expensive form, was largely confined to the years 1791-2. But for four minor and rare exceptions, it ceased publication in Britain for the next twenty-five years. One of these exceptions was a conflation of the two parts, written by Paine while imprisoned in France in 1794 and published, at three shillings a copy, by Daniel Eaton in 1795 under the universalist title The *Rights of Man for the Use and Benefit of All Mankind*.

The second exception was the inclusion of both parts of 'Rights of Man' (unexpurgated) in a so-called *The Works of Thomas Paine* that appeared in 1796. No publisher or printer was named. All that was given was the place of publication which was London. It differed markedly from *The Works of Thomas Paine Esq.* as published by D. Jordan in 1792. In the 1796 *Works of Thomas Paine* individual items were not given their own title page (thus preventing them from being sold separately), the pagination was continuous and the text on each page was arranged in double columns. Unlike the 1792 *Works of Thomas*

Paine Esq., its content was not just political but also religious, since it included 'The Age of Reason'. Although in small print and on inexpensive paper, it could not be regarded as a cheap production on account of its bulk, running to almost five hundred pages. Neither it nor the Eaton conflation could have had much of a sale, with very few copies surviving today.[84]

A third exception was also published in 1796. On the title page it declared itself to be 'printed for the people' and published in London. It was another cheap edition of *Rights of Man* but distinguished by running the two parts together in one continuous pagination. By doing so, it set a precedent for the cheap editions published in the nineteenth century. Today it is a work of great rarity (with only two known copies), and so not printed in large numbers at the time. The same could be said of a strange and surprising reprint in 1795 of J.S. Jordan's sixpenny edition of *Rights of Man* part I, of which only three copies are known to have survived.

How is one to account first, for the infrequency with which *Rights of Man* was published after 1792 and, secondly, its complete non-publication between 1797 and 1817? One factor was surely the absence of Paine himself, who fled the country in September 1792. Found guilty the following December, his status as a fleeing felon condemned him to exile for the rest of his life. Another factor was a consequence of the book's ultra-radical message and its exploitation by loyalists to present Paine as a leveller and an anarchist capable of arousing 'Lancashire troglodytes' and 'Irish bogtrotters' to seize all.[85] A government terrified by radical sentiments, as well as by their interconnection with revolutionary developments in France, was driven to extreme measures of suppression in order to set a stern warning to the British people against disobedience and disorder. Fearing that popular uprisings could be incited by news of the Paris mob as well as by reading Paine, the government established in late 1792 military garrisons in or close to large towns such as Sheffield, Manchester, Nottingham, Birmingham, Coventry and Norwich.[86] It prosecuted publishers and booksellers for printing or selling Paine's works: notably Symonds, Eaton, Ridgway and Spence of London, Daniel Holt of Newark and Richard Phillips of Leicester, the convicted receiving disproportionately heavy sentences of several years in prison and exorbitant fines.[87] Reacting to Paine's call for a national convention, first proposed in *Rights of Man* and affirmed in *A Letter to the Addressers on the Late Proclamation* - the purpose of which was to transform the political system by abolishing hereditary rule and by drawing up a written constitution authorised by the national will – the government's anti-

Paine measures also featured transporting to Australia in 1793-4 a number of Paineites (e.g. Thomas Muir, Maurice Margarot, William Skirving, Thomas Fyshe Palmer and Joseph Gerrald); a charge of high treason brought in 1794 for the same reason against members of the London Corresponding Society and of the SCI; another charge of conspiracy to overthrow the constitution brought against Thomas Walker and fellow Mancunians also in 1794; the suspension of the Habeas Corpus Act in the same year; and fresh counter-insurgency legislation in 1795 to suppress seditious speech and associated meetings and, in 1799, to prevent the circulation of cheap seditious publications.[88] Reducing demand for *Rights of Man*, radical reformers shied away from advocating its more extreme principles, partly out of fear of punishment and partly because either they did not believe in them or because, by doing so, they might endanger their preferred cause. Focused on universal suffrage and believing that it could be achieved by reviving the ancient constitution rather than by creating a new one, they rejected Paine's proposals for establishing a completely new political system by removing from it the hereditary element.[89]

Working contrary to this conservative tendency on the part of British radicalism, there emerged, following the Napoleonic Wars, two Paineite republican movements, one founded in 1817 by the teenage publisher William Sherwin and the former journeyman tinsmith Richard Carlile, the other embodied, during the early 1830s, in the National Union of the Working Classes under the leadership of the journalist Henry Hetherington. Significantly, both movements were against Christianity, suggesting that another factor in the radical aversion to *Rights of Man* was Paine's publication of *The Age of Reason* in 1794 and the reputation he thereafter acquired as an atheist. Between them, Sherwin and Carlile organised a spectacular republication of *Rights of Man*, publicising it, along with the other works of Paine, in weekly journals, the first called *The Republican* and edited and published by Sherwin (later to be called *Sherwin's Weekly Political Register*), the second, also titled *The Republican* that was edited and published by Richard Carlile and his wife Jane. The latter journal succeeded the former, running with one short intermission, from 1819 to 1826. Persistently, they promoted the ideas of Paine, notably his hostility to the polity of the blood. They also republished his works. In 1817 *Sherwin's Political Register* was interleaved with free instalments of *Rights of Man*. Yet the editions of *Rights of Man* that Sherwin and Carlile published were not particularly cheap, and the tendency to bind them up with Paine's other political works made them even more expensive.[90] Nonetheless, a strong demand existed, the result of a twenty-year prohibition. According to Carlile, a man prone to exaggeration, he and Sherwin 'circulated' 5,000 copies a year between 1817 and 1820.[91] Seeking to undercut them, William Benbow (the man who, along with Cobbett, dug up Paine's skeleton in New York State in order to bring it back to England for a proper burial) published in 1821 a cheap pocket edition of *Rights of Man* combined with *Common Sense*. But beset by financial difficulties, he was obliged to give it up, with only a few copies sold.[92] This second phase in the publication history of *Rights of Man* had fizzled out by 1822, its brevity resembling the original publication in 1791-2. Bringing it to an end was Sherwin's sudden retirement from radical publishing in 1819, the result of getting married and falling into bankruptcy. At the same time, Carlile started a lengthy imprisonment in Dorchester Gaol for publishing Paine's *The Age of Reason*, a six-year sentence accompanied by government confiscations of his printed stock.

Ten years passed until, in the early 1830s, another revival of Paineite republicanism occurred. Backed by the National Union of the Working Classes (NUWC), a third and final phase took place in the publication history of *Rights of Man*, with James Watson publishing in 1832 and 1834 sevenpence-halfpenny editions, the two parts united by a continuous pagination and therefore halved in price. At the same time, other editions of *Rights of Man* were published by John Brooks of Oxford Street London in 1830, John Sharp of Greenock in 1832, McGowan and Muir of Glasgow in 1834, Wighton of Kelso in 1836 and B.D. Cousins of London in 1837. However, in terms of sales this phase represented a trickle, not a flood; and the NUWC had folded by 1835. Watson's cheap editions continued to appear throughout the 1840s and into the 1850s, but, by then, it was becoming clear that Paine's political works were, linguistically and ideologically, losing their practical appeal. With radicalism (in the guise of Chartism, the Reform League, the Liberal and Labour Parties) continuing to distance itself from the republican sentiments of *Rights of Man*, and with republicanism (in the form of Mazzini nationalism, Owen-inspired communitarian socialism, Bradlaughite political reform and O'Brienite state socialism) adopting priorities that differed greatly from those of Paine, *Rights of Man* lost its relevance, even though a hereditary monarch remained head of state and a hereditary peerage remained ensconced in parliament.

b | Conclusion

Staggeringly high figures have been quoted for the sale of *Rights of Man*, notably by Paine himself who in 1802 claimed that, over the previous decade, 400-500,000 copies had been sold in the British Isles. For him, it represented 'the greatest run of any work ever published in the English language'. In a similar way, he had puffed up the sales of his earlier bestseller *Common Sense* (1776).[93] The tendency nowadays is, rightly, to propose that the higher sales figures given for *Common Sense* and *Rights of Man* were gross exaggerations.[94] But, because of the absence or inadequacy of evidence, and the generally held view that both were exceptional bestsellers, the reservations held by scholars in this matter might seem like academic quibbling. Moreover, the call for a more realistic estimation of sales carries the danger of belittling what was achieved in 1791-2. Consequently, the only practical way forward, with regard to *Rights of Man*, is not to pass an opinion on total sales but to identify, examine and evaluate the central features of its publishing history.

Notable and striking are the following restrictions placed on sales: i.e. the almost complete absence in Britain of editions published between 1793 and 1817; the virtual absence of English provincial editions; the complete absence of English cheap editions in 1791 (the first year of the work's publication); the inhibiting prosecution of Part II in 1792 (its second year of publication); the limited sale experienced by three of the four English cheap editions published in 1792; and the scarcity of abridgements. Furthermore, the original Jordan editions had a very short life, with part I not republished after 1791 and part II not republished after 1792. Yet, truly remarkable was the sale of the expensive editions of both parts as published by J.S. Jordan in London between March 1791 and May 1792 (66,000 copies), and of the cheap edition of both parts published in London by Symonds in late 1792. Equally remarkable was the sale of the cheap Irish edition of part I during the period 1791-2 (at least 40,000). Moved by these sales, Paine had felt in November 1791 that 'I have so far got the ear of John Bull' but that 'the tide is yet the wrong way'.[95] The question is: did the tide ever turn? Many were fascinated by *Rights of Man* when it first appeared but only a few were moved to accept its main message: i.e. to abolish the polity of the blood. Most of its supporters were swayed instead by its lively chastisement of the old regime: for being corrupt, for only serving the privileged few, for callously employing a fiscal system that switched wealth from the poor to the rich, and for relying upon a legislative system in which the House of Commons was as unrepresentative of the nation as the House of Lords. Consequently, the exceptionally large circulation figures attained by *Rights of Man* in 1791-2 cannot be simply explained as a popular upsurge in republican or egalitarian sentiment. They rather reflected the charismatic power of Paine's pen and his ability to expose issues that political reformers found useful for shaming the establishment and for promoting a radical remedy centred not on antipathy to the polity of the blood but upon support for the democratic principle of universal suffrage.

The Polity of the Blood

Chapter IV
Paine and the Tradition of Radical Reform

a | Richard Carlile's Promotion of Paine

In the 1820s two separate and distinctly different attempts were made to revive the reputation of Thomas Paine and his political reform programme: in a bid to terminate the government clampdown that had followed the publication of *Rights of Man* part II in 1792. One was led by Richard Carlile, a former tinsmith turned publisher and journalist, who had recently acquired a substantial following, thanks to his involvement in the republication of Paine's works after twenty years of effective prohibition. Also boosting Carlile's popularity was his part in publicising the Manchester Massacre of 16 August 1819 [i.e. Peterloo] and the sympathy he had gained from the unreasonably long imprisonment (1819-1826) imposed upon him for the minor crime of blasphemy, the result of republishing Paine's *The Age of Reason*.[1] The other attempt to promote Paine was a much more muted affair. It came of William Cobbett's recent return from the USA accompanied by Paine's bones.[2]

To begin with, Carlile's promotion of Paine operated from his shop at 55 Fleet Street while Cobbett's operated from across the road, just a stone's throw away, in his printing office where he had chosen to store Paine's bones: at 183 Fleet Street and later at 11 Bolt Court. Uninterested in Cobbett's reburial project, Carlile and his followers sought to advance the Paineite cause by making Paine's works readily available to the public, by holding feasts to celebrate his birth and by extolling his virtues in a weekly periodical entitled the *Republican* (1819-1826) which Carlile edited from a cell in Dorchester Gaol.[3] Carlile's promotion of Paine continued into the early 1830s through the pages of the *Prompter* (1830-31) and the *Gauntlet* (1833-4) – two republican weeklies, again edited by him, this time mostly from a cell in the Giltspur Street Prison, London. Both periodicals advocated the abolition of hereditary rule and the establishment, by physical force if necessary, of a republic. In an ironic celebration of William IV's coronation in 1831, Carlile issued a Coronation Handkerchief, printed in red on calico, that declared: 'This coronation is an entire mummery and a disgrace to the growing knowledge of the present time and... a consequence of having kings and priests and lords.' It went on: 'Its meaning is nothing more than to grease the king's body and the queen's head with a little oil – to put a tinselled bauble on each of their heads and some plaything in their hands – to sing a song – to say a prayer – and to declare "God save the king and queen" [when what was meant is] "God damn the people".' The handkerchief presented the coronation as no more than 'a festival at which the king, the priests and the lords celebrate their triumph over a conquered and degraded people and at a cost of £50,000'. It concluded: 'Down with kings, with priests and with lords.' Promoting the same Paineite cause was Carlile's so-called Temple of Reason at 62 Fleet Street which, presided over by a statue of Paine, served for almost a decade (1826-35) as a book shop and lecture theatre.[4] In the early 1830s Carlile also backed the cause of Paine by running a huge and well-attended infidel chapel, near Blackfriars Bridge, called the Rotunda. Finally, in 1833 he raised a substantial force of volunteers who pledged themselves to take action whenever he gave the summons.[5] Assuming command of this army, Carlile presented himself as 'the living personification of the political principles of Thomas Paine', with a commitment to 'resistance moral' where appropriate and 'resistance physical' if required.[6]

In response, throughout the 1820s and during the early 1830s, supporters organised themselves in the provinces, as well as in London, to discuss Paine's political and religious beliefs. They wrote enthusiastic letters to Carlile announcing their allegiance to Paineite republicanism and Paineite freethought (many of them printed in his periodicals), besides furnishing him with funds to continue the struggle against Christianity, monarchy and aristocracy. By the start of 1823, through Carlile's agency, large concentrations of Paineites had declared themselves in the Northwest (notably in Manchester, Stockport, Bolton, Ashton-under-Lyne, Oldham, Failsworth); in the Northeast (Leeds, Huddersfield, Dewsbury); in East Anglia (Norwich, Wisbech, Great Yarmouth); in the Midlands (Nottingham, Birmingham); in the Southeast (London, Portsmouth); and in Scotland (Edinburgh, Aberdeen, Glasgow, Greenock, Paisley).[7] Some were veteran Jacobins, who in the 1790s had become supporters of the French Revolution after reading Paine's *Rights of Man*; but many were recent converts to republicanism, having gained access to Paine's works thanks to their republication between 1817 and 1820.

In contrast, on the other side of Fleet Street very little happened. Paine's bones lay there throughout the 1820s and into the early 1830s, with nothing done to stage the spectacular funeral, originally planned by Cobbett to demonstrate, through the support he expected the event to attract, the British people's recognition of Paine as 'that illustrious patriot' and 'Noble of Nature'.[8]

b | Radical Reform's Antipathy to Paine

For the leadership of the Radical Reformers – the movement in support of universal suffrage headed by Henry Hunt – the return of the bones to England in 1819 had been a matter of acute embarrassment, exposing the party to the charge that it was badly infected by republican and anti-Christian sentiment, and that its proposed political reforms were not confined to the election of MPs but threatened a major violation of the constitution through advocating the abolition of the Crown and the House of Lords. In counteraction, a dissociation from the ideas of Paine occurred which, while also involving Cobbett, was mainly the work of Hunt, a man long lampooned as a Paineite republican and desperate to escape the attribution.[9] It first came to light on 8 December 1819 at the Crown and Anchor in the Strand when a celebration was held to welcome Cobbett back to Britain after three years of self-imposed exile in America. At the meeting the point was firmly made that Radical Reformers should have no truck with Paine's central principles, as Hunt, its chairman, followed by Cobbett, its principal guest, denounced republicanism. Hunt then proceeded to affirm his Christianity by condemning Deism, the religion of Paine.[10] Hanging over Hunt at the time was a charge of political sedition, the result of the prominent part he had played at the Manchester reform meeting of 16 August 1819. At his trial in April 1820, Hunt, as he stood in the dock, tearfully repudiated the Paineite reform programme of Richard Carlile. He told the court that 'none of the principles, professions and doctrines Carlile said I have espoused were ever, at any moment in my life, imbibed or believed by me'.[11] It failed to save him from imprisonment.

A year later, in a published letter to his followers from Ilchester Gaol in Somerset, Hunt continued his dissociation from Paine by denouncing 'A Declaration of Reform', the work of Joseph Brayshaw, a Radical Reformer of Leeds. Some residents of Leeds and its vicinity had demonstrated an allegiance to Paine's principles in January 1821 and again in January 1822 through holding, on each occasion, a dinner in celebration of his birth; and by the latter date a sizeable group had formed prepared to call themselves republicans and to reject Christianity.[12] Drawn up in March 1821, the Brayshaw Declaration gained some acceptance in Lancashire, Yorkshire, Derbyshire and Cheshire. It was clearly Paineite in tone, content and procedure.[13] Claiming that Britain lacked a constitution, a point made by Paine, it proposed that one needed to be formulated and put into writing. This constitution, it argued, should be based on principles selected by reason, not on historical precedent. For this reason, it should exclude the hereditary right to rule. Moreover, it proposed to follow Paine in regarding a national convention of delegates elected by universal suffrage as the best means of achieving this constitution. When Brayshaw sought Hunt's support for this scheme, he encountered a barrage of abuse. Hunt branded it one of the 'most sweeping acts of despotism that ever emanated from the brain of mortal man'. It was for him 'an open act of rebellion against the present form of government' and one that would inevitably entail the 'taking up arms'.[14] In other words, it went totally against the procedure of peaceableness that Hunt had constantly advocated, one reliant on remonstrance and petition and predicated on the belief that parliament could reform itself – a plan of action which Paine had dismissed as mistaken and futile.[15] Rebuffed by Hunt, Brayshaw sent the declaration to Richard Carlile who published it, endorsed with his full approval, in October 1821.[16]

Cobbett followed Hunt in distancing himself from Paine. Publicly he declared his support for monarchy and church, while shelving all his recently formulated plans to promote Paine's reputation as a patriot.[17] Such plans had entailed not only a grand public funeral but also the construction of a great monument, the holding of feasts on Paine's birthday and the formation of clubs to approve Paine's principles.[18] Under pressure from their leaders, by the end of 1823 the Radical Reformers had been largely purged of Paineite affiliations, allowing them single-mindedly to focus upon the task of making the House of Commons truly representative of the people.[19] Consequently, those Radical Reformers prepared to remain true to Paine shifted over to join the following of Carlile who, on the one hand, adopted and applied Cobbett's idea of holding Paineite dinners and running Paineite discussion societies but, on the other, refused to consider making political capital out of Paine's bones.[20] Carlile's attitude towards the latter was revealed in a letter to William Carver of New York. In response to Carver's enquiry concerning their whereabouts, Carlile claimed not to know.[21] He assured the American: 'I think so much about his principles, and so little about his bones, that I have never once made an enquiry about them'. He was not, he declared, 'captivated with them as relics'. In fact, 'I have no relics, keep-sakes, no rings, no miniatures'. First and foremost, it was 'the writings of Thomas Paine' that he valued, knowing that 'they are calculated to improve the condition of mankind'. He concluded: 'I admire the mind but not the bones of the man.'[22] Carlile's supporters felt likewise.[23]

A major schism thus developed within the movement for Radical Reform. It divided those led by Hunt, Cobbett, Cartwright and Wooler from the adherents of Carlile who, true to Paine, objected to the hereditary principle, repudiated the Christian religion, required a much more extensive reform of the political system than Radical Reform proposed, and were prepared to use force.[24] This republican group persisted in upholding the principles of Paine throughout the 1820s and into the early 1830s. Intensifying the schism was the bitter antipathy that developed between Hunt and Carlile as both vied for support from the pool of Radical Reformers (the same could be said for the relationship between Cobbett and Carlile), hurling personal abuse at each other in the bid to enlarge their share. Carlile accused Hunt of having caused the Manchester Massacre, principally through adopting a policy of peaceableness that had allowed the attack on the crowd to go unchallenged.[25] Besides exercising poor leadership, Carlile accused him of dishonesty, declaring: 'Of all the quacks who ever quacked since quackery commenced, Henry Hunt is the greatest.'[26] Hunt hit back by suggesting that Carlile was no more than a tradesman, peddling the causes of republicanism and infidelity for commercial profit.[27] Money was Carlile's concern, he claimed, not principles. He also charged him with cowardice. In contradiction to Carlile's depiction of himself at Peterloo as a courageous and chivalrous knight engaged in rescuing damsels in distress, Hunt and his followers alleged that he had, with quivering lips, fled the field.[28] A decade later, Hunt told an outrageous public lie in claiming that Carlile attended Peterloo not to promote political reform but to report on it as a government spy.[29]

Cobbett waded into the fray, snobbily dismissing Carlile as 'a poor, half-mad creature' who, locked away in Dorchester Gaol, was unable to pursue his original trade of making and mending kettles, and therefore should be released so that he could do something useful by resuming such plebian work.[30] He also sought to brand Carlile, on account of his advocacy of contraception and extra-marital sex, a monster of depravity intent on dragging the nation's maidenhood into prostitution.[31] Carlile retaliated, charging Cobbett with cowardly desertion of the radical cause when he fled to America in 1817.[32] He also accused Cobbett of being a crypto-Catholic for publishing his *A History of the Protestant Reformation* in 1824, a work alleging that Henry VIII had broken with Rome in order to take possession of church property.[33] He questioned Cobbett's powers of reasoning, claiming that trapped by 'deep-rooted prejudices... his reasonings and arguments are shallow and rarely useful to the working class of people'.[34] For Carlile, Cobbett was an opportunist rather than a man of principle, 'a political weathercock', 'a freebooter in politics', 'a trading politician', a man moved by 'a passion against persons', not a man the people could trust.[35]

c | Radical Reform's Republican Moment

Yet, despite its bitterness, this schism within the Radical Reform movement did not lead to a complete parting of the ways. In the following decade, two events provoked a radical rethink: first, the Revolution of July 1830 that terminated hereditary monarchy in France in such a way as to demonstrate that a revolution could occur without political or social chaos. Secondly, there was the failure of the Reform Act of 1832 to grant most of the changes Radical Reform required, with universal suffrage, the secret ballot and annual parliaments all denied. As a result, by the mid-1830s Hunt and Cobbett had followed Cartwright in displaying some sympathy, if not enthusiastic support, for a republican system of government, bringing all three of them close, politically if not in religion, to the Paineite reform programme advocated by Carlile.

Major John Cartwright was Radical Reform's most prominent and influential theoretician. His programme, although formulated as long ago as 1776, had recently been backed up by Bentham's *Plan of Parliamentary Reform*, a work first published in 1817 and followed by a revised and simplified version in 1818.[36] In contrast to Cartwright and Bentham, Hunt was little more than a brilliant orator and Cobbett, little more than a brilliant journalist. As effective demagogues, both had contributed leadership, spirit, energy, charisma and courage to the Radical Reform movement but not ideas. These had originated with Cartwright. Acting in the belief that the English constitution had an Anglo-Saxon foundation (a belief which he, in turn, had adopted and adapted from Sir William Blackstone, Obadiah Hulme and James Burgh), Cartwright proposed that, to reform the political system, all that was needed was a reinforcement of the representative element through broadening the electorate to encompass all adult males (which he termed universal suffrage), along with certain safeguards against misuse (namely annual parliaments and voting by ballot). Universal suffrage, he claimed, had flourished in Anglo-Saxon times but, following the Norman Conquest, the practice had declined to the point of extinction. By means of its restoration, he reasoned, the House of Commons could again be made directly answerable to the people as well as independent of control by the Crown and the Lords, allowing a balance between the representative and hereditary elements of parliament to be regained, and a course safely steered between despotism and chaos.[37] By the end of 1816 Cobbett and Hunt had come round to this way of thinking. They now accepted that the parliamentary franchise should be simply a right of every man rather than a privilege confined to men of property or wealth.[38] This left them aligned with Paine on the issue of representation, yet profoundly opposed in their continued willingness to accept an hereditary element in government.

Shortly afterwards, however, Cartwright began to shift in another direction, the result of his researches into Anglo-Saxon history coupled with his appreciation of the new American Republic and how well its democracy was working.[39] Reacting against Paine's provocative assertion that there was no such thing as a formal English constitution, Cartwright eventually produced one which, however, had much in common with Paine's basic political beliefs. It was published in 1823, under the title *The English Constitution Produced and Illustrated*. In it he confessed that, though he had once accepted, as a central element in the constitution, a legislature comprised of 'Kings, Lords and Commons', he had recently undergone a profound change of mind: 'lately I was able wholly to shake off the error [i.e. of 'hereditary legislation'] when fully convinced that it was a fallacy'.[40] Cartwright was now convinced that the true constitution had no role for government by birth right. The House of Lords and a hereditary Crown, he believed, were merely impositions of the Norman Conquest. Applying a metaphor used by Paine, he presented the House of Lords as therefore 'an excrescence' that required excision. As for the monarchy under the Anglo-Saxons, it was never more than an elected chief magistracy.[41] Removing the hereditary claims assumed after the Conquest, he proposed, would restore the constitution to its pristine purity. A major breakthrough in the political thinking of the Radical Reform movement was offered, then, but without effect: for Cartwright died the following year, his book dismissed, by radicals and conservatives alike, as the work of an elderly and demented crank.

As with Cartwright, witnessing the American model of a republic in operation caused Cobbett and Hunt to adopt a more open-minded attitude towards the political principles of Paine. In 1829 both, in a final joint venture – after which they became again embroiled in a bitter, irreconcilable squabble – produced a declaration of radical reform. Published in *Cobbett's Register* under the title 'To the Reformers of the Whole Kingdom', the piece was significantly dated 4 July (i.e., the Day of American Independence), although not issued until 11 July.[42] It recommended 'the great and glorious republic on the other side of the Atlantic that gave an example to the oppressed in every part of the world'. With reference to republicanism, Hunt on 16 June 1832 publicly admitted – at a meeting of the National Union of the Working Classes (a party with republican affiliations) in Pendleton, Lancashire – that, although hereditary monarchy was his preference, his primary concern was 'cheap government'. The patent inability of contemporary monarchs to achieve this goal, and the contrasting success of the USA in its attainment, had led him to think that it would be best for Britain to adopt 'a republican government' along American lines.[43] Two months later, in a letter written to the periodical *Cosmopolite*, he told the staggering lie: 'At no period of my life, since I read Paine's *Rights of Man*, did I ever utter a word against him or his admirers.' Instead, he claimed, he had always spoken of Paine 'in the terms of the highest admiration'.[44]

Cobbett followed in Hunt's footsteps. In March 1835, he questioned the commonly held fear that the termination of kingship would have dire consequences. Would the establishment of a republic in Britain, he asked, be such a 'hellish sort of thing' as to lead necessarily to anarchy or despotism? Look at the USA, Cobbett told his readers, where, thanks to its revolution, the people were free, equal and happy and the economy was in a flourishing state. For him the question begging an answer was not whether a republican government would be good or bad for Britain but how soon could it be introduced and how best could it be employed to solve the outstanding problems of the present: i.e. the high cost of government, the political corruption represented by the Civil List, the social injustice of the New Poor Law, and the military despotism embodied in the new police force.[45]

Nonetheless, when Hunt came to regard republicanism as a viable political system for Britain, he had reached the age of fifty-nine. Suffering from ill-health, he was well past his prime and about to retire from public life. The same was true of Cobbett, a decade older than Hunt. Having recommended republicanism as something to consider 'fully and frankly', Cobbett had to admit that 'the time was not ripe'; by which he meant that his health was no longer up to the massive task of its implementation and, by implication, that therefore the bones in his possession should be left in peace rather than used to inspire a destruction of the old order.[46]

d | The NUWC and its Promotion of Paine

In the early 1830s, the time seemed never more ripe for raising the republican flag. No longer was Carlile ploughing a lonely furrow. Independently of him and his followers, others were eager to embrace Paineite republicanism. This applied not only to the leaders of Radical Reform. Alongside the republican periodicals associated with Carlile – that is, the *Cosmopolite*, the *Isis*, the *Prompter* and the *Gauntlet* – there appeared several other low-priced weekly periodicals, all dedicated to the Paineite cause: the work of Henry Hetherington, James Lorymer, James Watson, John Cleave and Richard Egan Lee. Between 1831 and 1834, Hetherington published the *Republican*, the *Destructive* and the *Poor Man's Guardian*, while Lorymer brought out *Le Bonnet Rouge*, the *Reformer* and the *Laughing Philosopher*, Watson and Cleave provided the *Working Man's Friend*, and from Lee came the *Man*.[47] As well as republican newspapers, cheap editions of Paine's *Rights of Man* were published, printed by Watson, B.D. Cousins, Muir, Gowans and Co. of Glasgow, and John Brooks, while Hetherington and Lorymer produced *The Beauties of the Works of Thomas Paine*, published in a series entitled *Every Man's Library of Republican and Philosophical Knowledge*. Also issued in the early 1830s, in a series entitled *The Harp of Liberty*, was a selection of 'True Republican Songs and Toasts', the work of Clio Rickman and others. In addition, there appeared *Berthold's Political Handkerchief*, a broadsheet newspaper printed on calico which invited female subscribers to use the material, once read, to make dresses for themselves and their daughters, and thus become walking advertisements for the republican cause. Over and above all, a republican party came into being: the National Union of the Working Classes and Others (NUWC) was dedicated to establishing a system of government based upon not only universal suffrage but also the complete absence of rule by birth right.[48]

What is more, in the early 1830s Hunt's policy of challenging the establishment by peaceful means alone was losing its persuasive grip as it appeared to achieve nothing. Fobbed off or ignored, Radical Reformers became more inclined to recommend physical force, or at least the threat of it, and showed a greater willingness to perceive reform in terms of revolution. In 1830 Cobbett, in his Rotunda lectures, presented the French revolution of that year as a responsible and effective instance of popular physical force. The following year he, along with Carlile, publicly approved of the Captain Swing riots. In July 1831 Julian Hibbert, in chairing a meeting of the NUWC to commemorate the anniversary of the 1830 French Revolution, regretted that the working classes of Paris had not insisted upon the establishment of a republic as a prerequisite to putting down their arms.[49] In 1832 Carlile, under the pseudonym of 'John Smith', published Colonel Macerone's *Defensive Instructions for the People* which offered advice on street fighting and on weapons that could be effectively deployed against armed troops. Much cheaper editions of the same work were published by Hetherington and by Carlile's son Richard, with pointed illustrations of civilians, equipped with lances and guns, in successful combat against foot soldiers and cavalry.[50]

Cobbett in his Rotunda lectures of 1830 had urged Englishmen to acquire firearms. The same point was made in 1833 by Carlile and taken up by his followers.[51] The cry was raised that, to be free, men needed to be armed, in keeping with American example. The same call to arms had been made years earlier by Cartwright in his book *England's Aegis* (1804, 1806), accompanied by his own designs for appropriate weapons, notably a 'Britannick spear' and a 'boarding pistol'. His appreciation of the right to bear arms initially rested on the belief that it would exclude the need for a standing army to defend the realm against foreign attack; but by the 1830s the same right was seen as a device to protect against a despotism imposed from within: by not only the army but also a newly established police force.[52] In response to an attack by the 15th Hussars on an unarmed crowd in Clitheroe, and moved by memories of the Peterloo Massacre of 1819, recently recalled by the belated publication of Shelley's *Masque of Anarchy*, Hetherington exhorted, as editor of the *Poor Man's Guardian*, in August 1832: 'How long will Englishmen remain unarmed? Will you suffer yourselves to be massacred and trodden underfoot...and content yourselves with merely throwing a few stones in return?' 'An armed people can never be enslaved', he declared, proposing the establishment of pistol-shooting competitions and clubs to improve marksmanship among the working classes.[53]

Between 1831 and 1835 the leading advocate of universal suffrage ceased to be the Huntite Radical Reform Association. Replacing it in this role was the National Union of the Working Classes and Others, a party expressly affiliated to Paineite republicanism but not to the republican following led by Carlile.[54] This National Union was founded in April 1831, at a time when government plans for parliamentary reform were persuading political reformers to accept a property franchise, even though it would exclude the working classes from the vote. With Hunt's single-minded adherence to universal suffrage no longer sufficient to stop his following from draining away, his former supporters looked elsewhere, joining either the new National Political Union (NPU), which backed the government's Reform Bill, or the new National Union of the Working Classes (NUWC) with its Paineite belief in a totally elective government. At the same time, Carlile was perversely opposing all unions, political or trade, and even prepared to accept a restricted franchise. For his following, his capacity for self-contradiction was utterly baffling. On the one hand, he continued to call for the end of monarchy; on the other, he was playing with the idea of elective monarchy and making complimentary remarks about William IV.[55] His self-destructive tergiversations hinted at madness, perhaps the long-term effect of ingesting raw mercury.[56] By August 1833 even his loyal and tolerant patron, Julian Hibbert, had had enough, writing: 'You are at present the most unpopular man in existence.' In the same letter, he urged him to 'turn over a new leaf', 'cease to insult the unions', and refrain from applauding the duke of Wellington.[57]

The failure of Hunt to retain support, and the failings of Carlile to produce a practical programme of reform, persuaded many former Huntites and Carlileites to switch allegiance to the NUWC as it emerged under the direction of Henry Hetherington, Benjamin Warden, George Foskett, William Lovett, James Watson, John Cleave and Julian Hibbert.[58] This transference of support got under way a month after Hetherington in March 1831 had founded the *Republican, or Voice of the People*, and a month or so prior to his publishing the *Poor Man's Guardian*, which assumed the task of recording the new party's meetings.[59] In August 1832 Hetherington joined together a periodical entitled the *Radical* with his *Republican*, calling the new paper the *Republican and Radical Reformer* in a clear attempt to convert former Hunt supporters to Paineite republicanism.[60] Assisting the establishment of the new party was Carlile himself who, having denied, in December 1830, the Radical Reform Association, along with the Metropolitan Political Union, the privilege of meeting at the Rotunda (a large debating hall that he rented, and rented out, in Blackfriars), conferred its use in July 1831 upon the NUWC.[61] Shortly afterwards, a separate contribution to the promotion of republicanism – again through the medium of the NUWC – was made by William Benbow, the very man who had, as we have seen, helped Cobbett grub up Paine's bones and ship them to England in 1819 and who, along with Carlile, had also been engaged in the republication of Paine's works.[62]

In January 1832 Benbow published plans for a general strike in an emotive, exhortatory and extreme pamphlet entitled *Grand National Holiday and Congress of the Productive Classes*. It had a much wider remit than the simple withdrawal of labour. On the day of the strike a congress, in a manner reminiscent of Paine's national convention, would legislate a constitution aimed to establish 'equal rights, equal liberties, equal enjoyments, equal toil, equal respect, equal share of production'. Universalist in scope (i.e. 'for all mankind'), the pamphlet was, nonetheless, pitched at the British working classes who, as 'the drudges of society...do everything and enjoy nothing'. For remedy, Benbow proposed the people should acquire knowledge, specifically 'of our own power, of our immense might' coupled with an awareness 'of the right we have to employ in action that immense power'. This boiled down to forsaking an expectation of aid from the middle classes 'or from any other class than those who suffer'. Rather, the British working classes should take a lesson from the people of Paris and, accepting that 'kingship and privilege are incompatible with popular liberty', they 'shall strike for a republic'.[63] In other words, a Paineite message was conveyed of republicanism as the universal panacea, but addressed to the productive classes (i.e. the working classes) rather than the nation.

Benbow served as an active member of the NUWC. A fractious maverick, a thorn in the side of the Union's leadership, he was, nonetheless, someone who had to be taken seriously. With the closure of Carlile's Rotunda in March 1832, the result of his decision not to renew the expired lease, the Union adopted Benbow's Institute of the Working Classes on Theobald's Road, Red Lion Square, as one of its two main meeting places. Coincidentally, the other main meeting place was James Watson's Philadelphia Chapel on Windmill Street in Finsbury Square, with the 'western classes' assembling in the one, and the 'eastern classes' assembling in the other. Such an arrangement gave Benbow the opportunity to act as chairman of the Union meetings held at his Institute.[64] By now, the NUWC was a well-organised party. Directed by a permanent committee, it had a system of enrolment and a card-holding membership arranged in local classes. It ran weekly general meetings to debate issues proposed in advance. Procedures were in place for passing resolutions and keeping minutes of debates and transactions. The NUWC not only functioned over a large part of the metropolis but also reached beyond London to form provincial branches, all of them presented as unions of the working classes, with potent concentrations of support in the Midlands, notably in Birmingham, and in the Northwest, centring upon Manchester.[65] Holding the party together was the *Poor Man's Guardian* which provided a weekly report of the Union's current and forthcoming business, views and activities.

Subjected to the pressures of a dwindling following, a desperate and defeated Hunt – who, in December 1832, was about to suffer the humiliation of losing his parliamentary seat in the elections to the reformed parliament – began, as we have seen, to concede that republicanism was not an utterly bad idea. His aim was to reach an accord with the NUWC and enlist the allegiance of its members. Encouraging him to do so was the support he was still attracting in his own special domain, the 'Peterloo' regions of the Northwest, in spite of the following the NUWC had gained there.[66] In July, a few weeks after first speaking in favour of republicanism to members of the Union in the Northwest, a second meeting occurred, again in Pendleton, between Hunt and members of the same Union. On this occasion, a deputation from the Manchester Union of the Working Classes persuaded Hunt to visit the site of Peterloo, and 'on that fatal spot' to deliver an address. For that purpose, they took him, on 13 July, in a huge procession from Pendleton to Manchester, accompanied by a band and sporting banners, some with Paineite associations. Inscribed on one was 'The Rights of Man'; and on another the quote often attributed to Paine: 'For a nation to be free 'tis sufficient that she wills it'. After the address, a dinner was held at the Windmill Tavern overlooking St Peter's Field where several toasts were drunk to republican heroes: notably, 'To the immortal memory of Thomas Paine'; 'To the indefatigable advocate of liberal opinions, Richard Carlile'; and 'To Henry Hetherington' (currently editor of the *Republican*). A further toast, with Paineite and Carlile implications, proposed 'That the edifices erected to prolong the age of superstition, bigotry and oppression [i.e. churches] may become the halls of science and temples of real knowledge for the political improvement of the human race'. Hunt excused his absence from the dinner on grounds of fatigue; but there is no reason to believe that, if he had attended, the toasts would have been any different.[67] It seems, then, that the reform programme he now shared with the NUWC was an unabashed Paineite one; and that Hunt saw himself gaining massive working-class support simply by admitting a radical change in his attitude to monarchy.

In the course of 1831, the NUWC proceeded to publish two declarations of policy and principle, both imbued with Paineite sentiments.[68] The first, entitled 'Declaration of the Rights of Man' and consisting of eleven articles, was approved and made public in June 1831. It faithfully echoed Paine in a preamble which proclaimed the importance of the 'unalienable rights' of man, and in article 2 which defined one of these rights as 'equality before the laws'.[69] Article 8 was distinctly Paineite, in stating that one generation cannot subject future generations to its laws since 'a people have always the right of revising, amending and changing their constitution', an argument used by Paine to deny the validity of hereditary monarchy and to brand it an inevitable despotism.[70] Article 11 similarly reflected Paine in stating: 'when a government violates the rights of the people, resistance becomes the most sacred and indispensable of duties'.[71] Yet the declaration did not explicitly require the abolition of monarchy or the House of Lords. This omission was seized upon by Carlile as he subjected the document to minute analysis in the *Prompter*, critically observing that it did not relate the 'rights of man' to 'monarchical despotism' as Paine had done. On the other hand, Carlile commended the declaration for offering 'no promised support to kingcraft, lordcraft or priestcraft', alleging that, in this respect, it stood in sharp contrast with the promises made by Hunt, the previous year, to the Metropolitan Political Union.[72] The authors appeared to be Hetherington, Foskett, Warden and two others who introduced it to the NUWC membership on 25 May 1831. After some debate, it was approved on 4 June.[73]

The second declaration came in two versions, the earlier one approved on 5 October 1831, only to be replaced by the other a month later.[74] Accepted by the Union's membership on 4 November, this revised version was accompanied by ambitious plans to ensure its full support from the 'useful classes', not only in London but also in the provinces, through meetings to be held on 7 November.[75] In sharp contrast with the October version's willingness to 'rely on the honest intentions of a Patriot King', the November version was explicitly republican. It consisted of six principles expressed in seven articles.[76] Presented as coming from 'we the working classes of London', it asserted in article 4 the Paineite principle 'that all hereditary distinctions of birth are unnatural and opposed to the natural rights of man' and therefore to be abolished. This was preceded, in article 3, by a related principle laying down that all laws should be 'instituted for the common benefit in the protection and security of all the people and not for the emolument or advantage of any single man, family or set of men'. The November version also connected itself to Paine by declaring in article 1 that only property which had been honestly acquired should be regarded as 'inviolable', and by insisting in article 6 that membership of parliament should not be confined to men of property.[77] It was avowedly the work of William Lovett, a cabinet maker, and of the printer James Watson.[78]

In the late 1820s, Watson had gone to work for Julian Hibbert, classical scholar, republican and atheist, who nursed him back to health when he fell ill with cholera and provided him with a printing press.[79] This Watson used, from the 1830s to the 1850s, to republish Paine's works, thus taking up where Carlile had left off a decade earlier. He also followed in Carlile's footsteps by reprinting on three occasions (1833 with Hetherington, 1840 and 1847) Shelley's *Queen Mab*, a poem with essay-length notes which covered the whole gamut of radicalism by declaring itself republican, democratic, atheistic, pacifist, in favour of temperance, vegetarian, for animal rights, against marriage and appreciative of labour value.[80] Watson's republican affiliations were fully expressed in 1833 when he published *The Working Man's Political Companion*, a collection of Paine's major political works, and a weekly periodical entitled the *Working Man's Friend*, the latter replete with quotes and sentiments from Paine. And it was Watson who rescued Paine's bones when they came up for auction in 1853.[81] There can be no doubt about both his republican credentials and their Paineite provenance.

As for Lovett, he eventually became a leading Chartist, drafting in 1838 the six points of the People's Charter, none of which made any reference to republicanism.[82] However, seven years earlier, along with Watson, he was a close associate of Julian Hibbert. In his autobiography Lovett recorded how, at that time, Hibbert had visited him in prison and 'put me a few crumbs of biscuit through the wire grating on the door'.[83] At this time (i.e. 1831), Lovett's outlook had been very different. 'I belong to the republican party', he had declared: that is, the NUWC.[84] Apart from his role in drafting the Union's November declaration, his Paineite republicanism was revealed by an anecdote in his autobiography. It concerned a deputation sent from the Union to consult Lord Melbourne, the Home Secretary, about this particular declaration. Upon learning that 'police were posted in the next room with truncheons at the ready', Lovett sardonically commented: 'I suppose they thought that prime ministers could not be safely trusted with men who had declared that all hereditary distinctions ought to be abolished.'[85]

Both declarations (i.e. of June and November) were published in the first year of the Union's life. That it continued to abide by their terms is indicated by a third declaration, produced in May 1833.[86] This followed the content of the June declaration but made two significant changes. One was to place, as its very first article, clauses 2 and 3 of the November declaration. It thus began, in a Paineite manner, in calling for the abolition of 'all hereditary distinctions' and by affirming that the purpose of government was for the common benefit of all the people and not to favour 'any man, family or set of men'. It then proceeded to confirm its Paineite provenance, in a section headed 'Statement of Grievances', by condemning the law of primogeniture, the Funding System and 'hereditary and exclusive legislation passed by a corrupt and selfish few'. On the other hand, it omitted articles 10 and 11 of the first declaration which, true to Paine, had presented the people's right to resist government tyranny as 'the most sacred and the most indispensable of duties'. However, this did not detract from the third declaration's basic adherence to Paine. Essentially, it was an unambiguous demand for the removal of hereditary monarchy and the hereditary peerage, thereby requiring an end to the polity of the blood.

Yet it would be wrong to present the declarations made by the NUWC as simply expressions of political radicalism, their grievances and principles drawn wholly from Paine or Cartwright. The NUWC emerged from the British Association for Promoting Cooperative Knowledge.[87] Consequently tinged with the philosophy of Robert Owen, it was also influenced by ideas found in the works of Thomas Hodgskin and Thomas Spence. As a result, it called for radical social reforms that were far removed from the essentially political concerns of Paine.[88] It was not just taxation and lavish government spending that were thought to be at fault; and it was not just the replacement of hereditary rule and rank with universal suffrage, that was seen as the quintessential remedy. Paine's frame of reference was the oppression of the people or the nation by a tyrannical government; whereas the NUWC focused specifically on those providing the labour for the production of wealth as against those responsible for its circulation, accumulation and consumption.

Thus, article 2 of the Union's first declaration, a statement of the rights of man in society, required for the working man 'the full enjoyment of the produce of his labour'. Elaborating on this point, the same declaration, in its enumerated 'objects', expressed the wish 'to obtain for every working man...the full value of his labour and the free disposal of the produce of his labour' as well as to uphold 'the fair and rational opposition made by societies of working men... against the combination and tyranny of masters and manufacturers, whenever the latter shall seek, unjustly, to reduce the wages of labour'.[89] The second declaration pursued (if not so emphatically) the same theme, asserting the importance of labour and the need for its protection.[90] It started with the quotation 'labour is the source of wealth' and concluded by declaring its list of principles (among which was the abolition of hereditary government) 'to be essential to our protection as working men and the only sure guarantees for the securing to us the proceeds of our labour'. Indicative of the NUWC's opposition to gross economic inequality, the declaration also approvingly displayed a classical quote from Thales of Miletus (probably provided by the classical scholar Julian Hibbert) which stated: 'That commonwealth is best ordered when the citizens are neither too rich nor too poor.'

The Union's 1831 declarations, then, voiced a working-class point of view and adopted a class attitude towards employers of labour or owners of capital, emphasising their uselessness when compared with the providers of labour, the true producers of wealth. Hunt picked up this message from the Union. Eager to attract and retain the support of its members, he expressed his approval of not only its republicanism but also the value it placed upon labour. In October 1832, when addressing an inaugural meeting of the Birmingham Union of the Working Classes, he dramatically raised the question 'whether any reform will benefit the working classes that will not secure to them the fruits of their labour', providing the emphatic answer 'No, no' in anticipation of the audience's response.[91] In his search for support, Hunt was prepared not only to embrace Paine's political principles but also to reveal publicly his own appreciation of the value of labour and the working classes who provided it. In November 1832 he addressed a large, rain-drenched crowd outside Padiham. To immense cheering, he said that 'he wished the people to be well-remunerated for their labour whereby they would be well fed, well-clothed and [able] to educate their own children in their own way and not by charity.'[92] In December 1832, returning from electoral defeat in Preston, he addressed a huge crowd on the field of Peterloo, speaking for thirty minutes in 'a severe hailstorm'. Although no longer an MP, he emphasised that he would continue to serve the public, 'particularly the working classes'.[93] The following January, he was found chairing a meeting of the NUWC at its centre in Red Lion Square.[94]

The Union's plan in late 1831 had been to obtain a broad, popular authorisation of the principles expressed in its second declaration. This it hoped to achieve at a public assembly to be held on 7 November 1831 in front of White Conduit House in Islington. Here, it would seek to obtain a ratification of the declaration's seven articles and an approval of certain resolutions. The 'useful classes' in the provinces were instructed to follow suit on the same day: 're-echoing these principles...in public meetings throughout the country'.[95] The plan uncannily reflected one produced at the end of June of that year. It was presented as 'Letter from a Poor Man' and appeared in the *Poor Man's Guardian* but was probably written by the very rich and ardent republican Julian Hibbert. It called for a 'great council of the nation' which bore a strong resemblance to Paine's notion of a national convention in having a remit to agree, at a meeting of elected delegates, a legal code to be called 'the Constitution of the British

Nation'. Having performed this task, the council would be dissolved with the option of meeting again, with a fresh election of delegates, if an amendment to the constitution were required.[96]

Upon learning of the Union's plan, the government issued a proclamation banning the November meeting and made military preparations in case the meeting was not called off. Why was it so alarmed? Not long before, in July 1831, Hetherington had publicly revived Spencean demands for replacing private property by common ownership. Writing in the *Poor Man's Guardian*, he claimed that Richard Carlile's call for the abolition of 'kings, priests and lords' was perfectly proper but fell short of providing an adequate solution. What was needed as well, he claimed, was recognition that 'it is property which has made tyrants and not tyrants property'. 'Were there no property', he argued, 'there would be no kings, priests and lords'. Carlile's republicanism, Hetherington claimed, was simply exposing the effect of tyranny whereas, in contrast, 'we grapple with the cause, and would at once destroy it'. He concluded: 'Down then with property, and kings, lords and priests will go down for themselves.'[97] For the landowning establishment this raised a terrifying prospect. But interestingly, the Union's November declaration did not pursue the point. Instead, it sought to scotch it. Prominently placed, as its first article and in words that echoed Paine, was a defence of private property. It read: 'All property (honesty acquired) to be sacred and inviolable.' Moreover, while present in the November declaration, the appreciation of the importance of labour was confined to an opening quotation and a closing remark. This left, as its foremost message, an advocacy of Paine's antipathy towards hereditary succession coupled with a distinctively Paineite solution. The planned November meeting, and its role in approving a list of principles, resembled something Paine had proposed as a necessary step towards achieving the destruction of hereditary rule: i.e., a national convention.[98]

Paine had first proposed the embryo of a convention in *Common Sense*, calling it a continental conference. Its purpose was to frame a written constitution for the thirteen rebel colonies in the form of a continental charter that would set out the basic principles of government and establish a unity of agreement between the colonies with the aim of preventing some bandit, in the manner of Massenello, from 'leading a rebellion to make himself king'.[99] The charter would be accomplished by a continental conference acting in 'a cool and deliberate manner'. Having accomplished its task of formulating an acceptable constitution, it would then be dissolved.[100] That a national convention 'was to make a constitution', rather than to carry one out through acts of legislation, was made in *Rights of Man* part I.[101] In *Rights of Man* part II further clarification of its nature came, with Paine recalling that three years ago he 'pressed' Edmund Burke to propose a national convention, presumably in parliament. 'Fairly elected', its assigned task would be to consider 'the state of the nation'. This, he reasoned, would 'explode' the savage custom of settling governmental differences by civil war, the national convention allowing 'the general will' to arbitrate and ensure that 'order is preserved uninterrupted'.[102] The actual role of a national convention was finally set out in his *A Letter Addressed to the Addressers on the Late Proclamation*, published in 1792: it was to discover the general will of the nation on creating a constitutional code, as a first step to ascertaining the extent to which the system of government needed to be reformed in the eyes of the people.[103] Its second task was to review, and weed out, the existing laws, a task which Paine thought should be performed every twenty-one years or so. Otherwise, the convention would not need to be in session.[104] Unlike parliament, with its exclusivity and corruption, the convention would consist of delegates, one thousand of them, elected by all the people.[105] Such a procedure, Paine argued, would overcome the drawbacks of the present system in which it was left to a corrupt parliament to reform itself aided only by a system of petitioning that it could easily ignore.[106] Paine's idea was taken up by others, notably Joseph Gerrald, who published in 1794 *A Convention, the Only Means of Saving Us From Ruin*, by Richard Carlile in the *Republican* for 1 December 1820, and by Henry Hetherington in the *Poor Man's Guardian* for early 1831. Each contribution inspired an attempt to hold a national convention but without success.[107]

With Paine's intervention, two modes of parliamentary reform developed in the late eighteenth and early nineteenth centuries, one the work of so-called associations which emphasised their intention to restore an ancient constitution, not to create a new one, and to proceed by a method of complaint acceptable in law: either a written remonstrance, agreed at an open-air meeting, or a signed petition addressed to the monarch or to parliament.[108] This approach, first proposed by Obadiah Hulme and James Burgh in the 1770s, found favour, over the next seventy years, with Cartwright, then Hunt, and finally the Chartists. It confined itself to making the House of Commons answerable, by means of the introduction of universal suffrage, to the people while continuing to show respect for the existence of the Crown and the Lords. In contrast, Paine's approach repudiated associations and petitions, arguing that neither expressed the general will of the nation; nor were they effective in achieving reform.[109] He preferred a convention of delegates elected by the whole people, whose task was twofold: to create a new constitution, since the old one could hardly be said to exist, and to require the complete abolition of the polity of the blood, thereby establishing a system of government that was wholly representative of the people and completely answerable to the nation. As a result, two distinctly different types of national convention came into operation: the one created by the Chartists, specifically to formulate and present a petition sanctioned by a large number of signatures. Its goal was to preserve an ancient system of limited monarchy by restoring to it an electoral franchise of universal suffrage. The other type of convention, as promoted by Paine, was bent on political innovation. Its aspiration was to allow an assembly of the nation to establish a republican constitution. Whereas the former was acceptable to the government because it could be seen as functioning within the scope of the present constitution, the latter was seen as 'new-fangled', against the law and intent on a violent destruction of the existing system of government. Ignoring Paine's protestation that the convention was a means of avoiding civil war through allowing the settlement of political differences by peaceful means, the government adopted a highly repressive approach to it, as was evident not only in 1793-4 but also in 1831-3. This approach contrasted with the remarkable forbearance shown by the government towards the other type of convention, the one that, under the Chartists, had evolved from a tradition of parliamentary reform by association.[110]

That the convention planned by the NUWC in November 1831 complied with Paine's idea of a national convention was, in fact, made explicit in a circular produced at the time by James Baden Lorymer. Printed by Hetherington, it was entitled 'A National Convention: the Only Proper Remedy'.[111] Moved by the Lords' rejection of the Reform Bill, it condemned the monarchy and the House of Lords for employing their hereditary privileges to favour 'the borough-mongering, tyrannical, blood-thirsty, plundering, execrable anti-reform aristocrats', and called upon 'fellow citizens' to ignore the 'glorious damnable constitution' and 'represent yourselves'. It proposed how this could be done: 'Let every city, town and considerable borough elect delegates for each place and its vicinity, to be deputed to sit and legislate for their constituents in the place now occupied by the mock representative borough-mongers' creatures and nominees of the national nuisances of Lords.' In other words, let us replace 'mock representatives' by 'real representatives'. This could be achieved if the unrepresented took the matter of remedy 'in their own hands'. It concluded:

'That remedy, the sole, proper and decisive remedy, is the election of delegates to be formed into a NATIONAL CONVENTION.'

The banning of the November 1831 assembly by proclamation was followed by a consultation between the Union's committee and the Home Secretary. At this meeting Melbourne condemned the NUWC's November declaration as seditious and treasonable. In response, the Union delegation argued that the principles underpinning it were to be found 'in the works of many eminent men' (one of whom was undoubtedly Paine, another must have been Bentham) and, therefore hardly merited 'so serious a charge'.[112] Such reasoning was somewhat specious since, forty years earlier, as everyone knew, Paine had been convicted of political sedition for holding identical sentiments, consequently fleeing the country never to return alive. Through Lovett, the delegation pointed out to Melbourne the government's unfairness in allowing 'the middle classes' to have open-air meetings for their political unions while denying the same right to the NUWC. Unmoved, Melbourne presented the proposed meeting as 'highly illegal', adjudging attendance of it 'an act of high treason'.[113] The sticking point was clearly not parliamentary reform, since meetings calling for a restorative alteration to the parliamentary franchise were accepted as perfectly lawful. Rather, it was the fact that members of the working classes were blatantly subscribing to the extreme and innovatory reform programme advocated by Paine. Melbourne had his way. The same evening the Union's committee had 'a very warm debate' on whether to hold or delay the November meeting. Sensing that the government was in deadly earnest, it voted unanimously for an indefinite postponement.[114] Such a meeting – conceived to establish a new system of government by means of a national convention, all in accordance with what Paine had recommended – was not to be attempted again until May 1833.[115]

e | O'Brien Makes his Mark

In the early 1830s three political developments impressed themselves on the NUWC's outlook and its attitude towards Paine. First, there was the Lords' rejection of the Commons' Reform Bill in October 1831. This generated in radical circles an extreme hostility towards the peerage, provoking calls for its abolition. Secondly, there was the passing of the Reform Act in June 1832, but only after a long process of enactment reaching back to March 1831. In this time, it became clear that the principle of universal suffrage would become side-lined as large numbers of political reformers – chiefly drawn from the middle classes but also prosperous artisans and shopkeepers – shelved their support for Radical Reform. Instead they joined the National Political Union, a party prepared to approve a property franchise that would, in effect, deny the working classes the right to vote.[116] In this manner, the eventual passing of the Reform Bill created a class fissure within the parliamentary reform movement that rendered the universal suffrage lobby more exclusively working class than ever before, and consequently more intent on emphasising the value of labour as a major source of grievance. Prior to that, the complicated passage of the bill through parliament had incited a strong hostility to the hereditary element in the legislative process, the Crown and the Lords, who were blamed, as the Lorymer circular indicated, for ensuring the exclusion from the franchise of a large portion of the population.[117]

Compounding an intensification of social hostility was the politicisation of the trades union movement, the result of its failure to curb the exploitative practices of employers by demonstration or strike action.[118] Previously, taxation had been presented as the major man-made cause of poverty, a view consonant with Paine's arguments for governmental reform. But now, notably from 1832, poverty underwent a profound change of perception as it came to be blamed not only upon an unfair fiscal system but also upon the asymmetrical relationship between capital and labour; and political reform came to be appreciated as a means of imposing restrictions upon the owners of land and capital – something that had not featured in Paine's political philosophy – in order to limit the exploitation of labour through high rents and low wages. Previously, radical reform movements had been quintessentially political (as, for example, those associated with Cartwright, Cobbett and Hunt), or quintessentially social, emphasising the need for a redistribution of the benefits of landownership (as with Spence), or for improving, on a piecemeal basis, the working relationship between employees and employers (as with Owen). Now a party had come to the fore, the NUWC, that was prepared to embrace both facets of radicalism.

Under the auspices of the NUWC the main concern of the Radical Reform movement switched from defending the interest of 'the people' to defending that of 'the working classes'; the issue of exploitation came to be blamed on low wages, high rents and prices unfairly fixed by 'middlemen' (rather than simply on the weight of taxation falling disproportionately upon the poor); and 'the enemy of the working man' ceased to be just the government and its minions but came to include landowners, farmers, merchants, shopkeepers and manufacturers. The establishment of a republic remained on the Union's programme, alongside universal suffrage, but neither was seen as sufficient in itself to remedy what was thought to be the major injustice of the time: that is, the pitiful condition of those who, by virtue of their labour, could justifiably be appreciated as the major producers of wealth but who, nonetheless, lived in wretched poverty. This was explained in terms of the grossly unequal way in which wealth was distributed, and the law's inability to contain the opportunistic, conscienceless rapacity of the owners of property and capital. With the 'rights of labour' supplanting the 'rights of man', the issue of injustice came to be articulated in terms of a grievance that Paine had failed to address.

This social complaint was already evident in 1831: for example, in the two declarations produced that year by the NUWC, as well as in remarks made by Henry Hetherington concerning property.[119] It was also found in the already noticed 'Letter from a Poor Man'(probably Julian Hibbert) addressed to 'my dear guardian' and published in the *Poor Man's Guardian* for 30 July 1831, with editorial compliments from Hetherington. The letter opened: 'In every society the land, its produce and the producer of human industry belong, by an unalterable right, to the working people', so much so that 'to him who does nothing...nothing can belong' and whose wealth must therefore have been fraudulently acquired.[120] In 1832 the social complaint was made more prominent by Bronterre O'Brien, a lawyer brought up and educated in Ireland who in 1829 moved to England to practice law but became instead a radical journalist. Replacing Hetherington as editor of the *Poor Man's Guardian* in November 1832, O'Brien also became editor of the *Destructive* (another Hetherington weekly) in February 1833. His thinking was inspired partly by the social reformers Spence and Owen but also, and more unusually, by the social theorists Charles Hall and Thomas Hodgskin.[121]

Hall in his *The Effects of Civilization* (1805) had proposed that the process of civilisation created a basic division in society between the rich and the poor, the one comprising a small minority, the other, the great majority; the one, although useless, rewarded with wealth, the other, although useful, left in dire poverty. In this society the rich held great power over the poor because the poor had no alternative but to depend upon the rich who therefore could appropriate – by means of wages, rents, interest on debt and regressive taxation – as much as they wanted of the fruits of labour.[122] Such power was as great if not greater than that exercised by monarchs.[123] Furthermore, it could exist in republics as well as in monarchies since 'it is wealth that puts power into the hands that have it'.[124] In other words, Paine's solution of terminating the polity of the blood offered no remedy for the bulk of the population. It simply substituted one form of tyranny for another. Somehow or other, the labourer had to regain the full benefit of what he produced. If this were achievable, his happiness could be assured.[125]

Working along the same lines, but with greater sophistication, was Thomas Hodgskin who first declared himself, under the nom de plume of 'A Labourer', in *Labour Defended against the Claims of Capital; or the Unproductiveness of Capital Proved* (1825). Essentially, this tract was written as a counterblast to the political economists, Malthus, Ricardo and James Mill, who had argued that the immiseration of the working classes resulted from the tendency of a population to outstrip the resources available to it, causing a lowering of wages, an increase in rents and rising levels of unemployment.[126] Rather than accept a demographic explanation for poverty, Hodgskin placed the blame upon capitalism and its predatory attitude to labour. According to him, the claims made for the value of capital in the productive process were false since the latter, and the wealth it generated, was quintessentially the work of labour. A redefinition of the respective importance of labour and capital was necessary to expose the injustice of the present system and to pave the way towards a remedy which was beyond the scope of political economists, whom he saw as apologists of capitalist exploitation. For this reason, Hodgskin published his tract. With echoes of Hall, it opened by stating 'The capitalists and labourers form the great majority of the nation, so that there is no third power to intervene betwixt them', and closed with the call to seek 'the progressive improvement' of the nation by allowing 'labour to possess and enjoy the whole of its produce'. Hodgskin's other important work, The *Rights of Natural and Artificial Property Contrasted* (1832), pursued the same aim of elevating the social status of the labourer by arguing that to labour and own the product was a natural right of man, a right sanctified by the fact that it went back to the beginnings of society, whereas the possession of property, in the form of land, was not natural to man and must have been usurped or stolen since originally God had given the earth to man in common. The same could be said of the possession of capital, the accumulation of which had resulted from denying the labourer his natural right to retain the fruits of his work. Much of this was taken from Locke's *Two Treatises of Government* (1689), the original meaning of which had been obscured since, under exposure to aristocratic society, his concept of property had become corrupted to imply 'land' rather than 'labour', while the constitution had come to be regarded as a safeguard of landed property.[127]

In addition, O'Brien's ideas of social reform, especially land nationalisation, were derived from Thomas Spence. Spence had wished to remove individual ownership of land, in his case by placing it in the communal ownership of the parish, and his followers were the first to propose the idea of transferring land from private to public ownership by denying property owners a hereditary right to their land, so that, upon death, it passed into a public fund.[128] Otherwise, O'Brien's ideas of social reform were inspired by the French Revolution. Drawn from Robespierre and Babeuf, they proposed to award labour the right not simply to vote but also to enjoy protection from the rapacity of landowners and capitalists.[129] This was made evident in O'Brien's heavily annotated translation of Buonarroti's *History of Babeuf's Conspiracy for Equality*, eventually published in 1836 by Henry Hetherington. The point made by O'Brien's gargantuan footnotes was that Babeuf's system of equals had originated with Robespierre whose overthrow prevented it from being put into effect, as had the execution of Babeuf and his fellow conspirators. Central to Babeuf's political philosophy was the belief that 'private property is the source of all the calamities on earth' and that therefore the right of property should not lie with individual citizens but should be 'vested always in the Republic'.[130] The issue was clearly set out in Silvain Maréchal's emotive 'Manifesto of the Republic of Equals'. Included as a selected text in *Buonarroti's History*, it declared: 'We aim at something more sublime [than land redistribution]...We look to common property...No more individual property in lands. The earth belongs to no one. We claim – we demand – we will the communal enjoyment of the fruits of the earth; the fruits belong to all.'[131] By the late 1830s, these ideas had germinated into a proposal for land nationalisation which became number 4 of the seven propositions O'Brien sought, unsuccessfully, to add to the six points of the People's Charter.[132]

In the early 1830s O'Brien impressed his ideas on the membership of the NUWC in a series of provocative leaders for the *Poor Man's Guardian*, and in the pages of the *Destructive* (1833-4). Although he attributed them to Robespierre, some were not unlike Paine's. Both men were against kings, aristocrats and priests and utterly devoted to universal suffrage. Both advocated currency reform, making objection to paper money.[133] Both objected strongly to the National Debt not only because, by providing the necessary resources, it encouraged the government to go to war, but also because, in combination with the regressive tax system of the time, and the manner of funding the National Debt through the issue of high-dividend government bonds, it syphoned wealth from the poor to the rich.[134] In counteraction, both men formulated schemes to redistribute wealth downwards, with Paine advocating more public spending to benefit the poor through a 'national fund' financed out of death duties and other fiscal revenue, while O'Brien proposed a system of 'national credit' financed out of the rental revenues accruing to the government from a policy of land nationalisation.[135] These schemes for a redistribution of wealth were in outraged response to pronouncements by clergymen that poverty was socially useful and necessary, O'Brien objecting to Parson Malthus' appreciation of poverty, along with war and plague, for placing a natural check on population growth, and Paine objecting to Bishop Watson's pronouncement that poverty was God-given.[136] Both O'Brien and Paine urgently called for a reform of the tax system to make it more reliant on direct rather than indirect taxation, on the grounds that the former, as a property or income tax, fell appropriately on the rich whereas the latter, as excises on food and drink, fell disproportionately upon the poor.[137] Both, moreover, passionately subscribed to a belief in equal rights and equal laws for all.[138] And both opposed a policy of regicide simply because they believed the system was at fault, and so could not be remedied by the removal of one individual.

Yet profound differences distinguished the one from the other. O'Brien did not subscribe to Paine's belief that hereditary rule was the major problem. For him the old system could be most effectively reformed not by removing monarchy but by curtailing capitalism and ending private property.[139] Whereas Paine's focus was to provide remedy for 'the people' or 'the nation' or 'the poor', O'Brien's concern was specifically to transform the economic condition, the social reputation and the political importance of the working classes. Whereas Paine addressed a conflict between a tyrannical government and the people, O'Brien addressed a conflict between capital and labour. O'Brien passionately opposed the middle classes, whereas Paine appreciated them as a vital instrument in the destruction of the ancien regime. O'Brien's antipathy towards capitalism opened up possibilities unavailable to Paineites, notably in the form of an alliance between Radical Reform and organised labour.

In 1833 O'Brien sought to secure further support for the NUWC by appealing to the trades' union movement. This was done through a sequence of leaders in the *Poor Man's Guardian* urging the trades' unions to join the struggle for universal suffrage. On 14 December 1833 O'Brien observed that, in the 'struggle which is now in progress between labour and capital, we were grieved to find among the leaders of the Unionists [i.e. trades' unionists] a disposition to exclude politics altogether from their deliberations'. On 4 January 1834 he claimed that in the struggle between capital and labour 'labour – the sole fountain of wealth – must prevail in the end' since 'the capitalists have but one bulwark'. That was 'the exclusive power of law-making'. He continued: 'Destroy this [through universal suffrage] and their empire is at an end.' He concluded: 'With universal suffrage our emancipation is certain...Hurrah for the trades' unions! Hurrah for universal suffrage! God save the people!!'[140] As part of the same effort to politicise the trades' unions, he changed the title of a weekly paper he edited from the *Destructive* to the *People's Conservative and Trades Union Gazette*. One outcome of his persuasiveness was, ironically, a dramatic decline in the membership of the NUWC, as working men switched their primary allegiance to the trades' unions in late 1833. Another consequence was the massive working-class support offered Chartism at the end of the decade.

In contrast to Paine, O'Brien declared himself to be against the principle of hereditary landownership and therefore in favour of land nationalisation. Moreover, he was less sympathetic than Paine to the use of popular violence. In spite of his admiration for Robespierre, and his willingness to excuse the large numbers of public executions that Robespierre had authorised, O'Brien advocated a peaceable approach to reform.[141] Thus, land nationalisation was to be achieved not by forcible confiscation but gradually and lawfully: that is, by annexing private estates on the owner's death in return for a fair payment of compensation.[142] Moreover, while both shared a contempt for the priesthood and superstition, O'Brien retained a firm, if unconventional, belief in Christianity, to which he gave a distinctive radical twist by redefining original sin as 'the desire of one man to live on the fruits of another's labour' and by commending Jesus Christ for seeking to destroy 'this demon principle'.[143] O'Brien's emphasis on achieving an economic re-ordering of society made him less reverential than Paine of recent revolutions. For him, the American and French Revolutions were bogus in the sense that their beneficiaries were the few, not the many.[144] Whereas Paine held no grudge against the middle classes, O'Brien detested them for confederating with capitalists at the expense of the working classes.[145] Both men were inspired by the French Revolution but by different stages of it, with Paine appreciating its initial achievement, the successful overthrow of hereditary rule and titles, whereas O'Brien was especially moved by the failed plans to redistribute wealth and social respect that Robespierre had formulated in 1793 and Babeuf had sought to implement in 1796.[146] For addressing the real problems of the time, O'Brien regarded the reforms favoured by Robespierre as much more relevant than those proposed by Paine.

O'Brien first recommended Robespierre to the readership of the *Poor Man's Guardian* in November 1832: in the editorial leader to issue 77.[147] This was backed up by a further recommendation in December, in the leader to issue 81.[148] A year later O'Brien published in the *Destructive* his own translation of Robespierre's 'Declaration of the Rights of Man and Citizen'.[149] In a strikingly novel manner, he presented Robespierre not as an evil, blood-spilling tyrant but as a benevolent reformer whose radical plans to protect the interests of the working classes obliged the owners of property and capital to bring about his overthrow (or 'assassination' as O'Brien liked to call it). In this respect, O'Brien felt that the so-called 'reign of terror', for which Robespierre was held responsible by virtually all British radicals, should instead be seen as 'the reign of equality over privilege and monopoly', or as 'the reign of the plundered many over the plundering few'. According to O'Brien, Robespierre was the French equivalent of Robert Owen since both wished to establish 'an equitable distribution of the fruits of human labour among those who produced them, on the principle of rewarding each according to his work', with the difference that Owen eschewed reform by political means and Robespierre was bent on 'using political power' to achieve social revolution.[150] It was in this manner, then, that a spectacular reassessment of Robespierre occurred and was, through the *Poor Man's Guardian*, conveyed to working-class society in general and the membership of the NUWC in particular.

In reaction, a number of letters to the editor of the *Poor Man's Guardian* raised the matter of Robespierre's brutal treatment of Paine, asking how this reflected upon Robespierre's real character and reputation. For example, William Carpenter criticised O'Brien for omitting to mention it. He also levelled at him the charge: 'You are the first person that I have ever found to defend Robespierre', claiming that 'radicals, republicans and Spenceans have all asserted him to have been a 'horrible monster' whose 'name has been handed down to posterity as something expressive of all that is unjust, savage, cowardly and impious'. He cited how Robespierre had sought to have Paine executed after imprisoning him for eleven months, and how Paine's life had only been spared by Robespierre's own fall from power: that is, the very same Thomas Paine who was widely recognised in radical circles as 'a friend to mankind, a real philanthropist'.[151] Other letters, written in a similar vein, followed: one from William Fisher; another from a certain H.B., who defended Paine by saying that his plan for the removal of kings, priests and aristocrats would (contrary to what O'Brien was suggesting) promote 'the successful introduction of social principles uniting labour and capital for the benefit of all wealth producers'.

Another letter, from J. Coulthard, deplored the comparison O'Brien had made between Owen and Robespierre on the grounds that Owen 'wishes...to promote the happiness of the human race' whereas Robespierre was prepared 'to murder a part of mankind in order to secure the happiness of another part'.[152]

O'Brien retaliated, claiming that Robespierre was 'the best truly great and good man that ever existed', and that Paine was a middle-class stooge who had done nothing for the working man, since nowhere in his writings was there 'any place for a radical change in the social state'.[153] He also dismissed Paine's reform proposals as out of date. O'Brien was prepared to concede that Paine was 'a very able man for his day' but thought his 'views fell immeasurably short of the exalted destiny intended by Robespierre for mankind': so much so that, if all the reforms that Paine had advocated 'were realised tomorrow', it would make little difference and 'the world would soon be in as miserable a state as ever'. In his judgment, 'there was nothing radical in Paine'. Robespierre, on the other hand, had 'a thousand times Paine's depth and perspicacity' and was 'for ever purging society of the very germs of vice'. Paine, he pointed out, was an admirer of the middle-class French Republic of 1792 but 'no friend of [Robespierre's] democratic constitution of 1793'. As a friend of Girondists, O'Brien declared, Paine was not to be trusted. Consequently, his arrest and imprisonment by Robespierre had been perfectly in order.[154]

O'Brien did not succeed in evicting Paine from the NUWC's pantheon of heroes. Writing in March 1833, just after O'Brien's campaign to replace Paine by Robespierre, Henry Hetherington came out strongly in favour of Paine's attitude to landownership, arguing that, while the aristocracy's monopoly of the land was deplorable, private landownership was perfectly acceptable so long as the property in question had been honestly acquired.[155] On the other hand, O'Brien managed to persuade the Union's membership to adopt certain changes of approach towards reform that rendered Paine's solutions increasingly inadequate. The conflict between labour and capital had played no ostensible part in Paine's identification of the problems oppressing society. It had failed completely to feature in his programme of reform. True, an awareness of the conflict between labour and capital had emerged in the pages of the *Poor Man's Guardian* prior to O'Brien's appearance on the scene. For example, it was evident in Hetherington's fulminations against the evils of private property; and it was reflected in the social concerns of the two declarations produced by the NUWC in 1831.[156] But, thanks to O'Brien's elaborations upon the ideas of Thomas Hodgskin in the *Poor Man's Guardian*, the capital-labour conflict became a much more pronounced feature of NUWC policy.[157] Paine's central principle of reform, the termination of rule and rank by hereditary right, thus came to be downgraded to something of secondary importance. On the other hand, Paine's faith in a national convention, summoned to produce and sanction a written constitution, continued to have a potent appeal for the Union's membership: that is, until the disastrous Cold Bath Fields incident of May 1833.

f | The NUWC's Persistence with a National Convention

The Union's first meeting to prepare for a national convention – planned to be held in front of White Conduit House in November 1831 – had been called off, as we have already seen, under threat of military action from the government.[158] But the idea of holding a similar meeting resurfaced in the course of 1832, initially through a succession of advertisements printed in the *Poor Man's Guardian* for May and June.[159] All related to 'An Address on a National Convention', a composition by Henry Hetherington who, in indication of his Paineite affiliations, chose to describe himself on the title page as 'editor of the *Republican*'.[160] In the issue of the *Poor Man's Guardian* for 16 May, the address was announced as 'just published'. Although no copies have survived, its meaning can be worked out. Priced at one halfpenny, it must have been brief.[161] Its declared aim was to provide 'the only proper mode of settling reform' and justifying its publication was the conviction that 'the unrepresented ought to represent themselves'.[162]

Following its publication, the NUWC held several meetings to discuss the matter. They revealed that a national convention was regarded as the best means of dealing with the shortcomings of recent legislation, notably the Reform Act of 1832, which had denied the demand for universal suffrage, and the Coercion Act of 1833, which allowed martial law to be employed against the Irish for refusing to pay tithes and raised the fear among the Union membership that it might be extended to suppress their own cause in England.[163] But to the fore in these discussions was the belief that a national convention would be the best means of liberating the nation from hereditary rule through establishing a Paineite polity founded on 'equal rights and equal laws'. At one meeting, held on 4 June 1832 and chaired by the republican William Benbow, the proposer of the motion for a national convention, John George (a paper hanger by trade who claimed to have been a republican for forty years and who was also a Spencean), stated that he was moved to do so by news that the people of Paris were doing something similar in opposition to the elective monarchy of Louis Philippe.[164] At the same meeting, the journalist Henry Berthold affirmed his attachment to Paine by wanting 'to get rid of hereditary imbecility [i.e. kings and nobles] throughout Europe'. He was especially moved by news from France of 'a popular plan' to establish a republic and felt that 'a national congress was the best means of achieving it'. By such means he hoped 'a commonwealth' would be established superior to any that had previously existed.

Nothing further happened until February 1833 when Benbow revived the idea of holding a national convention. He argued that parliament's ability to improve 'the condition of the working classes' was hindered by 'a pampered monarchy, an indolent aristocracy and a bloated hierarchy'. Therefore, the members of the Union needed to prepare for a 'convention of the people' since this was 'the only mode by which they can devise means to extricate themselves from the grievous misrule under which they have too long and too patiently been suffering'.[165] The point was pursued further at a meeting held the following April when the journalist Richard Egan Lee, in Paineite parenthesis, declared: 'the government of kings, aristocrats and priests had never benefitted the people' and so the best way forward was 'to come immediately to a national convention' in which 'every man that chooses may have his representative in London from all parts of the country'. Put to the meeting, this motion was 'carried by acclamation'.[166]

Three further meetings were held to consider the matter, on consecutive Mondays in late April and early May 1833. At the first meeting, the Spencean carpenter James Mee claimed, when supporting a motion to 'found a system of universal equity' by means of a national convention, that some might call him 'a leveller' bent on abolishing 'the privileges of certain classes'. Instead of denying this charge, he brazenly declared: 'They were right who said so' since such classes were intent on upholding 'the hereditary privileges...brought into the country by that bastard of a fish-fag, William of Normandy'.[167]

At the next meeting, Citizen Lee elaborated on the same issue arguing that 'the middle classes were as much their enemies as the upper classes' and, as a result, kings, priests and nobles could not be pressured into alleviating the lot of the poor. Therefore, a national convention was required to authorise a radical reform of the system of government: one that was justified by 'the people's sacred right to remodel and alter any form of government in order to meet their wants'.[168] All this was true to Paine. Lee was supported by George

Petrie a Scottish tailor, a Spencean and keen trades unionist.[169] In a Paineite manner, he attacked 'the ancient institutions of the country', proposing that there was no reason to venerate monarchy which, thanks to its hereditary nature, would sooner or later place the nation under the rule of a fool or a rogue. Nor was there any need to respect the church which had become such an 'abomination of desolation' that no one, apart from the recipients of its patronage, could regard it as worthy of existence. Such Paineite sentiments met with 'immense cheering', to which Petrie responded by encouraging them to prepare for a national convention which would replace the present hierarchical system with one where 'all have an equal share of the government' and in which – a hint of the influence of Richard Carlile but not of Paine – 'females will be allowed to vote'.[170] At the same meeting a further Paineite contribution was made by the veteran republican John George who claimed that 'the destitute condition' of the people of England and Ireland called for action. He presented the problem as stemming from the exclusiveness of a political system in which 'kings, nobles and priests formed the nation'. The meeting was brought to an end with its chairman prescribing a national convention for remedy and receiving three cheers for doing so.[171]

A third and final meeting, held on 6 May, proceeded a step further by passing, rather than merely considering, a resolution to hold a national convention. That its purpose was to go beyond establishing universal suffrage was revealed by John George who closed the proceedings with a speech on the illegitimacy of hereditary monarchy.[172] In the universalist manner of Paine he claimed that 'the kingly office was the offspring of conquest in all ages of the world' and therefore no monarch could justifiably claim to rule by hereditary right. As for the 'boasted divine hereditary succession', this was not only a fiction but 'the source of most of all the evils under which the nations mourned'. Backing the resolution for a national convention, he presented its role as not only establishing universal suffrage but also disposing of monarchy. The passing of the resolution, and the fiery talk associated with it, was extensively reported in the *Poor Man's Guardian* where it was read not only by the Union's membership but also by government agents on the look-out for seditious activity.

In addition to the NUWC's threatened onslaught upon the old regime, there was published at the same time a series of articles by 'Publica' (a radical journalist named David Edward Williams) attacking the hereditary principle of government and specifically calling for the abolition of the House of Lords. Originally appearing in the *Weekly Dispatch*, these articles were reprinted in James Watson's *Working Man's Friend*.[173] Furthermore, two contributions, printed in the *Destructive* for late April 1833, were signed 'Brutus'. Hiding behind this nom de plume – like Publicola, a key figure in the termination of the Roman Monarchy and the foundation of the Roman Republic – was the classical scholar Julian Hibbert, generous patron of Richard Carlile and James Watson, at the time the two key promoters of the Paineite cause, and respected intellect of the NUWC.[174] Brutus's letter of 27 April mentioned his recent seven-week journey to the north of England which had left him convinced that the people there 'have emerged from reform into that of revolution' and that they were 'inclined to march to London'.[175] This signalled, he sensed, that 'a revolution is inevitable', but, to prevent a bloody one, he thought that 'some sort of constitution should be promulgated'. He therefore proposed that members of the NUWC should 'meet and escort' their northern friends into London, provide them with accommodation and 'proceed forthwith to form a national convention', whose task would be to frame a constitution, establish a provisional government, and make all necessary arrangements for 'well-feeding' the people until a 'national legislative assembly [i.e. a reformed parliament] and a firm government' had been formed. It was a plan dear to Paine, as was its international dimension: for Brutus claimed that the whole of Europe, likewise oppressed by monarchy, nobility and clergy, were looking to 'us' to provide 'the political lever by which they may regenerate themselves'. All that was needed was the establishment of 'a pure republic' in England. To achieve it, Brutus offered 'the outline of a constitution to be submitted to the national convention'.[176] Following Paine, it proposed that the forthcoming national convention should not only formulate and sanction a written constitution but also have the power to reassemble in order to make alterations to it. It reads like the sequel to 'A Letter from a Poor Man' (published by the *Poor Man's Guardian* in July 1831), which had proposed how and why to assemble a national convention. The similarity is so close that, if Hibbert had composed the one, he must have composed the other.[177]

'Outline of a Constitution' by Brutus ran to nineteen clauses. It endeavoured to provide the sort of written code that Paine had recommended, beginning with two principles, both close to Paine: the first, requiring 'all kingly authority, all hereditary titles and the law of entail and primogeniture [to] be abolished' and the second, requiring 'there shall be no state religion [and] all titles [presumably non-hereditary ones such as knighthoods and the intricate panoply of clerical honours] (to) be abolished'. Yet it went well beyond anything suggested by Paine, especially with regard to property. While including in clause 14 the Paineite principle that the rights of private property should be inviolable, along with rights of personal security and liberty, the code laid down, in clause 13, 'that all crown lands, church lands, waste land and whatever may...be constituted national property [and] shall be taken possession of in the name of the nation'. In clause 17 it suggested that 'all the land shall be let out in parcels from one to 100 acres at an equitable rent'. Amenable to Paine would have been clause 15 which declared that 'the people shall be armed, so that they may be prepared at all times to resist any oppression and assert their rights', and clause 19 which proposed 'that it is in the power of the nation, any time, to alter or vary the whole or any part of this constitution by assembling a national convention for that purpose'.

To fulfil such plans and hopes the NUWC announced an open-air meeting to be held on 13 May in Cold Bath Fields, not to hold a national convention then and there but 'to take preparatory steps for carrying [one] into effect' at some future date.[178]

g | The Fiasco at Cold Bath Fields

As in 1831, when the government had issued a proclamation banning a very similar meeting on grounds of illegality, it followed the same course in 1833.[179] But, whereas in 1831 the NUWC had complied with the government's order, in 1833 it chose to make a stand. On this occasion, the government's proclamation was issued on 11 May, two days before the Union's proposed meeting.[180] This was in response to a placard, signed by Secretary Russell, announcing a public meeting on 13 May at 2 pm in Cold Bath Fields.[181] The location was an enclosed waste ground in Clerkenwell, at the back of Cold Bath Fields Prison and at the end of Calthorpe Street which leads off Gray's Inn Road. Close by are Spa Fields where Henry Hunt had held his monster meetings in 1816-17. As the placard made clear, this particular meeting was not intended to be a session of the national convention itself but rather a meeting to determine 'preparatory measures' for holding a national convention. This it justified as the only means (parliament having failed in the task) 'of establishing and securing the rights of the people'. To prevent any misunderstanding of the placard's meaning, 'Public Meeting', 'National Convention' and 'Rights of the People' were printed in bold capitals, with 'Meeting' and 'National Convention' appearing in large lettering. Also by 11 May, the committee had identified in the *Poor Man's Guardian* two assembly points for Union members to meet prior to going in procession to Cold Bath Fields: thus, the classes (i.e. local branches) south of the Thames

Paine and the Tradition of Radical Reform

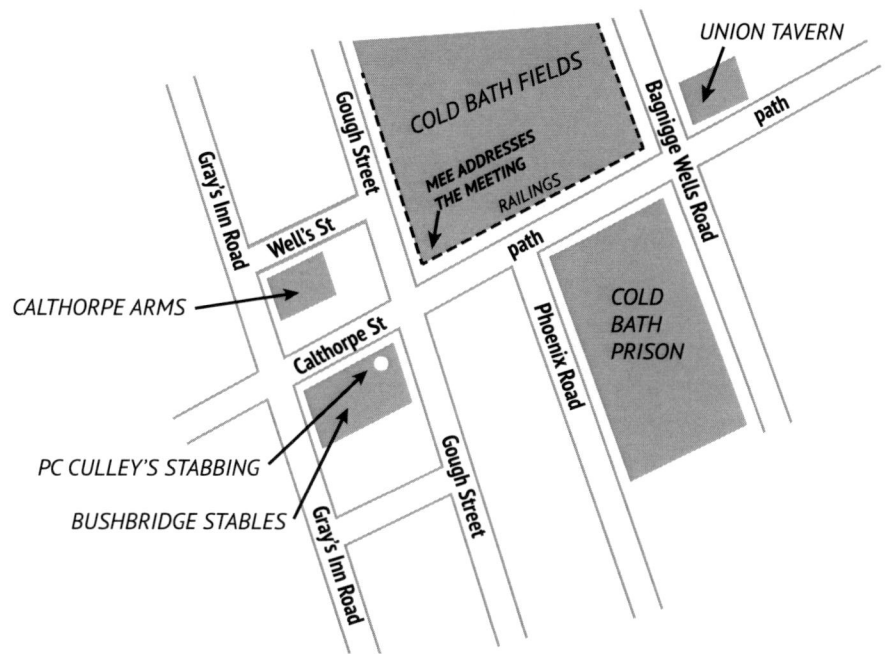

Site of the 13 May 1833 public meeting in Cold Bath Fields, an enclosed waste ground in Clerkenwell, at the back of Cold Bath Fields Prison and at the end of Calthorpe Street which leads off Gray's Inn Road.

were advised to gather on St George's Fields in Southwark, and the east and west classes located north of the river were asked to congregate in Finsbury Square.[182] Moved by the government's proclamation, the Union's committee decided that, rather than calling off the meeting (something impossible to achieve at such short notice) its members should make themselves available 'near the ground' on 13 May in the event of a large turn-out. Then, if the police sought to stop the meeting, they could step forward and adjourn it 'to some better opportunity'.[183]

A head-on clash with the police occurred on the appointed day: an incident lasting no more than a few minutes, a scuffle rather than a skirmish, and only a riot in the sense that a small number in the otherwise peaceful crowd retaliated when brutally attacked by units of truncheon-wielding police, killing one constable and injuring two others. The incident is very well documented, owing to the presence of several journalists (e.g. William Carpenter of the *True Sun*, James Courtenay of the *Courier*, Edward Moran of the *Globe*, James Grant of the *Morning Advertiser*, and an anonymous reporter from the *Times*).

121

Providing a host of further eye-witness accounts was a coroner's inquest on the death of P.C. Culley, a victim of the event, and a parliamentary report on the alleged brutality of the police as they disrupted the meeting and dispersed the crowd. A remarkable amount of eye-witness evidence has consequently survived, although much of it is contradictory, with many inclined to use the witness stand either to defend the actions of the police as necessary and fair, or to defend the claims made by the Union that its members were victims of police brutality.[184]

By ten o'clock on 13 May 'little knots of persons' had appeared and were 'conversing together on the ground'.[185] By eleven o'clock around 300 persons had gathered.[186] By one o'clock the crowd had increased to about 1,500 and, by two o'clock, the time when the meeting was meant to begin, about 3,000 were present.[187] The Union's Committee had yet to show its face, although its members had spent the morning close by – in an upstairs room of the Union Public House on Bagnigge Wells Road (i.e., King's Cross Road) – just the far side of Cold Bath Fields. On the table in this room was a set of resolutions prepared to be put to the meeting for its approval.[188] It comprised a preamble stating that, until the working people obtained universal suffrage, they will remain 'the dupes of designing factions'; a 'declaration of rights'; and a concluding list of grievances. The declaration largely reproduced the first declaration of June 1831 but omitted the final article that had acknowledged the people's resistance to a government intent on violating its rights as 'the most sacred and indispensable' of its duties. Two highly radical demands not present in the declaration of June 1831 were added: prominently placed at the head of the 1833 declaration of rights was a demand for the abolition of all hereditary distinctions (which had featured prominently in the second declaration of November 1831). Also included in the statement was a new demand objecting, in the Spencean manner, to 'individual appropriation of the soil' because the earth 'is the natural right of all'. This rejection of private landownership stood in complete contradiction of the first article in the November 1831 declaration which had asserted: 'all property honestly acquired to be sacred and inviolable'. It also went totally against Paine's attitude to the land. Nonetheless, the 1833 resolutions remained true to Paine in identifying among 'the most prominent of the evils under which we are now suffering' the law of primogeniture, the funding system and hereditary legislators, arguing that, between them, they had created a corrupt, parasitic and grossly expensive political system, the maintenance of which – since it was financed principally out of indirect taxes – fell unfairly 'on the labour and industry of the productive classes of the community'.[189] These resolutions were shown to the journalist William Carpenter when, around two o'clock, he visited the committee in its room at the Union Tavern. His aim, he said, was to persuade the committee to postpone the meeting in view of the government's proclamation banning it and the proximity of sufficient police to enforce the ban. In response, the committee explained that what they intended was perfectly legal – as could be seen from the Union's resolutions – and therefore they would only call off the meeting if required by the police to do so.[190]

At the appointed hour of two o'clock the committee had failed to appear on the ground and, as yet, no hustings had been erected. Disappointed by the committee's absence, and with doubts sown by the lack of hustings and flags – all of which suggested that the meeting had been cancelled – a segment of the crowd was already drifting off.[191] Also by two o'clock the Union's contingent from south of the river had yet to arrive. On the other hand, a large number of police, 1,800 in all, were in the area and armed with truncheons, along with an unspecified number of troops from the Horse Guards and the 1st Regiment of Life Guards, stationed in the adjacent prison. Two of their officers in plain clothes were keeping the crowd under surveillance with orders to report back.[192] The Home Secretary, Lord Melbourne, the very man who had issued the proclamation forbidding the meeting, was close by, concealed within the walls of the same prison.[193] The police had been in the vicinity from at least twelve o'clock, stationed very close to the ground, but out of sight, partly in Dawson's Riding School on Gray's Inn Road and partly in Busbridge's Livery Stables. The latter had a front entrance on Gray's Inn Road and a back gate on Gough Street.[194] Spying on the crowd were police in plain clothing.[195] At three o'clock, the crowd was reckoned at between 1,500 to 4,000 men, women and children.[196] Keen to emphasise the difference between the strength of the armed police and the weakness of the unarmed crowd, the *Poor Man's Guardian* put the latter at about 500 men and 1,000 old men, women and children.[197] An eye-witness sympathetic to reform described the assembly as small in size but 'very imposing' and with 'a great number of respectable women'. His estimate of around 2,000 seems about right, given that 3,000 were reckoned to have been present an hour earlier: that is, before many had been deterred from staying by the Union committee's failure to show up at the appointed time.[198] Like most contemporary open-air reform meetings it was difficult to estimate how many in the assembled crowd were attending out of conviction and how many were there simply out of curiosity.

To place the event in some perspective, it should be noted that, only twenty-six days earlier, the NUWC had held another reform meeting on Cold Bath Fields, with members coming to the ground in processions from different assembly points.[199] This had been a much more extravagant affair, the processions arriving with musical bands as well as banners and with an attendance amounting to 25,000. Three conjoined vans had served as the hustings. Several radical MPs were invited, but only Feargus O'Connor had turned up after Cobbett had promised to attend but then bowed out with a troublesome cough. The Irish Coercion Bill had been the issue, to protest against which resolutions had been approved and incorporated in a petition to the Commons. Although Richard Egan Lee had told the crowd that Magna Carta was broken and that consequently the people needed 'to make a constitution which shall never be broken', no specific mention of national conventions was made. Nor had there been an attempt to by-pass parliament or to question the principle of hereditary rule. As a result, the government made no attempt to declare the meeting illegal or to send in the police.

At the meeting on 13 May 1833 trouble broke out around three o'clock. So far, the police had taken no action, having no certain knowledge, in the absence of leaders, flags, hustings and placards, that the present assembly was in breach of the government's proclamation.[200] But at 2.45pm the committee members, five or six of them, joined the crowd, and ten minutes later a horse-driven van drew up in Gough Street North to serve as the hustings.[201] It parked alongside the railing enclosing Cold Bath Fields. But no sooner had several committee members jumped aboard than, following a brief dispute over the charge, the driver drove away, causing the committee members to jump off at the top of Calthorpe Street. Deprived of hustings, the crowd lifted two of the committee members, Richard Egan Lee and James Mee, onto the nearby horizontal railing that separated Gough Street from the waste ground. Both stood there, raised above the heads of the crowd, Mee supporting himself by leaning against a lamp post, Lee propping himself up with the long staff of a placard. This arris rail, about three foot from the ground and supported by a series of widely spaced posts, thus became an improvised hustings from which Mee, successfully proposed as chairman by Lee, delivered an address.[202] The journalist William Carpenter, who stood within hearing distance of Mee, observed that nothing in the address identified the meeting with the government's proclamation: in other words, it made no mention of a national convention.[203] He went on to say that Mee started his address by explaining why they were assembled: it was to consider the conduct of the government and to pass 'a resolution or two declaratory of the grievances of the working classes'. Instead of disclosing these resolutions, Mee proceeded to flatter the crowd, saying how honoured he was to address such a numerous and respectable assembly. Their respectability, he commended, lay not in the possession of 'coronets and splendid equipages', or in the enjoyment of government pensions, but in their 'industrious and peaceable' nature and in their generosity, for, although responsible for producing the country's wealth, they were 'desirous only to enjoy a fair and equitable share of it for themselves'.[204] Totally absent from his speech was the rabble-rousing rhetoric he had displayed at recent meetings of the Union when he had proudly admitted to being a leveller and had exhorted members to take matters into their own hands.[205] With the ban and police presence in mind, Mee warned the crowd that in its midst were agent provocateurs, all in the government's pay, who might try to induce them to acts of violence. For this reason, they ought to 'be on their guard' and 'to maintain the most perfect order'.[206] But then his tone suddenly changed, and he asked if it were 'expedient to go on with the business for which they had met'.

Before the crowd could answer, a procession of 150-200 men arrived, shabbily dressed like Irish labourers and carrying banners and flags.[207] They were recognised as the Union members from south of the river. Having crossed the river at Blackfriars they had marched to Cold Bath Fields via Holborn, Gray's Inn Road and Calthorpe Street.[208] On Gray's Inn Road, they were joined by William Gore, a solicitor from Worcestershire, who asked them if they were aware of the government proclamation banning the meeting. They said not but then contradicted themselves by declaring that, since it was not signed by Lord Melbourne, the proclamation had no legal effect. What is more, they were doing nothing illegal as their intention was not to disturb the government or the peace but merely to agree to a resolution for petitioning parliament on the issue of 'assessed taxes'.[209] Spotting the police as they passed Busbridge's Stables, they delivered a barrage of hisses, hoots, groans and catcalls of contempt.[210] As they approached the crowd assembled at the top of Calthorpe Street, they were met by a 'person more respectable than the rest' who doffed his hat and 'saluted them as friends'. Probably, this gentleman was Julian Hibbert.[211] The contingent's arrival was met with 'deafening acclamations' followed by a pregnant silence as those carrying the flags and banners gathered round Mee.[212]

Prior to the procession's arrival, there were no flags or banners on display.[213] Consequently, the purpose of the meeting remained unclear. Well before its start, a character in a white hat (redolent of Hunt) had been on the waste ground reading passages from the *Reformer* (a republican weekly recently published by James Henry Lorymer) and, it was reported, urging the people 'openly to carry arms'. But was he there on the authority of the committee? Then, there was the hearty welcome given to the Union committee upon joining the meeting. Yet, what could be read into that? There existed the Union's own placard announcing the intention to prepare for a national convention. But in spite of a print-run of 500 copies, the only evidence of its presence at the meeting was the one attached to the staff used by Lee to maintain his balance on the arris rail. According to a police report, a circular existed in praise of national conventions and against hereditary legislators. Hetherington had published it in 1831, the composition of James Henry Lorymer. Possibly it was reissued in 1833, yet it went completely unmentioned in all the eye-witness material. This would suggest that its use in 1833 was a police fabrication. Finally, there were the few words delivered by Lee and Mee to the crowd, although neither appeared to mention a national convention. [214] The uncertainty surrounding the meeting stood in sharp contrast to the clear-cut declarations of intent the Union's committee had previously made, raising doubt as to the illegality of the meeting and the relevance of the government's proclamation.[215] Now, however, with the flags and banners present and placed close to Mee, the meeting's purpose became explicit and its prohibition seemingly justified.

The four banners brought to the meeting by the south of the river contingent sported a range of mottoes and emblems: a very large one had 'Unite and Conquer', along with a beehive to represent industry, inscribed on the white stripe of the French tricolour. It must have been made of silk since, in spite of its size, the policeman who confiscated it was able to stuff it in his hat. A second banner displayed 'Liberty or Death' accompanied by a skull and crossbones, all on a black background with a red border. A third banner had 'Holy Alliance of the Working Classes' inscribed on crimson silk. On the fourth banner was the Paineite inscription 'Equal Rights and Equal Laws', also worked on crimson silk. Besides the banners, there were two flags, each a blatant declaration of republicanism: one, the French tricolour, inscribed with the motto 'Liberty and Equality', the other, the stars and stripes of America. In addition, someone sported a cap of liberty hoisted on a pole.[216] So far, the crowd had appeared unarmed, but now, following the arrival of the procession, it included a small number of men holding long spears that resembled Macerone lances, a weapon recommended for street fighting by Colonel Macerone's *Defensive Instructions for the People*. This work was first published the previous year and summarised in the *Poor Man's Guardian*, with an illustration of workers raising the banner

'Liberty or Death' and deploying lances to fend off the military. Only the previous month (April 1833) Watson's weekly the *Working Man's Friend*, a periodical closely associated with the NUWC, had advertised a version of Macerone's tract with three illustrations for the price of just one penny.[217] In the following issue was an article justifying revolution that thanked Paine for his role in creating the republics of France and America.[218] Concerned that they might destroy the impression of a peaceable gathering, Mee ordered the lance-bearers to remove the spear-heads; and this was promptly done.[219]

The sight of the flags and banners, along with the presence of the speakers, clearly revealed that the meeting had begun in earnest. Its resemblance to the one banned by the government's proclamation compelled the police to take action. As Mee repeated his question about adjourning the meeting, and with those in the crowd urging him to 'go on', 70 police of A Division appeared at the bottom of Calthorpe Street, their truncheons at the ready.[220] Spitting on their hands, they marched, in lines stretching from kerb to kerb, up Calthorpe Street from their station in Busbridge's Stables on Gray's Inn Road. At the same time, another body of 100 police from H Division appeared in Gough Street South, having emerged from the back gate of the same stables.[221] Without reading either the Riot Act or the proclamation banning the meeting, and without issuing an order to disperse, both police units, in a pincer movement, attacked the crowd gathered at the T-junction of Calthorpe Street and Gough Street, clubbing with their truncheons.[222] Their object was to seize the flags and banners and to arrest the ringleaders.[223] A brief scuffle ensued, with some resistance offered in defence of the flags. Most of the crowd sought to escape along the two ends of Gough Street, down Calthorpe Street and across Cold Bath Fields, only to find themselves running the gauntlet of other police units who used their truncheons to strike the shins of those fleeing past.[224] Along with them went Mee, in his pocket the resolutions he had failed to deliver to the meeting. A further scuffle occurred halfway down Calthorpe Street as police from C Division sought to stop men from escaping with the flags. This resulted in one policeman stabbed to death and two others suffering serious stab wounds.[225] From start to finish the affray lasted little more than five minutes.[226]

But, even though the crowd had dispersed, the police remained active for the next hour, clubbing and prodding individual men and women, partly to prevent a crowd from regrouping, and partly in reprisal for the injuries inflicted upon the three policemen.[227] Besides Union members, many were there because they lived in the area or had turned up out of curiosity. They also fell victim to the police.[228] Residents appeared on upstairs balconies and, shocked by the brutality, shouted: 'shame on the police'.[229] Down below, other spectators, who had sought refuge in the fronts of the houses lining Calthorpe Street, suffered cuts and bruises from being bludgeoned by an extremely angry police force.[230] The victims included William Gore, the solicitor from Worcestershire. Drawn to the meeting after encountering the Union procession in Gray's Inn Road, he had positioned himself as an observer in Calthorpe Street thirty yards or so from the speaker and away from the crowd. As the second wave of police (C Division) proceeded up Calthorpe Street, they bludgeoned him to the ground and trampled on his prostrate body, leaving him 'much bruised'.[231] As he looked around, he noticed, four yards away, an injured gentleman leaning groggily against some house railings. Gore sought to learn his name but the man refused to give it, saying that he was 'a person of respectability' and that to divulge his identity might lead the government to charge him with organising the meeting. The gentleman had arrived in a gig which his servant had parked close by. Gore helped him to the vehicle. Both agreed that they had not heard a reading of the government's proclamation or of the Riot Act; nor had they been called upon by the police to 'move away'. This gentleman was, in all likelihood, the anonymous correspondent who, in a report published in Carlile's *Gauntlet*, presented it as a carnage.[232] If so, he was probably Julian Hibbert, the very same gentleman who had greeted the procession from south of the river, just before it joined the meeting. The *Gauntlet* letter was entitled 'Testimony of an Eye-Witness'. It claimed that the author was assaulted by members of the C Division just after witnessing a man, assaulted 'ferociously' by a policeman with the words 'Now where is your "Liberty or Death"', stab his attacker with a macerone spear. Immediately afterwards, the correspondent allegedly received a blow to the shoulder that knocked him to the ground. Then, as with Gore, several policemen trampled on his body, causing him temporarily to black out. He closed his report with the bitter exhortation: 'Unless a people are armed, they never can be free.'

One surprising outcome of the Cold Bath Fields incident was the exoneration of the main perpetrators of the violence committed. This applied not only to the police, whose behaviour on the day was judged appropriate by a special committee of parliament, but even to those Union members whose violent resistance had caused the death of a policeman. They were acquitted in court with a remarkable verdict of 'justifiable homicide'. In fact, only a few stone-throwers underwent punishment.[233] Such leniency stood in stark contrast to what had happened in 1793-4 when men had been transported to Australia and charged with high treason for attempting to hold a national convention. The incident, however, did nothing for the reputation of the metropolitan police. The Union had been on the receiving end of police truncheons in the recent past. A year earlier on 21 March 1832, a royal proclamation had ordered the nation to support a Day of National Fast and Prayer, held in response to an outbreak of cholera, and the Union had expressed contempt for such a measure by instructing its members to make a peaceful, if provocative, procession from Finsbury Square to Westminster. Police in large numbers had sought to stop the procession, blocking its passage and attacking the participants: first at Temple Bar, and then successfully, close to Tottenham Court Road. The conduct of the police on this occasion led to the accusation that their recent creation was not principally to safeguard society from crime but to subdue radical reform.[234] The Cold Bath Fields incident appeared to justify the same charge.

The incident did nothing to promote the cause of Paineite reform. In the struggle to resist the Union's plan for a national convention, the government got its way. The Cold Bath Fields meeting itself had turned into a fiasco, predictably enough given the rash threats made by the Union's committee in the lead-up to the event (all of which were carefully noted by the police and reported to the government), as well as the indecisiveness and poor judgement of the meeting's organisers on the day. Bearing this in mind, the NUWC decided thereafter to steer a different course.[235] It did so by submitting to the direction of Bronterre O'Brien. Shortly afterwards, in a long editorial for the *Poor Man's Guardian*, O'Brien persuasively argued against a wide-spectrumed approach to political reform, recommending instead a single-minded effort to achieve universal suffrage. The guiding principle he proposed was: 'Seek no object that is illegal and seek no legal object by illegal means'. In keeping with this principle, he reasoned that they should steer clear of a national convention. This was necessary, he argued, because a national convention was an alien part of the constitution, whereas 'universal suffrage is long familiar to all classes', and because universal suffrage could achieve everything to be expected of a national convention while appearing 'less obnoxious'.[236] What O'Brien proposed was a revival of the Radical Reform programme of Henry Hunt. Its adoption by the NUWC led on to Chartism which, true, continued to employ the term 'convention' but only to designate an important meeting recruited from different regions for the purpose of producing a multi-signatured petition addressed to the crown or parliament and calling for some change not to the constitution but to current legislation. In contrast, the Paineite convention was meant to authorise a new constitution. Consequently, in dealing with the Chartists, the government was able to shelve its traditional opposition to what was termed a national convention since it was evidently very different in purpose from the convention recommended by Paine.

A final outcome of the Cold Bath Fields incident was an increase in the number of Union members favouring the carrying of arms. A call to arms featured in a letter, written soon afterwards and published in the *Poor Man's Guardian*. It was signed 'Palafox Junior', a pseudonym for Julian Hibbert, who, as we have seen, had probably published in the *Gauntlet* an anonymous account of the incident that had reached the same conclusion. The Palafox Junior letter recommended that every working man, when attending a public meeting, should carry a stout and sharp knife not only to cut his bread and cheese but also to provide a means of self-defence. If this happened, he claimed, the 'hired bludgeoneers' (i.e., the police) would cease to treat crowd control as a blood sport.[237] The necessity of physical resistance, if all other measures failed, became a recurrent theme in the following months. For example, in July 1833, at the third anniversary of the second French Revolution, an occasion attended by 3,000 Union members, the publisher James Watson made the point that the English working classes were no 'less courageous' than the Parisian artisans whose militant action had brought about the end of hereditary monarchy in France. This claim was met with cheers from the audience. He went on to say: 'when the proper moment arrived that they should be called into action', they would surely do so; for, if they could not succeed by moral means, then they should use 'any physical effort that might be necessary'. This aroused more cheers.[238] It was clear that, although Henry Hunt's demand for universal suffrage continued to be articulated, the peaceable means he had advocated for its achievement was losing its appeal. This development, and a persistence of the desire to eliminate government by hereditary succession, suggested that, among the Union's membership, Paine's guiding hand still remained on the tiller.

Yet the Cold Bath Fields incident undoubtedly marked a turning point in the history of British republicanism. Prior to Paine, it had been created and shaped by the struggle against Stuart despotism in the Civil War and the Glorious Revolution, the outcome of which was a form of republicanism capable of accepting a submissive crown, an ascendant aristocracy and a minute electorate. Thanks to Paine, however, republicanism came to be seen as predicated on abolishing the institutions of hereditary rule, coupled with the establishment of a wholly representative parliament based on universal suffrage. Thus, in place of the elitist republicanism of the late seventeenth and early eighteenth centuries was the egalitarian republicanism of Paine. Nonetheless, after the Cold Bath Fields incident, Paine's political philosophy fell out of favour. Consequently, the survival of republicanism in late nineteenth-century Britain owed a great deal to being attached to other concerns: notably, supporting the nationalist cause of Joseph Mazzini, extending the franchise, nationalising the land, adopting various forms of socialism and Irish independence. The general effect was to downplay the importance of terminating the hereditary principle, as the priorities defined by Paine were replaced by others, notably the welfare of the working classes and the liberation of nations. As a result, crown and peerage, except in much of Ireland, managed to survive, their wealth and social distinction intact but subjected, in the interest of self-preservation, to a long-drawn-out process of political etiolation.

As for Paine's idea of a national convention – his preferred means of transforming the political system – the Cold Bath Field's incident brought it to an abrupt end. Over forty years, it had been appreciated in British radical circles as a simple means of creating a new constitution. But invariably it had failed. No such convention was ever convoked in this country, and the meetings arranged as a preparatory step for holding one had led to nothing. This rather suggests that, in a British setting, Paine's convention was an impracticable device. His hope of using it to achieve peaceful radical change could, in fact, be regarded as equalling in naivety his plan in the late 1790s for an armed invasion of England in flat-bottomed boats.[239] Overlooked by Paine was the evident fact that the national convention could only operate successfully in a revolutionary situation, as was the case in America and France. Seeking to organise one without this revolutionary pre-condition was to attempt the impossible, especially since the government was strongly inclined to regard any attempt to hold a national convention as a threat to order, property and the traditional constitution, and therefore as something to be stamped out: unless, as was the case with Chartism, it could be proved otherwise.

b | Carlile's Last Stand

In 1833, the very same year in which Bronterre O'Brien sought to persuade the NUWC to confine its immediate goal to universal suffrage (and therefore to postpone attempting a disposal of the monarchy), Richard Carlile, archrepublican and principal upholder of the Paineite cause, was dismissing as misconceived and futile the Union's reliance on a national convention to achieve its republican goal. As he pointed out in the *Gauntlet* for 19 May 1833, a national convention of the Paineite sort could only work if it 'followed an overthrow of the old regime'. For him 'a national convention implies the absence of all other authority, and an appeal to the people for the purpose of beginning a new government'. In this respect, 'it cannot be [workable] until the old government is overthrown'. Therefore, 'it was a folly or a wickedness to talk about it and to make it a matter of public meeting'. Such was the impracticability of a national convention in the present circumstances, he concluded, that, if one sought to trace how the idea came to be adopted by the Union's committee, it might well turn out to be the underhand 'work of a government agent'.[240]

In his own bid to topple the old regime, Carlile was planning, at that very time, to raise an army of 'enrolled volunteers' pledged to do whatever he, their leader, commanded.[241] His announcement of this project in March 1833 was met by an enthusiastic response from over 3,000 men, women and children. Strong support was offered in the metropolis, the Midlands (notably Birmingham, Nottingham, Leicester and Coventry), in Yorkshire (Bradford, Huddersfield, Sheffield), in Lancashire (Manchester, Salford, Oldham, Bolton, Hollins, Royton), in East Anglia (Norwich, Great Yarmouth and Wisbech), and in Bristol.[242] The correspondence the project aroused revealed a popular enthusiasm for action, not just to establish universal suffrage but also to destroy the old regime, as embodied in hereditary monarchy and hereditary nobility.[243] For Carlile the problem in realising such a project was his current imprisonment in the Giltspur Street Compter, the result of a conviction for political sedition in 1831 after he had, in his republican weekly the *Prompter*, urged rioting agricultural workers to continue burning haystacks and destroying farm machinery. In the advice he offered on how to proceed, he recommended them to seek inspirational guidance in Thomas Paine, 'the greatest political friend of the labouring man'.[244]

Released from prison in August 1833, Carlile immediately sought contact with his enrolled following, first by holding a meeting for his London supporters in the Rotunda at Blackfriars and then, from September to November, by means of an extensive tour of the West Country and the North. Here was the golden opportunity to mobilise the men and women who had proved their worth by waiting so patiently for his call to action. He met up with the metropolitan volunteers in the large theatre of the Rotunda on 25 August when 2,000 came to hear him speak. But the occasion was wrecked by the intrusive presence of his flamboyant friend, the Reverend Robert Taylor. Thanks to his brilliant and entertaining oratory, Taylor monopolised the attention of the meeting so effectively that, at closing time, Carlile had yet to deliver his prepared address. When he sought a second attempt to deliver it, a few days later, he found that the building had been demolished. A month went by as he searched for another venue. One was eventually found at 8 Theobalds Road in Holborn, a place recently used by the NUWC for its weekly meetings. Here, he presented himself to his London supporters as 'the living personification of the political principles of Thomas Paine', and promised, in the manner newly adopted by the NUWC, to resort to 'resistance physical' if 'resistance moral' failed.[245]

During Carlile's 1833 tour of the provinces, he lectured not only on Paineite politics but also on 'morals and 'religion'. The lecture on politics was given an enthusiastic reception. In contrast, his lecture on morals met with outrage, especially when it became known that accompanying him on the tour was his young mistress Eliza Sharples – not his real wife Jane, a heroine of the Paineite cause in her own right. What is more, his lecture on religion proposed a bizarre form of 'true Christianity' that baffled his infidel supporters while failing to appeal to those republican Christians who had previously found his politics attractive but his atheism repellent.[246]

The volunteer enrolment project fell apart as it became clear that, with Carlile in charge (a man deranged by years in prison and the long term habit of ingesting crude mercury, and whose personal reputation had been seriously damaged by his published recommendation of birth control and of sexual relations outside marriage) the mobilisation necessary to implement a reform programme based on the ideas of Paine was rendered nigh on impossible.[247] Compounding the problem created by Carlile's mental and physical ill-health was the sudden death, in January 1834, of Julian Hibbert, the wealthy patron who had paid the rent on Carlile's shop at 62 Fleet Street and had provided the financial backing for a succession of republican periodicals.[248] Deprived of this support, Carlile abruptly retired from the political fray. In the course of 1834, he closed down his Fleet Street shop, terminated the *Gauntlet*, the last of his republican papers, and took up residence in the rural retreat of Enfield. His friends urged him not to desert the Paineite cause, but to no effect.[249] The remaining years of his life were spent as a licensed reverend, expounding a version of Christianity which few could understand and fewer cared to share.[250]

With Carlile's voluntary enrolment project failing soon after the incident at Cold Bath Fields, and because of the damage the latter inflicted on the reputation of the NUWC, the republican cause, after attracting so much vigorous support in the 1820s and in the early 1830s, sank into a state of quiescence and apathy. Paine's political philosophy, rendered distinctive by its opposition to hereditary rule and rank, accordingly lost its appeal for those who yearned for political reform and keenly sought the best means of bringing it about.

i | The Limitations of Paineite Republicanism Exposed

The NUWC, along with its official voice, the *Poor Man's Guardian*, had come to an end by the close of 1835, the former having faded away over the previous two and a half years. Concern at a fall in numbers was first declared in July 1833. This coincided with an announcement that the Union could no longer hold its meetings at 8 Theobalds Road, presumably the result of a falling-out with its proprietor, William Benbow.[251] By January 1834 the membership had contracted considerably, the result, it was thought, of a tendency among its members to join the trades' unions movement instead, an exodus the NUWC's executive committee recognised but did not seek to resist, wishing 'not to thwart, but rather to assist in the noble stand made by honest industry against domineering, despotic capital'.[252] Encouraging this transfer of membership was Bronterre O'Brien, editor of the *Poor Man's Guardian*, who, from November 1833, wrote favourably about trades' unions on numerous occasions. His claim was that the trades' unions allowed the working classes to take 'their affairs into their own hands' and, if they came out in support of universal suffrage, the workers would be able 'to deal with usurers, landowners and cotton lords' whose current control of the House of Commons ensured that the legislation enacted was in the interest of capital rather than labour.[253] Along with the fall-off in membership was the disappearance of the NUWC's provincial branches and, in London, a reduction in the number of its weekly class meetings, an end to the monthly general meetings and a frequent postponement of the quarterly meetings.[254]

As for the *Poor Man's Guardian*, it had maintained an impressive circulation under the direction of O'Brien, and was only terminated, so it was claimed, to allow O'Brien the opportunity to establish a new interpretation of the first French Revolution. This he hoped to accomplish by publishing an English translation of Buonarroti's *History of Babeuf's Conspiracy for Equality* and by writing a life of Robespierre. O'Brien also aimed to produce a 'genuine' history of the French Revolution which would dismiss its initial stage (lasting from 1789 to 1793) – the one in which Paine had been much involved – as having done very little to improve the material needs of the French people. The same work would express regret for the failure of the second stage (lasting from 1793 to 1794) since, if successful, it might well have made up for the defects of the first stage.[255] This reinterpretation was meant to confirm a theme already pursued in the *Poor Man's Guardian*: one that played down the importance of Paineite republicanism by emphasising the point that the pressing problems of society stemmed from the misery permanently suffered by the majority in spite of the wealth generated by a flourishing economy; and, therefore, could not be solved simply by bringing the polity of the blood to an end.[256]

Responsible for debunking Paine's essentially political solution to the problem of poverty was, then, Bronterre O'Brien. Throughout the 1830s – first, as editor of the *Midland Representative and Birmingham Herald* (1831-2), then as editor of the *Poor Man's Guardian* (1832-5) and, after that, as contributor to the *London Dispatch* (1836-9) and as editor of the *Operative* (1838-9) – he repeatedly called for a policy of social revolution in order to protect the working classes from middle-class exploitation. In this manner, O'Brien created a scenario of reform that, contrary to Paine, transferred the blame for the major problems of the time from the monarchy and nobility to the middle classes. For Paine, the middle classes were seen as agents of reform and liberation, whereas, for O'Brien, they were the agents of reaction and tyranny. For Paine, the people's distress was caused by a regressive tax system acting in conjunction with the way royalty and nobility drained the public revenue through the extravagance of their life-style and a proclivity for war, while failing to make an appropriate fiscal contribution in return.[257] For O'Brien it stemmed from the advantages that holders of capital or property enjoyed over the providers of labour in annexing the nation's wealth. In this manner, and at that time, Paine's achievements were continually being undermined and belittled. As part of this process, O'Brien was intent on providing a new interpretation of the political revolutions that had occurred, over the last century, in the Americas and in Europe. His particular focus was on those of North America and France. Contrary to Paine, he argued that, by dispensing with kingship and nobility, they had achieved very little in the sense that, for the bulk of the population, the social situation in both countries was no different from that of Britain where the hereditary principle remained intact and untouched.

During the early 1830s, support for the establishment of a British republic had been promoted by the realisation that the successful revolt of the American colonies had created a political system that, although without hereditary rulers, worked extremely well. This was revealed not only in a change of attitude on the part of Hunt and Cobbett towards republican systems of government,[258] but also in the pages of the *Poor Man's Guardian*, notably when recording the weekly debates held by the NUWC. In November 1832, for example, George Edmunds had claimed that 'everything was hastening to a republic'. This would do no harm, he reasoned, 'as America abundantly proved'. His observation earned applause from the audience. In commending it, he noted that, in Cincinnati 'there was not a single pauper'. Nor was there 'a rich man'.[259] Evidently, the gross inequalities of the old world were disappearing in parts of the new. At another Union meeting, held in the same month, William Reeve made a related point, observing that 'the glorious republic of the USA' was distinguished by its orderliness.[260] In other words, the removal of the old order had not resulted in chaos and Paine's point had been proven that the cause of popular disorder normally lay with the government, not the people.[261] In March 1833 Henry Hetherington had invoked the 'Glorious Republic' that the American Revolution had produced, expressing the hope that 'in England a like glorious consummation may result...and that a republic may arise' in which 'the rich and the poor be placed in an equality in the eyes of the law'.[262] Providing further evidence for the superiority of a republic over a monarchy, especially in financial matters, a Mr Jackson, at a quarterly meeting of the NUWC in January 1834, had praised the USA for having almost cleared its national debt, while in England, 'groaning under our monstrous load of debt', we might well exclaim: 'Oh kings and priests, how have you robbed and plundered us and our fathers, and what an immeasurable load of misery have you in store for ages yet unborn?'[263] At a weekly meeting of the Union, held the following month, a Mr Charles, to much applause, made a telling comparison between the USA president and the British monarch, the former receiving an annual income of £5,000 in return for extensive duties, the latter receiving £800,000 p.a., even though he was unable to compose his own speech to the nation.[264]

The 1830 revolution in France had been likewise appreciated by the membership of the NUWC, especially for terminating hereditary monarchy by undoing the restoration of 1815. Every July, between 1831 and 1834, the so-called Second French Revolution was celebrated by Union members. Wearing a tricoloured cockade, following banners and accompanied by bands playing the 'Marseillaise March', they went in procession through the streets of London to assembly points in Copenhagen Gardens or at White Conduit House where speeches were delivered and entertainment was provided.[265] At the 1833 event, Paine's portrait topped a flag with the inscription 'Justice and Reason'.

All this had redounded to Paine's credit: the man who had not only condemned the hereditary principle in his writings but, through his active participation in the American Revolution and the First French Revolution, had played a vitally important part in ensuring that both nations broke decisively and systematically with the past by completely rejecting all attachment to a polity of the blood.

Yet, by mid-1834, doubts were creeping in as to what the American and French Revolutions had actually achieved. The current condition of the French and American working classes was a matter of concern, raising the question of whether or not the two revolutions had lived up to Paine's expectation that, simply by sweeping away the society of orders, the lot of the people would be much improved. Such doubts were largely sown by O'Brien who, as we have seen, had already sought to demote Paine by comparing him unfavourably with Robespierre.[266] Thus, in March 1834 an editorial in the *Poor Man's Guardian* branded the French political system 'a government of usurers'.[267] A month later, another editorial declared that the working-class 'conquest' of Paris in 1830 had already been undone by the middle classes, thanks to their control of the legislature and the military.[268] This, O'Brien felt, exposed the true nature of tyranny which was not the creation of kings but specifically of 'those who rob the labourer of his hire'. Kings should therefore be regarded as 'mere instruments of despotism' not as actual despots. In the same piece the real despots were identified as the middle classes, with government presented as the means by which they legitimised their exploitation of the workers.[269] This thesis was carried a step further in another editorial of May 1834. Here, the middle classes were accused, on the one hand, of starting the revolution of 1789 in order to take possession of the nobility's and clergy's landed estates and, on the other, of halting it in order to prevent the working classes 'from sharing its benefits'. Similarly, and for the same reason of greed, O'Brien saw the middle classes as proceeding against the revolution of 1830.[270]

By late 1834, the editorials of the *Poor Man's Guardian* had turned against the American Republic as well, arguing that, in spite of its democratic claims, with most public officials elected on a wide franchise, the system of government remained a despotism in so far as the working classes were concerned. Kings and aristocrats had gone, but that made no real difference, for in their place was the even more oppressive tyranny of the middle classes.[271] Consequently, as elsewhere, the 'useless classes' got richer and richer while 'the producers' became poorer and poorer.[272] True to Paine's *Common Sense*, monarchy had been rejected but, according to O'Brien, below the level of government, monarchical practices persisted: notably in the factory and the workshop, thanks to the prevalence of the belief that it was perfectly acceptable for one man, in the capacity of employer, trader or banker, to 'appropriate the fruits of another's labour'.[273] This was the 'major evil' in society and prevailed, irrespective of the nature of the political system, in both Britain and the USA. In both, a 'monied aristocracy' held sway, comprised of 'bankers, merchants, factory owners, store-keepers, contractors, land jobbers and profit-hunters'.[274] According to O'Brien, the USA 'is overrun by these vampires'.[275]

Paine's programme of political reform was therefore dismissed as belonging to the past. O'Brien made this doubly clear in refusing to print, in the *Poor Man's Guardian*, an article condemning hereditary monarchy, arguing that 'the subject is...too trite to warrant our publishing it to the exclusion of other matter'.[276] To deal with the problems of the present, in both republics and monarchies, he called instead for 'a social revolution'.[277] And that had nothing to do with Paine. Nor did it have much to do with the socialism of Robert Owen. This O'Brien rejected as impracticable and inadequate, partly because it was apolitical and partly because it merely sought to restrict capitalist exploitation in a piece-meal manner, not to banish it completely.[278] Essentially, O'Brien was proposing a system of socialism promulgated by the state but one which, in contrast to Paine's political reform programme, allowed no role for physical force. Distinctively, it involved a major alteration in the system of property. O'Brien envisaged a policy of land nationalisation, to be achieved gradually and with compensation to the landowners. Eventually, he was prepared to abolish monarchy and the House of Lords; but, in terms of priorities, the very first step was peacefully to establish a system of universal suffrage.[279] The failure to achieve this first step for the next eighty-four years placed on hold every other radical reform considered beneficial for the working classes. In this manner, and because such a policy of prioritising the suffrage was adopted by Chartism and the political reform movements that followed, Paine's radical relevance was pushed to the back of the cupboard, along with the bones.

j | The Chartist Aversion to Paine

Three years after the termination of the NUWC, Chartism took over the cause of radical reform, likewise advocating universal suffrage. Following in the footsteps of Hunt and his Radical Reform movement of the late 1820s (which happened to be in accordance with the organisations projected by Burgh and

Cartwright in the 1770s), Chartists regarded themselves as an 'association' engaged in persuading the government to reform itself by means of a monster petition or a written remonstrance approved by a monster meeting. The most important Chartist association, in terms of numbers and impact, was Feargus O'Connor's Great Radical Association. O'Connor revered Hunt and adopted his method of enlisting the working classes, especially in the north, to sign a petition or sanction a remonstrance by the display of a handsome, gentlemanly presence on an open-air platform and a demagogic approach to the assembled crowd: a combination of rousing oratory, relatively conservative principles and a preference for non-violence.[280] Averse to advocating the abolition of monarchy or the House of Lords, strictly focused on subjecting the House of Commons to a system of representation resting on one-man-one-vote, and inclined to abide by the Christian religion, this approach was far removed from Paine's. That Chartism adopted Hunt's approach was evident in the People's Charter and its provisions for universal suffrage, and in the Declaration of Rights, adopted unanimously by the General Convention of the Industrious Classes of 1839. Opening with the declaration that 'the sovereignty of this United Kingdom is monarchical, not despotic but limited', it proceeded to elaborate that 'the prerogatives of the imperial crown of the United Kingdom are a constitutional trust vested in the person of the monarchy for the benefit and service of the people, and may be controlled, modified and limited by the will of parliament'; and concluded by declaring that 'the legislative power is essentially and rightly vested in the monarch, the peers and the duly elected commons of the realm, in parliament assembled'. This was perfectly in keeping with Hunt's Radical Reform programme and totally opposed to the political philosophy of Paine.[281]

In the late 1830s, two other associations emerged, both connected with the origins of Chartism but also heirs to the republican and distinctly Paineite NUWC. One was the London Association of the Working Classes, led by William Lovett; the other was the East London Democratic Association, led by George Julian Harney. Neither, however, declared itself republican. By 1836-7 Lovett was drifting away from the republicanism he had professed in the early 1830s.[282] A resolution adopted by the London Association of the Working Classes in June 1837 focused on universal suffrage and made no mention of monarchy (although it did include a proposal for a 'Bill of Reform' to make the House of Lords 'responsible to the people').[283] Lovett then proceeded to have an important hand in drafting the People's Charter, which likewise steered clear of calling for a republic.[284] Unlike Lovett, Harney remained for many years a keen republican: over a decade later, for example, he was editing a succession of republican periodicals, in the form of the *Democratic Review* (1849-50) and the *Red Republican* (1850-51). But this made little difference for, while working for the *Poor Man's Guardian*, Harney, having fallen under O'Brien's spell, was converted to the belief that the removal of Crown and Lords, although a worthy aspiration, was less important than the need to transform the relationship between labour and capital.[285]

As for Harney's East London Democratic Association, it did issue, in January 1837, a prospectus that was explicitly Paineite.[286] It opened with the declaration that its object was 'to promote the moral and political condition of the working classes' by 'disseminating the principles propagated by that great philosopher and redeemer of mankind, the immortal THOMAS PAINE'. To honour Paine's principles and character, the prospectus set out arrangements for monthly meetings, presumably to discuss matters pertinent to Paine, and also for an annual meeting, to be held on the anniversary of Paine's birth, along with a celebratory supper. Nonetheless, in defining what was to be discussed at the monthly meetings, the Association's prospectus made no mention of either republicanism or religion. Instead it declared that the goal was 'the principles of cheap and honest government', to be achieved by implementing the five 'grand principles of Radical Reform': i.e., the Cartwright/Hunt programme of universal suffrage, the secret ballot, annual parliaments, and the removal of a property qualification for membership of the House of Commons. This approach to reform was affirmed in the spring of 1838 when the party changed its name to the London Democratic Association and produced a constitution supposedly true to the NUWC but offering universal suffrage as its central political goal while making no mention of the hereditary principle and the need for its abolition.[287]

Furthermore, the London Democratic Association pulled away from Paine's philosophy by adding to the political issue of the suffrage the desire to destroy a social system which encouraged a gross inequality in wealth through allowing the fruits of labour to be requisitioned by those with property and capital.[288] This goal was vividly expressed by Harney. Echoing a remark made earlier by a member of the NUWC, he wrote in July 1838: 'We are generally branded as levellers,' a charge to which 'we plead guilty' if it means 'the destruction of inequality occasioned by the enactment of bad laws'.[289] The same point was expressed in even more extreme terms by J.C. Coombes, another member of the London Democratic Association, who in June 1839 claimed that the establishment of the Charter would achieve nothing of value. He went on to declare: 'Your whole social system requires "revolution", your commercial system requires "revolution", and nothing short of actual convulsion will effect a cure.'[290] This threat of revolution fell within the scope of Paine's political thinking, but a social and commercial revolution did not, thus representing another retraction from his reform programme. Thanks to O'Brien's influence and its purveyance by Harney, the London Democratic Association focused on reforming parliament in such a way as to make social equity achievable by benevolent legislation. A House of Commons, representative of labour rather than property and capital, seemed to offer the perfect remedy. The importance attached to establishing universal suffrage was, therefore, no different from what was set out in the People's Charter. Rather than providing Chartism with an independent lead, the London Democratic Association had become, by 1841, absorbed within its ranks.[291]

Chartists, certainly, were capable of recognising Paine as a radical hero, naming their children after him and holding convivial dinners to honour his birth. But their reform programme was firmly rooted in the Radical Reform movement created by Cartwright in the 1770s and doggedly applied by Hunt and Cobbett from 1816 to the mid-1830s.[292] The Chartist Association would have no truck with removing the Crown or the House of Lords; and nor would Chartism's principal leader, Feargus O'Connor. Its chosen course of action, nonetheless, did feature the summoning of conventions. Could this suggest a Paineite affiliation? Not so. The specific purpose of the Chartist convention – designated a 'general convention of the industrious/working classes' – was to produce a monster petition, to make arrangements for its spectacular presentation to parliament, and to pose a threat of further action if pressure was required to persuade the government to accept its terms.[293] As Linton neatly put it in his *James Watson, A Memoir*, the role of the Chartist convention was 'to watch over the Charter and Petition when presented to parliament'.[294] In fact, the Chartists' general convention of the industrious classes bore little resemblance to the national convention (i.e. convention of the nation) recommended by Paine and adopted in the early 1830s by the NUWC.[295] The one differed from the other in three basic respects. *a:* Paine had no faith in petitions, dismissing them as useless. *b:* For Paine, a convention was meant to represent the nation, whereas for the Chartists, it was meant to represent the working classes. *c:* Echoing the examples of revolutionary America and France, Paine's convention was designed to provide not a submission to, but a replacement for, the existing constitutional order. Thanks to operating within the bounds of the constitution – made evident in the Chartists' declaration of rights of September 1839 – their conventions were consequently shown much greater tolerance by the political establishment.[296]

Coincident with the emergence of the Chartist Association, which acted as heir to Henry Hunt, the Cobbett Club was founded to keep Cobbett's name and reputation alive. Both men had died in 1835, but their attitude towards political reform lived on, to the exclusion of Paine. A key figure in the Cobbett Club was its honorary secretary, the tailor Benjamin Tilly, who had owned the surviving piece of Paine's brain and a lock of his hair since the early 1830s, and, from the mid-1840s, took possession of Paine's skeleton with a view to giving it a worthy public burial.[297] However, the political reform programme that Tilly favoured was very different from Paine's. This was made evident in the petitioning activities of the Cobbett Club. Between August 1838 and July 1842, it presented six petitions to parliament, one of them to the Lords, the rest to the Commons. It also published in this period a pamphlet entitled *A Political Tract by the Cobbett Club of London* which defined its attitude towards political reform.[298] Like the Chartists, the members of the Cobbett Club regarded a very limited electoral franchise to be at the heart of the problem. For this reason, the Club proposed to concentrate on making the franchise fully representative of the male population. Once that was established, and the control of parliament consequently made answerable to the people (and so wrested from the aristocratic grip of Whigs or Tories), its interests could be served and furthered simply by a process of corrective legislation. Paine may have accepted this much, but his main complaint against the existence of birth right to political authority and social status went ignored by the Club members, largely because they were intent on restoring a damaged tradition. Running through the papers of the Cobbett Club was a firm belief in the ancient constitution: a reverence for King Alfred and a system of Anglo-Saxon government thought to be based on universal suffrage. It was also seen as a system of elective monarchy, one that ruled out primogeniture but not dynastic succession, with the people having the right to vote for the next king on condition that he came from the same family line. The Cobbett Club thus sought the restoration of a polity of limited monarchy which, from the Norman Conquest onwards, ruthless kings and nobles had innovatively altered in their own interest.[299] Paine was seen as another innovator, offending what had survived of the ancient constitution by proposing to remove the birth-right element. In adopting this attitude to political change, the Cobbett Club was as anti-Paine as the Chartist movement.

Paine's political writings were republished several times in the 1840s, by men such as James Watson and William Dugdale, but only once under the auspices of the Chartist movement. This was the work of T.M. Wheeler, secretary to the Chartist Land Company, who eventually published *The Political Works of Thomas Paine, to which is added a copy of the people's charter.* However, this did not happen until 1846. The preface to the Wheeler edition, a pronouncement from the executive committee of the National Charter Association, revealed exactly where the Chartist movement stood in relation to Paine by condemning his willingness to accept revolution as a genuine means of political reform.[300] It did so, rather in the manner of O'Brien, by presenting the French Revolutions and the American Revolution as having failed to alleviate the lot of the working man. Thus: 'Kingly dynasties have been hurled to destruction, but the harvest nourished by the blood of patriotism has been reaped by ambitious, crafty and designing knaves.' It went on to say: 'France still writhes under the lash of a despotism as flagrant as any upon the face of the globe!'; and 'even Paris, the scene of so many brave struggles for liberty, is now environed with a wall of fortification not to resist assaults from without, but to maintain, uninterrupted, the stillness of slavery within'. As for the USA, 'evils yet afflict it'; even though its citizens, thanks to the franchise and the ballot box, possess 'the power of redressing every grievance', and the means to correct every abuse. The preface also made it clear that Chartists were not prepared to subscribe to Paine's religious views, emphatically stating that, when commending his writings 'we speak of his political works only'.

Why then republish Paine's political works at all, given the large number of cheap editions that had already appeared in the 1830s and 1840s? While noting that, in the political works of Paine, there is 'everything to commend; nothing to condemn', the preface failed to mention the central tenet of Paine's political philosophy, namely the repudiation of hereditary right to government authority. Instead, it applauded him for making 'the heart glow with the holiest philanthropy' and for firing the soul 'with the purest patriotism'. 'In Paine', it claimed, 'liberty finds an ardent friend, despotism a relentless foe'. All this could have appeared in the dedication made to any political reformer of the time. Indeed, it would have suited Edmund Burke, or anyone else bent on preserving the ancient constitution. It would appear, then, that Paine had become acceptable to the Chartist movement as a legendary hero, but with the uniqueness of his radicalism filleted out. In other words, the Chartists respected him principally for his adherence to universal suffrage, a cause that had failed to feature prominently in his major works. It is not that Paine disbelieved in the principle. Rather, this omission came of his obsessive fixation with hereditary succession and that, by the time he composed *Rights of Man*, a system of universal suffrage, and how best to operate it, could be taken as read (the result of Cartwright's *Take Your Choice*, a work published in 1776, the same year as the publication of *Common Sense*). Significantly, the one work of Paine's to stress the importance of universal suffrage, that is, the tract *Dissertation on First Principles of Government*, was placed first in the order of items included in the Chartist edition of Paine' political works.

It would be presumptuous to think that the Chartists' emphasis upon universal suffrage, and their strict adherence to the six points of the People's Charter (all of which related to parliamentary reform), meant that their concern was simply a political one. Given the range of grievance articulated by the movement, some sort of hidden agenda must have existed: one to be revealed only after universal suffrage had been achieved. Yet it does not necessarily follow that, with the control of parliament transferred from a social elite sustained by education and the ownership of land and capital to classes sustained by their handicraft skills, their labour and their experience of life, the next step would be to establish a Paineite republic. Matthew Roberts writes of a 'veiled republicanism' present within the Chartist movement, but there are two good reasons for doubting that the veil would ever be cast off.[301] Especially among the Chartist leaders, there endured a faith in the Crown, with some of them moved by a variant belief in Bolingbroke's concept of 'the patriot king' who would, benevolently and paternally, take the interests of the people to heart and intervene to curtail their exploitation by usurers (i.e. bankers) 'feudal lords' (i.e. rentier landowners) 'cotton lords'(i.e. factory owners) and the 'shopocracy' (i.e. shopkeepers).[302] Imbedded in the radical belief that the constitution with its rights and liberties was founded in Anglo-Saxon times by Good King Alfred, this faith in monarchy had undergone a revival in 1830 on the accession of William IV, even among supposedly die-hard republicans like Richard Carlile.[303] It resurfaced in 1837 with the accession of Queen Victoria, a distant echo of a reforming alliance between royalty and people raised by Queen Caroline's Cobbett-assisted bid to have her regal title recognised in 1820.[304] Backing up this hope of a benevolent monarch in the mid-nineteenth century were a number of modernising reforms in the tax system, the effect of which was to upend the Paineite theory that the major cause of poverty in Britain lay with a system of regressive taxation (the weight of which fell upon the poor rather than the rich), combined with the extravagance of the Court and the Crown's propensity to go to war. Among these fiscal reforms were: the creation from 1842 of a regular income tax; changes in customs and excises following the repeal of the Corn Laws in 1846; the removal of other taxes which had been a source of bitter radical complaint (such as the window tax in 1851 and the newspaper tax in 1855); and the introduction of Estates Duty in 1889. It thus became possible to argue that an alleviation of the tax burden was not necessarily predicated upon terminating the polity of the blood.[305]

The second reason for doubting the Chartists' capacity to promote a Paineite republic was their concern for 'the defence of labour against the claims of capital': something that had been very much to the fore in radical circles from the early thirties, and which had become firmly lodged in the mentality of the working classes by several key events. Notable among them were conflicts between the government and trade unionism that led to savage sentences of transportation passed on the Dorchester farmworkers in 1834 and on the Glasgow cotton spinners in 1837. In addition, the New Poor Law of 1834 was seen as another device designed to oppress labour by keeping wages down. Chartism became, in conceit and following, very much a working-class movement. Its conventions were termed 'of the working classes', its impact was dependent upon the support that leaders such as O'Brien and O'Connor could muster from those who dressed in fustian and worked with their hands. The defence of labour thus became of vital importance, not to protect it against the fiscal exactions of the state (as conceived by Paine) but against 'the claims of capital' (as conceived by Robespierre and stated first by Hodgskin and then by O'Brien). As a result, the second step taken by the Chartist movement would, in all likelihood, have been a policy of social reform to protect the working classes from capitalist exploitation.[306] Ruling this out was its failure to achieve the first step, one exclusively confined, as we have seen, to political reform. On the other hand, a number of political reforms occurred in compensation for the failure to obtain universal suffrage: notably the introduction of a secret ballot in 1872, the extensive broadening of the franchise in 1867 and 1884, the removal of the property qualification for MPs in 1857 and the payment of salaries to MPs in 1911. All of these reforms accorded with long-term demands and offered some assurance that the Radical Reform movement, as expressed through Chartism, had not been a total failure, and that it was only a matter of time for one-man-one-vote to come about. A persuasive message was in this way imparted: that, to achieve democracy, a sudden and complete overthrow of the old order, along Paineite lines, was not required since a process of political reform was moving, if slowly, in the right direction.

k | Democracy versus Democracy

Thus, two types of democracy found favour with radical reformers in early nineteenth-century Britain, the one created by John Cartwright, the other, by Thomas Paine. The former emphasised the importance of universal suffrage; the latter, the importance of abolishing hereditary succession. The supporters of Cartwrightian democracy concentrated upon a just representation of the people in the House of Commons; the supporters of Paineite democracy focused on the abolition of crown and peerage.[307] Overall, in the competition between the two for popular support, the Cartwright system of reform, although not so sophisticated as Paine's (on account of the willingness to accept, despite its primitiveness, rule by right of succession), possessed the greater appeal. Its advantages over the Paine system of reform lay, first, in its open-endedness. With the House of Commons rendered answerable to the working classes, social as well as political grievances, arguably, could be remedied simply by appropriate legislation. Secondly, its foundation by peaceful means seemed within the realm of possibility, whereas the establishment of Paine's reform programme had been associated with violent overthrow. To achieve what Cartwright proposed, parliamentary reform was the only requirement, and this was presented as obtainable merely by a constitutional process of restoring the *status quo ante*. The drawbacks against founding a Paineite system lay in Paine's explicit contempt for a tradition of ensconced liberty and, viewed in terms of American and French example, in the necessity of revolution and innovation for its achievement. Such a revolution had to be popular rather than aristocratic, otherwise it would simply elevate the noble order at the expense of the Crown. This charge could be held against the Glorious Revolution, normally revered by radicals but rejected by Paine as a trick played upon the people by those who ruled by right of birth. Moreover, in contrast to the Cartwright system of reform, which was in no danger of going out of date thanks to the slowness with which it was being realised, it became increasingly clear, as the nineteenth century wore on, that Paineite solutions to the problems of the time were inadequate at best; so much so that to put them into practice would leave the basic problem of society untouched: that is, the destitution to which the majority was subjected. Furthermore, the Paine system was inextricably associated with a man whose reputation had been indelibly sullied by his own unpatriotic behaviour, both in siding with the enemy (in the war against the American colonies, as well as in the following war against revolutionary France), and by curtly rejecting the historical (i.e. Anglo-Saxon) foundations of British liberty.

Widely held against Paine was his repudiation of Christianity.[308] As his *The Age of Reason* (1794) made clear, for him the Christian religion was not only fiction but also a political trick played by the old order to maintain its ascendancy. Republicanism in nineteenth-century Britain was at its most potent when its supporters could subscribe to both his religious and political principles. This was true of Richard Carlile's following in the 1820s and early 1830s, of the membership of the NUWC in the 1830s, and of the Bradlaugh movement in the early 1870s. But in a Christian society, infidelity was bound to be a handicap. In sharp contrast, the Radical Reform associations led by Cartwright, Cobbett, Hunt and O'Connor abided by, and benefited from, some form of Christianity. Seriously undermining any chance of a republican movement within Chartism, for instance, was the prevalent Christianity of most of its members and all of its leaders.

Finally, since the Radical Reform movement occurred within a patriarchal society, it must have been assisted by its leaders' determination to confine the electoral suffrage to men: as was the case with Cartwright, Hunt, Cobbett and O'Connor. Paine appeared to hold the same view, but in Britain his political philosophy came to be filtered through the lens of his principal promoter Richard Carlile, who chose to extend the vote to women.[309] More respectful of the orthodoxies of the time, and presented in terms of restoring lost liberties rather than creating new rights, Cartwright's system of democracy stood a greater chance of being appreciated for its own sake. Even so, its complete realisation was obliged to wait until after the First World War. It is, then, quite misleading to explain the failure of Paine's project for abolishing the polity of the blood simply in terms of the strength and tenacity of conservatism. Also contributing to its defeat was popular support for other expressions of radicalism. Just as his proposed reforms were excluded by alternative forms of republicanism, blocking the way was also an alternative form of democracy.

The Polity of the Blood

Chapter V
General Conclusion

An instructive contrast distinguishes the return of Paine's bones from the USA to England in November 1819 and the return of the body of Terence McManus from the USA to Ireland in November 1861. McManus had suffered transportation to Tasmania for his contribution to the Young Irelanders' Uprising in Tipperary of 1848. Escaping to San Francisco, he died at the age of forty-one, and was initially buried there in 1861. By this time the Irish Republican Brotherhood had emerged with Fenian cells in America as well as in Britain. Arrangements were made to exhume the body and send it, via the Panama Canal, to New York so that it could receive a lying-in-state and a requiem mass in St Patrick's Cathedral. With that accomplished, the next step was to take it to Ireland, in the hope of a requiem mass in Dublin Cathedral. However, this was disallowed by the archbishop. Instead, a service was held by the grave side in Glasnevin Cemetery where, despite the rain, the slush and the mud, a large crowd of 20-30,000 gathered to honour the body. McManus' burial signalled a turning point for the Brotherhood in Ireland, with James Stephens, the organiser of the funeral arrangements, suddenly finding himself the leader of a flourishing republican movement in his home country.[1]

Something similar might have happened with the return of Paine's skeleton to England in 1819, but for the fact that there was no equivalent of Stephens to exploit the republican opportunity and, given the strength of loyalty to the Crown, not much of a constituency to arouse. And whereas in Ireland republicanism and Christianity went hand in hand because of Catholic opposition to an imposed Protestant state religion, in England Paineite republicanism had to face the repressive authority of the Anglican church. Moreover, led by Henry Hunt, the Radical Reformers, although incensed by the government's responsibility for the Peterloo Massacre, were predominantly monarchists and Christians and therefore little inclined to resurrect Paine. In fact, given their central aim (to extend the parliamentary franchise to include all adult males), they were more inclined to distance themselves from his doctrines so as not to damage their own political cause. In this hostile environment, the keepers of the bones, namely William Cobbett and later

Benjamin Tilly, chose to hide them away. Instead of the spectacular funeral and impressive monument that Cobbett had promised, they were simply stowed away in the chest used to convey them to England and kept well out of public sight.

Paine's legacy was not just a skeleton but also a celebrated book: a teach-yourself-treatise on how to define and establish a true republic. *Rights of Man* was a best seller when first published in 1791-2 but thereafter suffered many years of government suppression, a period of persecution only terminated by William Sherwin's boldness in republishing it in 1817. Paine's political beliefs belonged to a British radical tradition reaching back to the revolutions of the seventeenth century. Yet they were distinguished by their unrelenting antipathy to rule by hereditary right. Previously, kingship had been condemned but only for being autocratic, its critics having no deep-seated grudge against aristocracy as a right of birth. Alternatively, within the same radical tradition, the principle of hereditary rule had been found wanting but not to the extent of justifying its abolition. All that was required was a parliamentary limitation of its authority. Paine's stand was distinctly different; as were its implications. Essentially, a new political system had to be created resting solely upon principles justified by reason. This meant the rejection of not only monarchy and aristocracy, irrespective of what form they took, but also the basic beliefs that upheld them: notably the ancient constitution and the theory that rule was by divine (hence natural) right. The latter, the original justification for the principle of hereditary succession, had been effectively challenged by leading philosophers from Thomas Hobbes onward; but, well beyond Paine's time, presenting monarchy as a calling from God exercised through the hereditary principle remained the means by which the Anglican priesthood upheld royal authority. Moreover, belief in the ancient constitution, with its dependence upon hereditary authority and the coronation oath, remained intact and inviolable until Paine declared there was no such thing and that this would continue until one was popularly approved in writing. Also challenged by Paine was the belief that political reform could only be achieved through the king in parliament. Paine argued that parliament was no fit body for the purpose and that a convention expressive of the nation's will was required to put matters right. The latter device was mentioned in both parts of *Rights of Man* but too briefly, in view of its importance.[2] For this reason, a third part of *Rights of Man* was published in 1792, just before Paine fled into exile never to return. Entitled *A Letter Addressed to the Addressers on the Late Proclamation*, it confirmed the vital role of a national convention in Paine's scheme of things: not to serve as a part of everyday government but simply to create a new constitution in which monarchy and aristocracy had no place.[3] The snag with this procedure was that, from a practical point of view, it presupposed a revolutionary disruption of the state. Thus, it was applied successfully in the USA and in France, but only following an overthrow of the old regime. In itself, it was not a workable prelude to such a momentous event, only a consequence of it. Moreover, the Paineite idea of a national convention tended to provoke a severe counteraction, as was evident in the early 1790s when attempts to hold one in Scotland and England led to sentences of transportation for sedition and trials of high treason. The same scenario was re-enacted in the early 1830s, leading to the fiasco on Cold Bath Fields and an end to the idea as envisaged by Paine. When the Chartists employed the term it was to signify a device with a different purpose: their 'convention' aimed not to create a constitution but merely to approve a petition calling upon the government to permit the reform of the House of Commons by making its members answerable to the people through a system of manhood suffrage.

Paine's objection to hereditary right was not all-inclusive. Notably, it did not apply to property. His egalitarianism therefore did not make him a leveller in the material sense since it related only to removing differences of inherited degree. On the other hand, objections made to his reform programme were not simply in defence of hereditary rule. They also stemmed from other issues, especially his reputation as a revolutionary, his anti-patriotism and his dismissal of Christianity as a poisonous concoction of biblical fable and clerical deceit. Cobbett brought Paine's body back to England in order to secure the country's recognition of him as 'the illustrious patriot', but that was an impossibility in view of Paine's absence from the country for the last seventeen years of his life, his association with French attempts to invade the country, and his earlier role in persuading American colonists to fight for independence. Realising the error of his ways, Cobbett quickly abandoned the project. Another source of alienation was Paine's view that Britain's past had not established liberty for the people but only for its aristocracy whose capacity to resist the monarch – as with Magna Carta in 1215 or the Bill of Rights in 1689 – had enlarged its own political authority at the expense of both commonalty and crown. Paine's contempt for Christianity was made crystal clear in *The Age of Reason* (1794). Its impact was evident in the fact that those who supported his type of republicanism were predominantly deists and atheists. This bond was broken in the mid-nineteenth century by the Christian W.J. Linton, under the influence of Mazzini and in the pages of *The English Republic* (1851), but re-established by Charles Bradlaugh in the early 1870s in the pages of the *National Reformer*.

Because Paine made himself an alien by provocatively promoting such a wide range of contentious issues, the opposition he encountered was not simply the predictable reaction of king worship. Moreover, sustaining such opposition was support from traditions of radicalism, notably the movement to establish universal suffrage. Founded in the 1770s and finally successful only in the twentieth century, this movement deplored Paine's theology, his 'foreignness' and his apparent sympathy for revolutionary violence. Another strand of anti-Paineite radicalism argued that Paine's emphasis upon taxation as the main cause of poverty, and his consequent provision of a political solution to society's problems, was misguided and insufficient. Its spokesmen were Robert Owen and Bronterre O'Brien, both advocates of socialism: 'communitarian' in the case of the former, 'state' in the case of the latter. Their criticism of Paine overlooked the welfare reforms first suggested in *Rights of Man* part II and repeated with some revision in *Agrarian Justice*.[4] In proposing an old-age pension and an apprenticeship annuity for all, and other forms of relief specifically for the poor, such as matrimonial, funeral and educational allowances, Paine was not reacting against capitalist exploitation. Instead he was making compensation for the loss of natural rights that had followed the establishment of private property, as well as providing remedy for the injustice created by the gross imbalance that existed between the proportion of government revenue dispensed to the rich and what was currently offered to the poor. Paine's welfare reforms therefore were quite different from the concerns and solutions of socialism. Promoting state socialism, O'Brien in the 1830s waged an extensive campaign in the press to demonstrate the superiority and relevance of Robespierre over Paine. The outcome was to show that Paine's political reforms had always been out of date and that removing crown and aristocracy would leave the condition of the working classes unchanged. This gave birth to a strand of socialism that was republican in spirit but not prepared, in the manner of Paine, to prioritise abolishing the polity of the blood.

The course taken by radicalism, whether parliamentary or socialist, tended to by-pass the central tenet of Paine's political reform programme, indicating that Paine's republicanism *per se* was not totally to blame for its non-establishment. A greater responsibility, arguably, lay with Paine himself who was proud to declare 'independence is my happiness' but failed to realise that, in leading him to promote so many intrinsically distasteful causes, it was also his Achilles' heel.[5]

Finally, central to Paine's programme of reform was a basic impracticability. Quintessentially, the programme required a national convention for its implementation. This proved impossible to summon without the precondition of a successful revolution. For Paine, it was not enough to produce, on two occasions (i.e. in *Common Sense* (1776) and in *Rights of Man* (1791-2)) a brilliant condemnation of the polity of the blood, or for both works to become astounding best sellers. Sinking his cause in Britain were his own indiscretions; while the failure of the British to achieve a popular revolution, despite a remarkable and durable capacity for creating unrest, rendered his proposed solutions not so much common-sensical as a visionary pie in the sky.

The Polity of the Blood

Appendix
The Tale of Tom Paine's Bones

a | Flawed Versions of the Story

The bizarre and macabre story of Thomas Paine's bones has been told a number of times.[1] Yet the notion prevails that we do not know where the bones went and that, given the limitations of the surviving evidence, we have no chance of ever finding out. In 1958 Leo Bressler declared that, from the mid-1840s, 'the records are vague', and as to what happened to the bones, 'no one knows'.[2] This note of despair is echoed in recent accounts. In 2004 Paul Pickering, for example, stated that 'Paine's bones were lost not long after they were disinterred' (i.e., in 1819).[3] His sentiments were echoed by James Grande in 2014: moved by William Hazlitt's claim that the bones 'were left to shift for themselves', he presented them as 'misplaced' by Cobbett and consequently lost for good.[4]

In 2006, a whole book appeared on the history of Paine's afterlife on earth. Written by Paul Collins and entitled *The Trouble with Tom*, it revealed that much could be added to the subject. Unfortunately, it was pitched at the public as an historical comedy. As such, it offers an amusing read but not one to be taken too seriously. It concludes by answering the important question 'Where is Tom Paine?' with the facetious rejoinder 'Reader, where is he not?'[5] Marring the study is not just its adopted tone but also a host of errors and omissions. For instance, the central character in the tale of the bones – second only to William Cobbett, the man responsible for removing them from a grave in New York State and conveying them to England – was the tailor Benjamin Tilly, custodian of the bones from 1844 until his death in 1869. Collins mistakes the place where Tilly first took possession of them as Bedford Square West (i.e. in Bloomsbury) rather than Bedford Square East (i.e. in Stepney).[6] He then fails to track the trail of the bones as Tilly conveyed them, for the rest of his life, from one address to another. There is no excuse for this since such information can easily be found in the basic family history sources, notably Trade Directories, Census Returns and the General Register of Births and Deaths. Furthermore, in relating Tilly to the story of the bones, he gets wrong the date of death of both Tilly's wife (she died in 1860, not 'by 1853') and Tilly himself who died not in 1860 but in 1869.[7]

Another key figure in the tale of the bones was the republican and infidel publisher James Watson, a well-known disbeliever in religion whom Collins incorrectly identifies as a Quaker.[8] He also wrongly attributes to him the authorship of the very first account of the bones: Watson was but the publisher; in all likelihood, the true author was Tilly.[9] Further confusion is caused by Collins' failure to realise that Watson's acquisition of the bones in 1853 marked only a brief hiatus in Tilly's custody of them, since shortly afterwards he returned them to Tilly. As a result, Collins' speculation that Watson was probably responsible for their reburial is complete and utter nonsense.[10]

Yet another key figure in the tale, in this case a vital witness, was Edward Truelove, like Watson a publisher of infidel republican literature, including the works of Paine. He was also owner of the writing table at which Paine had proof-read part II of *Rights of Man* and had composed *Letter Addressed to the Addressers on the Late Proclamation*.[11] In Collins' book he is the man with no name, receiving mention only as a London bookseller.[12] An important correspondence exists between Truelove and Moncure Conway, both keen collectors of Paineite relics. Now located in Thetford Public Library, this correspondence throws light on what happened to Paine's skull once it became detached from the body.[13] Yet Collins failed to consult it. Another key figure was the Unitarian minister, Alexander Gordon, whom Collins assumes was a resident of Manchester when involved with the bones.[14] But, at that time, Gordon lived and worked in Norwich, making it most likely that he had the bones buried in Rosary Cemetery, a burial ground on the outskirts of that city.[15] Several key figures in the story of the bones Collins completely overlooked. They include the wealthy republican Joseph Cowen, who in 1853 was complicit with Watson in seeking to secure for Paine a reburial in Kensal Green Cemetery and, in all likelihood, provided the financial means for Watson to acquire the bones when they came up for auction in that year.[16] Nor did Collins mention Mrs Ball, of Harrow-on-the-Hill, a friend of Tilly who allowed him free accommodation in her house following his wife's death and who, after Tilly's death, provided information on his final years. He also omitted Edward Smith of Hale End, Walthamstow, who managed to acquire a lock of Paine's hair and who provided important evidence on John Chennell of Guildford, one time owner of Paine's coffin and a few of his smaller bones.[17]

For these reasons, then, a further reworking of the surviving evidence is due. This can best be done by means of a critical and comparative study of the earliest attempts at telling the true story of the bones. The first to appear was

Tilly's own account, entitled *A Brief History of the Remains of Thomas Paine*. Published in 1847, it was only able to deal with their early history. Essentially, it charted how they passed from Cobbett to Tilly. For the later history, there are the findings of two clergymen who, from the late 1870s, sought to solve the mystery of Paine's lost remains. One was the American Moncure Conway, a Unitarian minister of the South Place Institute, Finsbury. He was not only a keen collector of Paine material but also a determined tracker-down of the bones. Incorporated in his research was the evidence he had gathered from his own communications with Truelove, Watson, Cowen, Smith and the lawyer Oliver Ainslie, who briefly owned Paine's skull and his right hand. Conway's research was eventually published in *The Adventures of Thomas Paine's Bones* (1902).[18] Although strewn with errors and unfounded speculation, it is, nonetheless, a highly informative source.

The other detective on the case was George Reynolds, a Baptist minister of Stepney and, like Conway, a keen collector of Paineite relics. His research included an interview with Tilly's friend, Mrs Ball, in 1896 and his own encounter in 1878 with Mr and Mrs Ginns, Tilly's last landlord and the couple to whom he had given the bones by the time of his death. Of Mrs Ball, Reynolds claimed to have spent a whole day conversing with her about Paine and Cobbett. He found her 'well posted up in the matter' as she 'explained to him many points needing elucidation'. She revealed herself to be a great admirer of both men. His own findings were first made public at the Thomas Paine exhibition of 1895. They were described in the catalogue (item 427) as 'Rev. Geo. Reynolds. The Light of Day. Remains of Thomas Paine, 1879-81'. Eventually they were published as *Thomas Paine's Bones and their Owners by an Old Daylighter* (Norwich, 1908), with Reynolds acknowledged as 'the chief authority for the statements made' therein.[19] The aim here is to collate these three sources and resolve their differences. In the process other independent sources of evidence, taken from communications in the press, are considered. The end-purpose is to provide the most accurate account possible of the bones and their disappearance.

A fourth source entitled 'Exhumation of the Remains of the Immortal Thomas Paine', and written 'by an eye-witness' who must be William Benbow, fails to live up to the expectations raised in the *Poor Man's Guardian* when, in an advance-notice, it promised 'a history of the disinterment of Thomas Paine with a faithful statement of the motives that led to the disinterment and of the contemplated consequences', written by the very person who had directed the operation.[20] The newspaper in which it was to appear, Benbow's monthly *Agitator*, printed the first two instalments in the issues for November and December 1833 but then abruptly closed down. As a result, all the promised details about the exhumation and its aftermath were never revealed.[21]

If the bones had remained together the story would be simpler to relate. Their dismemberment and dispersal, however, means that within the one story there are several tales to tell. Thus, the history of the ribs is quite different from that of the skull and right hand. The same could be said for the rest of the skeleton. And the portion of brain and the two surviving locks of his hair followed trails of their very own. The inevitable outcome is a highly complicated account of what happened to one man's remains: one that reflects upon how Paine and his philosophy of reform were regarded at several points in nineteenth-century Britain.

b | Paine's Repatriation and its Problems

In June 1809 Thomas Paine – despite achieving great fame as author of *Common Sense* (1776), *Rights of Man* (1791-2) and *The Age of Reason* (1794), and notwithstanding his leading role in impressing republicanism on both the American and French Revolutions – had received a quiet and private burial abroad. He had left his native land hurriedly in 1792 to escape arrest for seditious libel. Found guilty in his absence, he had never returned. He remained in France until 1802 when he moved to the USA. His hope was to be buried there in a Quaker cemetery, but, alienated by Paine's reputation as a non-Christian, the Friends turned his request down. In consequence, he was laid to rest in an unconsecrated corner of his own small farm at New Rochelle in New York State.

A decade later, in reaction to this miserly send-off, William Cobbett, once his fiercest critic but now a devoted and apologetic fan, resolved to give him a funeral worthy of his greatness. Aided by the shoemaker-turned-publisher, republican and radical Christian, William Benbow, he dug up the body, now a skeleton, in September 1819 and brought it to England the following November. Cobbett's account of the exhumation claimed that he 'took up the coffin entire', adding: 'just as we found it, it goes to England'.[22] In fact, the remains came over in a chest. Cobbett, however, did not abandon the coffin but brought it over as well. It was made of mahogany and had a silver plate attached to its lid. The plate, now badly tarnished after so many years in the ground, identified the body by name and date of death but added a couple of years to Paine's actual age.[23] The coffin and plate were important to Cobbett since, once back in England, both would be needed to prove the authenticity of the bones. Cobbett's plans for Paine were made clear and explicable before he set sail: 'We will honour his name, his remains and his memory with a tomb' that would serve as 'an object of pilgrimage with the people.' Paine deserved as much, Cobbett claimed, through being 'our famous Englishman' and 'an honour to his country', the result of having distinguished himself by exposing the inadequacy of both the parliamentary system and the system of public finance. On the other hand, he took care to stress that 'we do not look upon ourselves as adopting all Paine's opinions'. Singling out his republicanism as totally unacceptable, he gave his full approval to Paine's support for universal suffrage. In his opinion, to establish universal suffrage, an act in keeping with tradition and the law and therefore a restoration rather than an innovation, would make England 'the best country in the world'. In contrast, to create a republican government – that is, to get rid of hereditary rule – would render it 'a poor, base, contemptible thing and the people the most distracted and miserable the world ever saw'. For this reason he regarded anyone advocating such a breach with the past as 'nearly mad'.[24] Presented in this selective manner, he thought Paine's 'political economy' would have a special appeal to the people of England and, as a means of promoting political reform, his repatriation could be fully justified. To absolve himself of responsibility for an exhumation which, dubiously, had taken place 'at peep of day' and without official authorisation, Cobbett proposed: 'Let it be considered the act of the Reformers of England, Scotland and Ireland', for 'in their name we opened the grave and in their name will the tomb be raised'.[25] Seen in this light, how could anyone of a reformist persuasion object to what he had done?

Further ideas for honouring Paine were proposed by Cobbett upon reaching England in November 1819: notably a spectacular funeral, with twenty waggon-loads of flowers strewn before the hearse; a monument at either Thetford, Paine's birthplace, or Botley, Cobbett's country residence, to be funded by selling to the public, at one guinea a time, gold rings, each with a strand of Paine's hair attached and a certificate of authenticity signed by Cobbett himself. Cobbett also envisaged a public exhibition of Paine's remains, placed in the original coffin, to allow the people the chance to display in public an appreciation of their hero. In addition, he proposed to rent or purchase a large hall in which annual celebrations of Paine's birth could be held. To perpetuate Paine's name, he also promised the construction of 'a colossal statue in bronze' and the foundation of Paine Clubs to discuss his principles.[26]

None of this happened. Cobbett came to realise that his possession of Paine's bones placed him in a very vulnerable position, especially because of the harm it could inflict upon his political reputation; so much so that the enthusiasm for the project that had sustained him in New York, gave way, following his disembarkation at Liverpool in late November, to a blustering defence of what he had done coupled with a deliberate policy of inaction.[27] Cobbett's appreciation of Paine had rested on Paine's denunciation of paper money, the National Debt and the Sinking Fund, his condemnation of political corruption and his support for universal male suffrage.[28] But this represented only the more innocuous parts of Paine's programme of political reform. The rest of it went totally against Cobbett's basic beliefs, as well as offending the beliefs of all loyalists and most radicals.[29]

For Paine, a genuine representative system of government could not be mixed with an hereditary one. In Britain, he argued, the two only managed to work together thanks to the prevalence of political corruption and the way it allowed the hereditary to control the representative element.[30] The establishment of true and pure representative government would therefore have to entail not only the introduction of one-man-one-vote in the election of MPs but also an abolition of monarchy and a termination of the House of Lords. To be achieved, it was not a matter of reviving the ancient constitution but of creating a completely new one. For Cobbett, Paine was also a dangerous companion because of a message, conveyed by his political career and in his writings, that, if the old regime could not be ended by negotiation, its violent overthrow was necessary. In addition, Paine had made an explicit and brazen stand against Christianity by rejecting the Bible as an absurd and obscene compound of fable and superstition. In commending Paine, therefore, Cobbett was obliged to protect himself against the damaging charges of being a republican, a disbeliever and a revolutionary, and, what is more, of seeking to persuade the people to follow suit. This he did by stressing his own unassailable support for monarchy and Christianity and by assuring the public that his prime concern was a reform of the House of Commons to make it 'fairly chosen by the whole of the commons', and to attain this goal by peaceful means alone.[31] The latter point was made in an address to the reformers 'in or near Manchester' shortly after reaching Liverpool. Thanking them for the welcome they promised to give him, he declared that he was 'extremely anxious that [it] should be attended with no one circumstance, however slight, tending to produce violence or even discord'. He closed the address by wishing that his entry into Manchester be 'unalloyed by anything calculated to give pain to any real friend of peace, order, the king and the laws'.[32]

Appendix

In self-defence, Cobbett proceeded to blame the original idea of repatriation upon his publisher and accomplice, William Benbow, to whom Cobbett in 1819 was closely attached, so much so that he warmly dedicated to him the first edition of his *English Grammar*, published that year. There may have been some truth in this charge. Benbow admitted as much in the early 1830s in his short lived newspaper the *Agitator*, declaring that the inspiration for bringing Paine's remains home came of a plan on the part of the British government to repatriate the body of a certain Major John André, an English spy arrested and hanged by the Americans.[33] At the start of February 1819 Benbow and some of his New York associates, were reasoning that, if this patriotic honour could be granted to André, surely it could be extended to Paine.[34] Nonetheless, if not its originator, Cobbett had, at least from May 1819, enthusiastically embraced the plan to return the body of Paine, and had continued to do so until his arrival in England with the bones in his baggage.[35] And, if he can be trusted, the plan was something he had 'vowed' to carry out ever since going to America in 1817.[36]

Upon reaching England, the rashness of his actions began to sink in. The time for Paine's return, he realised, was far from propitious, what with political tensions following the Peterloo Massacre of August, and the harsh sentence imposed upon Richard Carlile in mid-November for publishing Paine's *The Age of Reason*. Such a critical situation, intensified by fears of disorder and prospects of savage reprisal, was bound to 'put public opinion, and especially with regard to myself, to the severest test'.[37]

His arrival in Liverpool on 21 November received massive acclaim from the people of the north, in the form of written addresses with long lists of named supporters attached. Yet, it also encountered a barrage of abuse and ridicule from the press.[38] The addresses made no mention of Paine while the press reports mentioned little else. The outrage expressed by the press was partly in response to Cobbett's own brief account of the exhumation and its purpose, composed the previous month in New York and first published in England on 13 November.[39] But, in all probability, it was also provoked by William Benbow, who had reached Liverpool a few days earlier than Cobbett on 11 November.[40] Benbow provided the first announcement in England of what had happened, adding matter not present in the Cobbett account. According to Benbow, the skeleton was 'in a perfect state' and that, once it was in England, Cobbett intended to 'parade' it through the principal towns of the north.[41] This generated the rumour (later dismissed by Cobbett as absurd) that, starting in the Peterloo regions of the North-west, Cobbett intended to raise a revolutionary army with himself and the bones at its head.[42] Cobbett, however, proceeded with circumspection. The only display of the body, in fact, occurred in front of the officials at the Liverpool Customs House who uncovered the bones as they searched Cobbett's luggage. Unphased, Cobbett declared: 'There, gentlemen, are the mortal remains of the immortal Paine.'[43] But he made no mention of the bones to the large crowds who turned up to meet him.

From Liverpool Cobbett intended to visit Manchester, a diversion on his journey to London; but at Irlam he was stopped by a letter of warning from the boroughreeves and constables of Manchester and Salford, who feared his arrival might ignite another Peterloo. This appeared to provide an ideal opportunity to display the bones; but Cobbett kept them under cover. Instead of proceeding to Manchester, he retreated to Warrington and continued his journey south. On the journey to London, the bones were kept out of sight; and no mention was made of them in the speeches Cobbett delivered to the crowds of supporters encountered on the journey, or in the addresses to reformers that he published en route.[44]

Nonetheless, yielding to insults went totally against Cobbett's nature. Consequently, on several occasions in the following two months, he threw caution to the wind and, under provocation, either mentioned the bones or extolled Paine: notably in early December 1819, when he encountered disapproval from Radical Reformers (i.e. advocates of universal suffrage) at a welcome-home dinner in the Crown and Anchor; in early January 1820, after Lord Grosvenor had suggested in the Upper House that the bones in Cobbett's possession did not belong to Paine, and, even if they did, the people would despise them because of Paine's hostility to Christianity; in late January after the Bishop of Llandaff, also in the Lords, had attacked Paine as a blasphemer; and again in September 1821 after the bones of André – having been brought back from America – were buried in Westminster Abbey.

The dangers inherent in the bones project, and the lack of support for it, were strongly expressed at the dinner held for Radical Reformers in the Strand on 4 December 1819.[45] Its purpose was to honour Cobbett's return to England. Henry Hunt, as chairman, impressed upon the meeting his reservations about Paine in his opening toast: 'The British Constitution, composed of King, Lords and a House of Commons elected by the free voice of the whole People' and in a later double-edged toast: 'The memory of Thomas Paine, and may his calumniators imitate his virtues, and his admirers avoid his errors.' At the

Appendix

same meeting, Hunt took the precaution of denying any connection with Deism, the theology advocated in Paine's *The Age of Reason*, while Cobbett declared his indifference to Deism and his hostility to republicanism. For him 'Petty tyrants were the worst of tyrants, and they were often to be found in republican governments'. But he also asserted that his appreciation of Paine had nothing to do with the latter's republicanism or his anti-Christianity, and that his plan to construct a huge statue of Paine in bronze was partly to atone for previously abusing him in print and partly to honour the memory of a great man. This drew a sardonic response from Thomas Wooler who told the assembly that, alongside such a statue of Paine, a statue of Cobbett should surely be 'placed... for they were worthy of each other in the eyes of their country'.[46] In reaction to Grosvenor's remarks that the bones were spurious, Cobbett threatened to put them on display, encased in the original coffin, in order to prove him wrong. 'How many applications have I had', he declared, 'to permit the applicants to see these bones: hundreds upon hundreds; and this desire shall be shortly gratified'. And as for Grosvenor's charge that Paine's anti-Christianity would alienate the people, Cobbett exclaimed in repudiation: 'Oh no! my Lord, it is the politics' of Paine that would attract their support.[47]

In reaction to the Bishop of Llandaff's charge of blasphemy, Cobbett argued at length that, although no Christian, Paine was not a blasphemer since 'he offers no indignity unto God himself'; and that the appeal of his writings to the people lay not in crude assertions but in subtle and persuasive arguments fully understandable to them because of the enlightenment they had undergone since the early 1790s when, in a state of ignorance and egged on by the clergy, they had burnt him in effigy.[48] Commenting on the burial of André in Westminster Abbey, he claimed that, in bringing André home, the person responsible, the Duke of York, was just as much a 'grave robber' as himself, with the difference that Cobbett had become one in order to show respect for an illustrious patriot, whereas the Duke of York had merely acted to honour a man executed as a spy.[49]

Otherwise, Cobbett was inclined to distance himself from the project. After seeking to arrange a dinner, chaired by himself, to celebrate Paine's birth in late January 1820, only to find it thwarted by his inability to hire a public room, he dropped the idea for good.[50] The same was true of a proposal to establish Paine Clubs.[51] In the same month, having described the intended funeral in extravagant terms, he had to admit: 'I do not say when this shall take place.'[52] Then, in September 1821, he appeared to abandon plans for an imminent burial, with the vague promise that it would take place 'in due time'. Meanwhile, he announced, the bones would remain in his care.[53]

Several considerations combined to persuade Cobbett to shelve the project. Besides the need to protect his political reputation from the taint of republicanism and infidelity, it was clear that the project was far from popular with other Radical Reformers. This even applied to radicals who accepted Paine's reform programme in full and presented themselves as infidel republicans. By 1823 there were at least 4,000 of them, concentrated in Manchester, Leeds, London and Edinburgh but also scattered over many parts of the country.[54] Led by Richard Carlile, they had no desire to back Cobbett's project. Publishing Paine's works was more to their liking than honouring his bones. Carlile told Cobbett: 'I do not grudge them [i.e. the bones] to you; they are dirt in my eyes; I would not be troubled with them.' First and foremost, it was 'the writings of Thomas Paine' that he valued, knowing that 'they are calculated to improve the condition of mankind'. He concluded: 'I admire the mind but not the bones of the man.'[55] His supporters felt likewise. In 1823 they held a Paine dinner in London attended by 300. At it a certain Mr Grainger called upon the company to thank Cobbett for returning Paine's body 'to his native country'. He went on to urge those present to require of Cobbett the date of its re-interment so that, in connexion with this event, they could contribute funds towards the erection of 'a monument to his memory'. In the absence of Carlile, who was still serving time in Dorchester Gaol, the veteran Jacobin and radical orator, John Gale Jones, spoke 'eloquently' against Grainger's motion, obtaining a large majority in favour of its rejection.[56]

This general lack of support left the project totally reliant upon Cobbett's own financial resources. However, constantly mired in debt, he became bankrupt in July 1820.[57] A few months earlier he had proposed raising a 'reform fund' of £5,000, refusing to disclose its purpose; but it transpired that this had nothing to do with Paine but was to finance a campaign to secure for himself a parliamentary seat.[58] At the same time, it became clear that the government planned a major crack-down on popular movements engaged in political and religious reform. Following Peterloo, this was signalled by the passage of the Six Acts in December 1819, a device to stop the monster meetings of 1819 and to rule out a cheap penny press critical of the government in matters of church and state.[59] There followed an onslaught in the courts against Paineites associated with Richard Carlile; the conviction for political sedition of all the major leaders of Radical Reform but for Cobbett; and the execution of the Cato

Street conspirators, to whom Cobbett was maliciously linked, for attempting to assassinate the Cabinet. In these circumstances, Cobbett was obliged to rethink his approach to political reform.[60]

Faced by a government seemingly bent on crushing political dissent, Cobbett was persuaded to distance himself from Paine and proceed by other means. Hence his plan to seek membership of the House of Commons. This ambition was announced in December 1819: 'For my part, I have always been for the ancient establishments of the country…I am for those establishments still. I am for no new, wild, visionary schemes; and therefore, it is that I wish for a reform of the Commons' House of Parliament; and therefore, it is, also, that I wish to be myself in that House.' He sought to realise this ambition in March 1820 when he stood for Coventry, the opposition making much of his recent dealings with Paine to sink his chance of victory.[61] His second resort was to promote the cause of Caroline of Brunswick who, following the death of George III in January 1820, returned to England to re-establish her right to be recognised as George IV's wife. Cobbett assumed the position of Caroline's secretary in a successful and popular campaign against the government's attempt to have the marriage annulled. In return, it was understood that, as Queen, she would exert influence in support of parliamentary reform, a project scuppered in July 1821 by her exclusion from the coronation and her death three weeks later.[62] Adapting to these changes in political circumstance, Cobbett abandoned his championship of Paine completely.

For Cobbett, the aim of the bones project had been to prove that Paine was 'the illustrious patriot', a difficult enough task in view of his absence from Britain in the last seventeen years of his life, his close associations with America and France, and the unpatriotic implications of his refusal to accept that the liberties of Englishmen were upheld by an ancient constitution founded in Anglo-Saxon times and preserved by the signing of Magna Carta in 1215 and, following the Glorious Revolution, by the enactment of a Bill of Rights in 1689. But proving him to be a great countryman was rendered virtually impossible when it became known that he had been deeply engaged in plans for a French invasion of England.[63] Thus, a final deterrent to proceeding with the bones project was the publication of 'To the English People on the Invasion of England', a long letter originally composed by Paine in 1804. It was published in Sherwin's *The Political Works of Thomas Paine* (November 1818) and republished in Carlile's *The Political and Miscellaneous Works of Thomas Paine.* (November 1820). The letter outlined 'a descent upon England' by means of flat-bottomed gunboats rowed across the North Sea from Belgium to the east coast of England, landing either in Essex, Suffolk, Norfolk or Lincolnshire, where 'the shore is a clean firm sand' allowing a flat-bottomed boat to be easily beached, and where inland the terrain 'is as level as a bowling green, and approachable in every part for more than two hundred miles'. If carried out shortly after a storm or in a fog or in a calm, Paine reckoned, the crossing (taking no more than thirty-six hours) would be well protected against attack from the British navy, whose capacity for action would be impeded by the shoals and shallows off the English coast. Paine envisaged an invading force of 100,000 men, brought over in 1000 shallow-drafted gunboats. They were to be led by Napoleon and accompanied by himself. He reasoned that such an invasion would be much easier than in Roman times since 'the mass of the people are friends to liberty': in other words, the invaders would be welcomed and assisted by an oppressed people longing to be free.

Paine's plan had first surfaced in 1796 when he composed 'Observations on the Construction and Operation of Navies with a Plan for an Invasion of England and the Final Overthrow of the England', sending copies to the American and French governments. It was worked upon in 1797 and into 1798. Revived in 1804, it remained a preoccupation for Paine in 1807. Much of what he wrote on the subject, although first published abroad, was brought together by Carlile and published in 1820.[64] It could not be excused as a passing whim. Contrary to Cobbett, it presented Paine as an irredeemable alien, a deadly enemy to the country of his birth.

c | A Public Funeral Denied

For thirteen years Paine's remains – a complete skeleton plus a portion of brain lodged in the skull and two locks of hair – were stored in the chest used in 1819 to bring them to England. For most of that time, they lay in Cobbett's Fleet Street printing office: that is at 183 Fleet Street in the 1820s and 11 Bolt Court in the early 1830s. Exceptionally, and for a short while in 1820, they were removed to the house of a friend somewhere in Hampshire who was, in all likelihood, Lord Peter King, Cobbett's friend and co-protester against paper money.[65] The occasion was, probably, the crisis created by Cobbett's self-declared bankruptcy in July 1820, the result of the expenses incurred when he stood as parliamentary candidate for Coventry in the general election of that year. If so, it was probably a safeguard taken against the seizure of the bones by bailiffs in the event of an order for the sequestration of Cobbett's effects. With the bankruptcy threat called off in October 1820, the bones were returned to Fleet Street.[66]

In January 1833, it was decided, with no reason given, to dispatch the chest and its contents to Normandy Farm, close to the village of Ash in Surrey where the elderly Cobbett had taken up residence, after choosing to live apart from what he called his 'monstrous family'. Responsible for their shipment was the tailor Benjamin Tilly, Cobbett's current companion, secretary, amanuensis and factotum.[67] He and two others set about the task. When doing so, Tilly pocketed the surviving portion of brain, having poked it out of the skull, and one lock of hair.[68] He thus inflicted upon the remains the first of a series of appropriations which, over the next forty years, led to their dispersal and almost complete disappearance. Sealing up the chest, Tilly sent it on its way.[69] At the same time the original mahogany coffin was also transferred to Normandy Farm where Cobbett, having abandoned the idea of a public exhibition of Paine and having lost all enthusiasm for a public burial, unscrewed the name plate from the lid and put the coffin to practical use as a grain bin.[70]

Upon Cobbett's death in June 1835, the chest was opened in Tilly's presence by Cobbett's eldest son and sole executor. In an act of crude, but unintentional, desecration – his aim was simply to declare ownership and provide a means of future verification – he scratched his own name on the larger bones as well as in four places on the skull. Tilly bore witness to the deed in writing.[71] Shortly afterwards, in January 1836, another financial crisis hit the Cobbett family, this time the result of a bankruptcy order served on the son for the repayment of his father's debts. It enforced the sale by auction of Cobbett's effects. Jesse Oldfield (Cobbett's main creditor, former friend, financial agent and the man responsible for securing the bankruptcy order) was keen to have the chest of bones included in the sale.[72] But Thomas Piggott, the auctioneer – arguing that he had never previously sold human bones 'and did not intend to begin now' – refused to comply. Nonetheless, a few of Paine's bones were inadvertently sold at that auction, thanks to their concealment in the original coffin. Unknown to the auctioneer, they went to the man who bought the coffin: that is, the corn merchant, John Chennell of Guildford.[73] A day later, another piece of Paine was removed, with Oldfield purchasing a lock of his hair. It was wrapped in an envelope upon which was written in Tilly's hand 'Mr Paine's Hair'. It remained in that envelope for the rest of the century as it passed from Oldfield to Edward Smith and eventually to Moncure Conway.[74]

Following Cobbett's funeral Paine's bones became divided into two groups: on the one hand, the bones in the coffin; on the other, the bones in the chest. The former remained with Chennell until the late 1840s, while the latter went to George West, whose farm lay next to Cobbett's and who was appointed official receiver of Cobbett's effects. Then, in the mid-1840s, they passed to the London tailor and Cobbett's former friend, Benjamin Tilly. The remains in Chennell's possession were a few small bones (possibly ribs) kept in a porcelain jar inside the coffin; those in West's custody, and kept in a chest, comprised the rest of the skeleton. Eventually, the two collections were buried in secret and in unmarked graves, both in sacred ground, the one in the churchyard of the Surrey village of Ash, the other in Rosary Cemetery in Norwich.

Throwing plausible light on what happened to the bones in the jar and the coffin is the evidence of Edward Smith of Walthamstow, a biographer of Cobbett, who made what he called 'a pilgrimage' to Guildford in 1876-7 in an attempt to 'trace the bones'. By this time John Chennell was dead but Smith was able to gather some information from his son.[75] It was the Chennell family's belief that the bones in its possession were acquired when the coffin was purchased at the Cobbett auction of 1836. Confirming and elaborating on this belief are two pieces of evidence: one a contribution signed 'A Native of Guildford' and published in *Notes and Queries* for 1868; the other, an anonymous contribution to 'Surrey Notes and Queries', published in the *West Surrey Times* for 1889.[76] The former recounted a meeting with John Chennell in 1849. It suggested that he had acquired the bones at the auction of Cobbett's effects in January 1836 when he successfully bid for Paine's coffin and, to his surprise, found inside a few small bones contained in a pot. As the *West Surrey Times* revealed, the pot was a porcelain jar with a parchment cover inscribed upon which was 'the great Paine's bones'. This indicates that a small cache of bones had been separated from the rest of the skeleton by Cobbett himself, presumably prior to the sealing of the chest in 1833. In confirmation was a story told by James Wyatt, a geologist, who, when a boy, met Cobbett and asked him if he kept Paine's bones in his house at Normandy Farm. In response, Cobbett took him upstairs and revealed some bones placed 'in a chest or pot'.[77] However, by 1849, according to 'A Native of Guildford', this pot of bones had disappeared. Chennell took him into the cellar of his store in Guildford High Street and showed him an empty coffin. 'What became of the bones, I do not know' he admitted. But, in all likelihood he had sold them to the West family for a payment of seven shillings and sixpence.[78]

Having yielded up the main skeleton to Tilly, the Wests, it seems, proceeded to give the bones bought from Chennell a proper, but not a public, burial. For this purpose, they must have later acquired the coffin. That these bones were buried secretly at midnight in the graveyard of Ash parish church was revealed in two letters published by the *Observer* for 14 February 1937, one from Hannen Swaffer MP, the other from George Williamson, Remembrancer to the Corporation of Guildford. According to Swaffer, whose information was taken from an old carpenter via William Bennett MP, both with Guildford connections, the box buried with the bones in Ash churchyard was made of mahogany, suggesting the original coffin and that Chennell had passed it to the Wests. If so, the burial could not have occurred before 1849, for in that year the coffin was still in Chennell's cellar. Supporting the idea of a burial in Ash is an article by John Whitbourn entitled 'A revolutionary lays down his bones in Ash'. It appeared in the *Surrey Advertiser* for 22 September 1989. However, his claim for the burial of the whole skeleton is wrong since it is known for certain that, at this time, most of the bones resided with Tilly in London. Also throwing light on the Ash burial is an anonymous email, dated 15 November 2014, sent in response to an internet piece by Pam Keyes entitled 'Cobbett the body-snatcher, or what happened to Thomas Paine's corpse'. The email's author claimed that 'a direct ancestor worked for William Cobbett' and that he 'buried Paine's bones in the graveyard of the church he was sexton at', which was situated 'in a small village in the south of England'. In connection with the rest of the evidence, this suggests that the ancestor was West and that the 'small village' was Ash.

But what happened to the bones in the chest? For the next eight years (1836-1844), they resided with George West, a neighbouring farmer and receiver appointed to administer the insolvent Cobbett estate.[79] Although his receivership expired in 1839, he continued to hold the bones, following a decree by the Lord Chancellor ruling that they were neither part of the Cobbett estate nor the rightful property of anyone else.[80] However, in March 1844, according to Tilly, West was obliged by poverty to hand them over to Tilly, now that the loss of his farm had reduced him to earning a living as a day labourer. Tilly stated that West had brought the chest of bones to London where he 'gave them into [Tilly's] possession', and this account was accepted by Conway and Reynolds.[81] For the next twenty-five years (i.e. from 1844 to 1869), most of the remaining bones – tucked away in the chest, along with the burial plate, and reunited with the piece of brain and the lock of hair removed in 1833 – lay in the possession of Tilly, first at 13 Bedford [now Ford] Square, Stepney, and later at a succession of addresses in the London area.[82] In fact, they remained with him until his death in 1869. In 1821 Cobbett had predicted that, if he were to die before fulfilling his pledge to rebury Paine, men 'will be alive' ready to 'perform the sacred duty in my stead'.[83] Tilly was one such man. As his *Brief History* of 1847 put it: Tilly intended to retain possession of Paine's bones 'until a public funeral of them can be arranged'.[84] Like Cobbett, Tilly was neither a republican in the Paine sense nor an infidel. Whereas Paine had rejected the notion that the rights and liberties of the people could best be protected by restoring the country's ancient constitution, and had advocated instead the creation of a brand-new polity based on principles resulting from reason and nature rather than historical precedent, Tilly, on the contrary, thought the people could best be served by restoring to 'its pristine purity' a constitution founded by the Anglo-Saxons. This could be done, he argued, by removing the innovations imposed upon it over several centuries, and recently confirmed by the Bill of Rights of 1689 and the Reform Act of 1832. For this reason, Tilly, along with Cobbett, saw the constitution as best comprised of three estates, Crown, Lords and Commons.[85] Republicanism for him meant either a Paineite expunction of the hereditary element, something he deplored, or it signified something that met his full approval: a struggle against despotism aimed at regaining the constitutional balance in existence under Alfred the Great. The latter was to be achieved principally by reintroducing a system of parliamentary election based upon universal male suffrage.[86] Tilly's political thinking, then, would appear to owe more to Major John Cartwright than to Paine.[87] On the other hand, he followed Paine in his willingness to countenance physical violence as a means of achieving political reform.[88] He also shared with Paine a contempt for the Glorious Revolution of 1688, regarding it as yet another device whereby the aristocracy had usurped power at the expense of the people.[89] And, following Cobbett, he supported Paine's objections to paper money.[90]

Thus, Tilly's aim in taking care of the bones was to honour Paine as a political reformer but not to subscribe to Paine's own brand of republicanism, with its characteristic rejection of government by hereditary right. To fulfil Cobbett's pledge required money which Tilly, a poor tailor, lacked. By the mid-1840s a committee had been formed to raise a subscription for the construction of a monument to Paine, yet *A Brief History* suggested there were divisions among its membership preventing anything from being done. In imitation of the monument erected to the universal suffrage advocate, Major John Cartwright, the plan was to attach to the monument a long inscription. It was the content of this inscription which divided the committee, especially its inclusion of the claim that Paine's return to England was inspired by the British government's repatriation of Major André, executed by the Americans for spying against them during the War of Independence. Responsible for proposing such a causal connexion was the extremely fractious William Benbow, Cobbett's collaborator in bringing the bones home. To the fore in opposing it was Tilly.[91] Moreover, following Cobbett's death in 1835, the fundraising for Paine found itself in competition with a scheme to build a monument to Cobbett.[92] Nothing had been achieved by 1853 when another financial crisis led to a further dispersal of Paine's remains.

In that year Tilly fell badly into debt, his possessions seized to settle a matter of rent arrears. As a result, the bones went to auction a second time. Rescue came in the form of two keen Paineite republicans, James Watson, the radical publisher, along with Joseph Cowen, a radical journalist from Tyneside and, the son of a mine-owner, a man of considerable wealth. They had a plan for a public burial of Paine in Kensal Green Cemetery.[93] Having fallen under the spell of Paine in the early 1820s when employed as a warehouseman for a drysaltery business in Leeds, Watson came to London to work for Richard Carlile, receiving an eighteen-month prison sentence for his pains.[94] After acquiring a printing press from Julian Hibbert, a wealthy freethinker and republican, he had become, by the early 1830s, a prolific publisher of radical tracts, including the political works of Paine.[95] Although falling out with Carlile, he nonetheless remained a highly committed Paineite republican for the rest of his life. In the early 1830s he was active in the formation of the National Union of the Working Classes and Others, the only national party in British history to avow a Paineite system of government. This was made explicit in its second declaration of principles, produced in October 1831 and formulated by Watson acting in conjunction with William Lovett.[96] Its article four left no doubt as to its Paineite provenance, declaring 'that all hereditary distinctions of birth are unnatural and opposed to the natural rights of man' and therefore should be abolished. Watson went on to print several republican periodicals, notably Harding's *Republican* (1847-8), Linton's *English Republic* (1851-5) and Holyoake's *Reasoner* (1846-61), as well as to produce several editions of Paine's *Rights of Man* in the 1830s, 1840s and 1850s, plus editions of Paine's *Theological Works* in 1833, 1840 and 1851. He was also the first to publish in English an address made by Paine to the French nation in the form of a pamphlet entitled *On the Abolition of Royalty* (1843): a powerful piece first published in Brissot's *Le Patriote Français* of 17 October 1792 in justification of the French republic created the previous month.[97] Moreover, it was Watson who published Tilly's

A Brief History of the Remains of Thomas Paine in 1847 and W.J. Linton's *The Life of Paine* in 1851. At the time he worked from a shop in Queen's Head Passage next to St Paul's, a short distance from Tilly's premises in Gresham Street. Joseph Cowen, a much younger man of twenty-three and still resident in Tyneside, revealed his commitment to the republican cause in the 1850s by editing the *Northern Tribune* (1854-5) and by collaborating in 1855 with George Julian Harney to found the Republican Brotherhood of Newcastle-upon-Tyne and to publish the *Republican Record*.[98]

Intent on reburying Paine, some time in 1853 Watson and Cowen called upon Tilly, now living at 40A Gresham Street in the City. On a previous visit, Watson had found him actually seated on the chest of bones as he worked away at his tailoring. On this occasion he was not at home. Moreover, soon afterwards, when they paid him another visit, they were shocked to discover his business no longer trading from that address.[99] They also learned that Tilly's goods, including the chest of bones, had been seized and carted off to Richard's Auction Rooms in Rathbone Place, close to St Giles' Circus. Stepping in, Watson, with help from Cowen, was able to make a successful bid for the chest and its contents, only to find, upon opening it up, that the skull and right hand were missing.[100]

Removed from the chest at this auction and sold separately, Paine's skull and hand were purchased by the Reverend Robert Ainslie, a so-called 'independent minister' of Regent's Park London.[101] Ordained in 1823 for the Anglican Church, he had become a congregationalist minister three years later. Eventually he switched to Unitarianism, becoming in 1860 pastor of Christ Church, the Unitarian chapel in Brighton.[102] Before acquiring the skull, he had lectured publicly against infidelity, especially the type associated with Robert Owen who had, like Paine, sought to bring anti-Christianity to the people. In doing so, Ainslie was acting as a member of the London City Mission, an inter-denominational organisation for Protestants founded in 1835 to spread knowledge of the Gospel among the East End poor. It subscribed to doctrines based not upon 'man's wisdom' (i.e. Paine's recommended 'reason' or 'plain truth') but upon 'the Holy Spirit' as expressed in the Scriptures and through the example of Christ. Ainslie had an important role in the Mission, as secretary of its steering committee and as editor of the *London City Mission Magazine*.[103] He also played a leading part in the crusade the Mission waged against infidel socialism (i.e. Owenism) in January and February 1840.[104] A series of ten lectures were delivered in the space of a month, with Ainslie giving the opening lecture entitled 'Is there a God?' and the closing lecture entitled 'An examination of socialism'. In the audience were many Owenites including Edward Truelove.[105] Although Ainslie's tone was one of extreme politeness, he gave no quarter as he sought to flog the subject to death, the closing lecture lasting for three hours and ten minutes. Within the same year all ten lectures were published in a volume entitled *Lectures against Socialism* and presented as 'under the direction of the Committee of the London City Mission'. Such beliefs and activities, and the light they throw upon his passionate hostility to infidelity, raise the question of why he should want to acquire two vital pieces of Paine, the author of *The Age of Reason*, a work which Ainslie must have regarded as steeped in sin, reeking of evil and blasphemous in the extreme.

Evidently pleased with his purchase, Ainslie could not resist the urge to boast about it to the infidel republican publisher, Edward Truelove, when, shortly afterwards, he visited his bookshop in the Strand. However, a decade later reticence had set in. Around 1863 Truelove wrote to Ainslie asking why he thought the skull and hand to be genuine and why he had acquired them and were they still in his possession and, if so, would it be possible for a cast to be taken of them, but received no reply.[106] George Jacob Holyoake was given a similar brush off. In speaking to Ainslie about the matter, the latter told him he did not wish it to be made public.[107] Oddly enough, a few years later Ainslie appeared a second time in Truelove's shop, now situated in High Holborn. It must have been in or after 1867, the year in which Truelove moved to this new address. Ainslie gave no indication of having previously met Truelove, but the bookseller reminded him of the earlier encounter and what had been said. Truelove again asked after the bones but Ainslie's 'answer was evasive'.[108]

In view of his involvement with the London City Mission, Ainslie could not have acquired the skull and hand on account of being a Paineite. In the course of time, however, Ainslie's religious beliefs lost their rigour as he turned towards Unitarianism. The process of conversion occurred between 1856 and 1860. In the former year he was still caught up in the christocentric, evangelical world of the London City Mission, and was able to declare that 'the old philosophers of Greece and Rome are placed in the shade by the wisdom, power, glory and supremacy of Jesus Christ'; while in the latter year he had become minister of a Unitarian chapel in Brighton that resembled an Athenian temple.[109] His conversion meant that most of the extant remains of Paine eventually fell into the hands of men who, as Unitarians, could be sympathetic of Paine despite his infidelity: that is, Gordon, Conway and himself. This suggests that, in his case, the motive for retaining the bones differed from the motive for originally acquiring them.

Conway first met Ainslie in 1863, but, at that stage, had no knowledge of the bits of Paine in his possession. Later in 1876, when Truelove had put him in the picture, Conway thought that Ainslie's acquisition of the skull might have reflected an interest in phrenology, although he then ruled this out, perhaps unfairly, on the grounds that Ainslie had acquired the right hand as well.[110] This left the possibility, implied by Truelove, that Ainslie had acquired these vital parts in an act of vindictiveness for Paine's dismissal of the Scriptures as fiction and for his rejection of Christianity as a malevolent force designed to subdue and exploit the people.[111] If this were so, it made sense to confiscate the skull, the container of the organ that had conceived *The Age of Reason*, and to remove the right hand, the instrument responsible for its composition. As trophies of the war against blasphemy they could not be bettered. Yet, following his conversion to Utilitarianism, Ainslie's retention of the bones probably had a less malignant motive. As for the secrecy he sought to impose upon his possession of them, this may well have sprung from a fear that, if known, it could be used by fellow Christians, as Holyoake suggested and Conway confirmed, to cast doubt upon his orthodoxy as a Christian minister and to brand him a heretic.[112] In the manner of Cobbett, Ainslie's association with the bones may well have assumed the potentiality of a poisoned chalice and therefore something to be concealed from the public.

Paine's skull and hand remained with Ainslie from 1853 until his death in 1876. In all likelihood, they were kept in his London residence at 71 Mornington Street, next to Regent's Park, although, coincidentally, he rented a large country residence, Trowmer Lodge in Bromley, Kent, where they may, at times, have lain.[113] In 1876 they were at his Regent's Park address but then, following his death, were moved to the house of Oliver Ainslie, his barrister son, at 48 Lincoln's Inn Fields. Oliver immediately commissioned Professor John Marshall of the Royal College of Surgeons – its offices were conveniently next door – to examine and assess them. The outcome was a disparaging report in which Marshall declared the hand to be remarkably feminine and the skull to be unusually 'small for a man': suggesting either that they were not Paine's or, if they were, his physical appearance was distinctly unmanly and therefore intellectually inferior. To underline these findings, Marshall's report also described the skull as having 'more cerebellum than frontal development' and to be 'somewhat conical in shape' and 'of the Celtic type'.[114]

Shortly after that, both skull and hand disappeared, following a room clearance at Oliver Ainslie's home by a mysterious Mr Penny, probably a rag-and-bone merchant. This Conway discovered when, tipped off by Truelove, he sought in 1876 to contact Ainslie and, finding that he had just died, approached his children instead.[115] Perhaps because of its attribution to Paine, perhaps because of its unusual features, perhaps because skulls were in demand for use in physicians' surgeries, perhaps because of the popularity of phrenology, the skull may well, as Conway suggests, have been acquired by a doctor or ended up in a craniological museum.[116] Whereas the hand disappeared for good, the skull seemed to re-emerge in 1987 when one purporting to be Paine's was acquired by a Sydney businessman while on vacation in London. Returning to Australia he sold it to John Burgess, an Australian claiming Paine descent. In view of the engravings upon it and their resemblance to the marks made by Cobbett's son in October 1835, its authenticity appears to be proven, if not placed completely beyond doubt. A DNA test was on the cards but was it ever carried out?[117]

As for the remaining bones, Watson returned them to Tilly's custody, along with the chest and its other contents, shortly after acquiring them at the auction in Rathbone Place.[118] In the process, the bones were taken along High Holborn to St Paul's and probably stored in Watson's shop at 3 Queen's Head Passage, close to Paternoster Square, before their transfer to Tilly's new address at nearby 38 Gresham Street where they remained until 1860. Why should Watson have acted in this way, given his plan to provide a public burial? That he was perturbed by the removal of the skull is evident in Truelove's report to Conway which claimed Watson 'smiled incredulously' upon learning it was in Ainslie's possession.[119] Watson and Cowen's reason for calling off the funeral is unknown, but perhaps the matter was decided as it dawned upon them that, without the skull, the remains were, in a very obvious sense, far from complete.

Reunited with the chest and its contents, Tilly clung to them for the rest of his life as he moved from residence to residence. Until 1860 Tilly and the bones remained in Gresham Street where he continued to work as an independent tailor.[120] But in that year two events transformed his life: the death of Mary, his wife, and the business failure of Job Swain, Tilly's former employer, a merchant clothier and a fellow member of the Cobbett Club. For much of the

1850s Swain had flourished, thanks to acquiring a clothing shop in Oxford Street and his appointment in 1858 as tailor to the Queen. Yet in the following year he abandoned this prestigious business to become, in 1860, publican of the Waterloo Arms in Marylebone High Street, his daughter Emily serving as barmaid.[121] Accounting for this sudden change of occupation, and the fall from grace that it must have signified, was possibly his public exposure as a former radical and the consequent boycott of his shop by high society.[122] A likely outcome of Swain's departure from the clothing trade was the collapse of Tilly's tailoring business, now deprived of the work Swain was once able to put its way.[123] Significantly, no occupation was given for Tilly in the Census Return for 1861. Still in possession of the chest of bones, now an elderly widower of sixty-five, and with no children to offer him shelter or support, he went to lodge first with his niece at 35 Camomile Street in Spitalfields, then with his friends, Mr and Mrs Ball in Roxborough Road, Harrow-on-the-Hill, and finally in the house of Charles Ginns, a wood merchant, at 3 Chester Place, Bethnal Green.[124]

Much of what we know about Tilly for the late 1830s and early 1840s comes from the scrapbook he kept as secretary of the Cobbett Club. For the later years, it derives from Mrs Ball who in 1896 was interviewed at length by George Reynolds, the Baptist minister of Stepney and keen collector of Paine memorabilia.[125] The information she provided sheds light on Tilly's financial difficulties in the early 1850s; while her admission of having given Tilly free board and lodging implies that his poverty continued into the 1860s.[126] What she failed to explain is why and when and how Tilly left her free accommodation to rent rooms from Mr Ginns.[127] Shortly before dying from stomach cancer in August 1869, Tilly gave the chest and its contents to Mr and Mrs Ginns, an act of gratitude for looking after him in his final days and, in all probability, a thank-you for keeping him out of the workhouse, an institution he had railed against in a long composition initially entitled 'Grinding the Poor' and published as *Robbers Detected by One of the Cobbett Club* (London, 1842).[128] From the early 1850s, then, Tilly was reduced at times to great poverty, even more so after 1860 when, with the failure of his tailoring business, he became reliant not only upon the goodwill of the Balls but also upon the generosity of Mrs Henry Vincent, wife of the Chartist orator and daughter of the radical publisher John Cleave.[129] She, it seems, helped him to pay the rent he owed the Ginns. In spite of all this adversity, he largely succeeded as guardian of the bones but failed to honour them with a fitting funeral.

Appendix

Upon Tilly's death the bones he had so dutifully conserved disappeared for ever. Nine years later, in 1878, George Reynolds, minister of the Cave of Adullum, a small Baptist chapel in Stepney, came in search of them, having learned from Ginns' daughter, a member of his congregation, about a chest of Paineite relics in her parents' possession.[130] Going round to the house, he offered Mr Ginns £25 for the chest and its contents. Upon opening it in Ginns' presence, Reynolds uncovered certain manuscripts and a scrapbook (concerning the transactions of the Cobbett Club) compiled by Tilly, its secretary. In addition, he came across a piece of blackened brain, the size of a fist, and a lock of hair, both separately wrapped in waterproof paper along with a note of explanation signed by Tilly. But the bones had gone and so had the original burial plate.[131] Ginns said he was already aware that the skull and right hand were missing, but expressed surprise at the absence of the rest of the skeleton. He assured Reynolds that his wife, presently out, would know of its whereabouts. Upon returning, she admitted that, some time ago, and not long after Tilly's death, she had discovered, when clearing out his room to make way for another tenant, lots of bones in a large bag. She claimed to have given them to a rag-and-bone man.[132] Reynolds, supported by Conway, sensed she was lying. They suspected she had sold the bones to the Rev. Alexander Gordon, a Unitarian minister, who, in corresponding with Conway, claimed to have 'seen' the bones in 1873 and to have 'heard' about them in 1876.[133] From this correspondence, one Unitarian to another, Conway gathered that Gordon had 'secured' for the bones a 'quiet burial'.[134] The question is where. Conway believed that it was in the town of Thetford, close to the grave of Paine's parents.[135] But another distinct possibility was Norwich where from 1872 to 1877 Gordon served as minister of the Octagon Chapel in Colegate, his authority extending to the Rosary Cemetery, a non-denominational burial ground near Thorpe Station.[136] In all likelihood, it was here, in this leafy, uphill cemetery, that Paine, or what remained of him, was quietly and secretly laid to rest.

When exploring Rosary Cemetery in the autumn of 2017, the sunlit air bright but cold, the grass twinkling with dew, the falling leaves either clattering quietly on lichened tombs or silently fleeing along the path, I encountered Mark Shopland. As he hurried past, my companion impulsively called after him, asking if he knew anything about the burial of Thomas Paine. He had to admit that he did not, but his interest was nonetheless aroused. He turned out to be a 'Friend of the Rosary Cemetery' and said he would look into the matter. In this way, I suddenly found that, although the teller, I had tumbled into the story as a participant, and that my meeting with Mark recalled those meetings recurrent in the nineteenth century between individuals questing for the bones and people who may well have had some association with them, only to find their initial excitement dashed by disappointment as the outcome proved to be elusive and inconclusive.[137] I had no expectation of finding a grave with a monumental inscription bearing Paine's name. But Mark made the point that not all buried in the cemetery were identified by name, either on the grave itself or in the burial records. A possibility raised by him was that Paine might have been quietly and anonymously slipped into one of the named plots, especially one belonging to a family with a radical past. One would have expected this to have been done on the authority of Gordon and in connection with a burial that he administered. The burial records indicate that in the period of Gordon's ministry, 1872-77, only a small proportion of the burials were carried out by him: no more than 21. Another possibility, raised by me, was that Paine had been interred without headstone in a part of the churchyard reserved for suicides or blasphemers. Normally, this would be north of the church. Resourcefully, my companion produced, from her ancient but fine leather handbag, a compass whose quivering needle indicated, alongside the chapel and to the north, a significant green space totally empty of marked graves. Could Paine be buried there? If so, his skeletal remains might still be recognised by the presence of the original coffin plate which is known to have lain with the bones until Tilly's death in 1869 but disappeared in the 1870s, perhaps because Gordon took possession not only of the bones but also of the evidence that indicated them to be Paine's. Having taken that step, it would surely have made sense to bury the two together.[138]

With the skeleton gone, all that knowingly survived of Paine was the lock of dark, reddish hair acquired by Oldfield in 1836 and passed on, in an envelope, to Smith and then to Conway. There was also the portion of brain, with a second lock of hair, taken by Tilly in 1833 and conserved by him until his death in 1869. By 1878, the latter two relics had passed, along with the original chest, to Reynolds.[139] But then Reynolds suffered the fate of previous custodians: a financial crisis. He fell heavily into debt, the result of becoming, as he put it, 'involved in ruinous litigation'. This arose from a pamphlet he published in 1877 entitled 'Dr Barnardo's Homes: Containing Startling Revelations'. It followed a war waged between the two over several years, as Barnardo threatened the ministry of Reynolds by establishing not only his East End Juvenile Mission in Stepney but also the spectacular British Working Men's Coffee Palace in the Edinburgh Castle at Limehouse, formerly a notorious gin palace and now a respectable temperance hall. On Sundays it doubled as the Mission Church

Appendix

of Working Men, the unqualified Barnardo assuming the office of pastor and administering a Baptist-type service to large and eager congregations. Unable to compete, the Baptist minister George Reynolds, with a small chapel and a minute congregation nearby, was not surprisingly aggrieved. Reynold's pamphlet alleged that Barnardo had consorted with a prostitute; had syphoned off funds, given as charitable donations, for his own personal use; was unqualified to use the title of 'Dr'; had made money out of the sale of suggestive and staged photographs of destitute, thinly clad children; and had allowed the black-holing and flogging of juveniles in his care. With the consent of both parties, the matter went to arbitration in the Court of Exchequer which in 1878 found, with reservations, in favour of Barnardo.

The litigation put both parties to enormous expense, obliging Reynolds to sell off, probably in 1878, what he had newly acquired from the Ginns.[140] As a result, O'Connell's letter and the 'Wright versus Cobbett' papers went to the British Library, raising 11 guineas, while James Paul Cobbett bought 'the Life of Cobbett' and 'The Westminster Rebellion' for £25. The rest, including the chest, a lock of Paine's hair, a piece of his brain, the Cobbett Club scrapbook, 'The Poor man's Bible' and 'The Monster Register' passed, for an undisclosed sum, to Louis Breeze of Stratford-by-Bow, a medical herbalist and proprietor of a public bathhouse. He displayed the brain and hair for a time in his shop window under a glass cover.[141] He also loaned them to Moncure Conway for display in the Thomas Paine Exhibition that Conway held at the South Place Institute Finsbury on 2 and 3 December 1895. The 485 items on show were presented by forty-five exhibitors but half came from Conway's own collection. They included only three bits of Paine: that is, two locks of hair and a part of his brain.[142] Also exhibited was Paine's death mask, coupled appropriately with the death mask of Burke, many books, manuscripts and illustrations, and several objects intimately associated with Paine such as his snuff box, his writing table and a 'small piece of timber from the birth-house of Paine, Thetford'.[143] Cobbett's project to make Paine physically manifest to the people, then, was finally realised but not in the spectacular manner he had originally planned.

A circular conclusion to the tale saw the return of what remained of Paine to his original place of burial in New Rochelle, New York State. With the death of Breeze in 1897, Reynolds regained possession of Paine's brain and the 'Tilly' lock of hair, now placed, thanks to Breeze, under a glass cover pasted to which was Tilly's note of admission that he had taken them in 1833.[144] Both, moreover, were still in the original chest, the very one used by Cobbett to bring Paine to

England in 1819, along with the manuscripts of 'The Poor Man's Bible' and 'The Monster Register' and the scrapbook kept by Tilly to record the transactions of the Cobbett Club. After failing to sell these items to a grandson of Cobbett, Reynolds found a buyer in Charles Higham, a Farringdon Street bookseller, who placed them in his sales catalogue for 1900.[145] Troubled by the prospect of the great man's brain being 'hawked about', or so he said, Conway bought it and the lock of hair for £5. By 1902, he had dispatched both objects to the USA.[146] He did likewise with the other lock of hair, the one bought by Oldfield in 1836 and passed on to Conway by Smith.[147] In 1902, to commemorate the return of the living Paine to the USA a century earlier, this particular lock was respectfully placed in the New Rochelle Thomas Paine Museum, while in 1905 the portion of brain and the lock of hair, originally taken by Tilly in 1833, were securely set in cement under the bronze bust of Paine which stood, and still stands, on a marble pillar outside the cottage (also in New Rochelle) where Paine had lived from 1803 to 1806.[148] As for what became of the chest, 'The Poor Man's Bible' and 'The Monster Register', nothing is known. However, the Cobbett Club scrapbook, which had lain alongside Paine's skeleton for so many years, surfaced in 2013, when it came up for sale in Galway, Ireland. Purchased by the historian M.L. Bush, it inspired him to pen this piece.

The Polity of the Blood

Select Bibliography

Guides to Sources

Copac [Jisc Library Hub Discover]: online listing of Paine's works in UK and Irish Republic Libraries.
The Thomas Paine Collection at Thetford (Norwich, 1979).
Richard Gimbel, *Thomas Paine: a Bibliographical Check List of Common Sense, with an Account of its Publication* (New Haven, 1956).
The Thomas Paine Collection of Richard Gimbel, compiled by Hildegard Stephans (Delaware, 1976).
The Warwick Guide to British Labour Periodicals, 1790-1970, compiled by Royden Harrison, etc. (Hassocks, 1977).

Primary Materials Consulted: Newspapers and Periodicals

Agitator (Benbow, 1833).
Berthold's Political Handkerchief (1831).
Black Dwarf (Wooler, 1817-24).
Bonnet Rouge (Lorymer, 1833).
Cobbett's Political Register (1804-20).
Cosmopolite (Pilgrim, 1832-3).
Democratic Review (Harney, 1849-50).
Destructive (O'Brien, 1833-4).
Drakard's Stamford News (1822-3).
English Republic (Linton, 1851-5).
Friend of the People (Harney, 1850-2).
Gauntlet (Carlile, 1833-4).
Hone's Reformists' Register (1817).
Labourer (O'Connor and Jones, 1847-8).
Lion (Carlile, 1828-9).
London Dispatch (O'Brien, Hetherington, 1836-9).
Midland Representative and Birmingham Herald (O'Brien, 1831-2).
Movement (Holyoake, 1843-5).

National Reformer (Bradlaugh, 1860-93).
Northern Tribune (Cowen, Harney, 1854-5).
Northern Star (O'Connor, 1837-44).
Notes to the People (Jones, 1851-2).
Operative (O'Brien, 1838-9).
Philanthropist (Eaton, 1795-6).
Political Examiner (Watson, Holyoake, 1853-4).
Politics for the People [i.e. Hog's Wash] (Eaton, 1793-5).
Poor Man's Guardian (Hetherington, O'Brien, 1831-5).
Prompter (Carlile, 1830-1).
Reasoner (Holyoake, 1846-61).
Red Republican (Harney, 1850-2).
Republican (Sherwin, 1817).
Republican (Carlile, 1819-26).
Republican or Voice of the People (Hetherington, 1831-2).
Republican and Radical Reformer (Hetherington, 1832).
Republican (Lorymer, 1834).
Republican (Harding, 1847-8).
Republican (Land and Labour League, 1870-2).
Republican Chronicle (Strandring, 1875-8).
Republican Record (Cowen and Harney, 1855).
Sherwin's Weekly Political Register (1817-9).
Tribune (Thelwall, 1795-6).
Working Man's Friend (Cleave, 1832-3).

Primary Materials Consulted: Texts

Barclay, Robert, *An Apology for the True Christian Divinity* (London 1736).
Barlow, Joel, *Advice to the Privileged Orders in the Several States of Europe* (London, 1792).
Baxter, John, *A New and Impartial History of England* (London, 1796).
Benbow, William, *Grand National Holiday and Congress of the Productive Classes* (London, 1832).
Bentham, Jeremy, *A Fragment on Government* (London, 1823).
– *Plan of Parliamentary Reform, in the Form of a Catechism*, ed T.J. Wooler (London, 1818).
Bolingbroke, Henry, *Letters on the Spirit of Patriotism, on the Idea of a Patriot King, and on the State of the Parties at the Accession of King George the First* (London, 1749).

Select Bibliography

Boulanger, Nicolas Antoine, *The Origin and Progress of Despotism in the Orient and other Empires of Africa, Europe and America* (Amsterdam, 1764).
Buchanan, George, *A Dialogue on the Law of Kingship among the Scots* (London, 1680).
Burgh, James, *Political Disquisitions* (London, 1774), 3 vols.
Burke, Aedanus, *Considerations on the Society or Order of Cincinnati lately Instituted* (Hertford, 1783).
Burke, Edmund, *Reflections on the French Revolution* (London, 1790).
– *Vindication of Natural Society* (3rd edition, Dublin, 1766).

Carlile, Richard, *An Effort to Set at Rest Some Little Disputes and Misunderstandings between the Reformers at Leeds* (London, 1821).
Cartwright, John, *Take Your Choice* (London, 1776).
– *An Appeal Civil and Military on the Subject of the English Constitution* (London, 1797).
– *The English Constitution Produced and Illustrated* (London, 1823).
Cooper, Thomas, *A Reply to Mr Burke's Invective against Mr Cooper and Mr Watt in the House of Commons* (Manchester, 1792).
Crome, J., *An Illustration of the Rights of Man* (Sheffield, 1792).

Defoe, Daniel, *The True-Born Englishman* (London, 1701).
– *Jure Divino* (London, 1706).
Dragonetti, Giacinto, *Treatise on Virtues and Rewards* (London, 1769).

Elwall, Edward, *A Declaration against all the Kings and Temporal Powers under Heaven* (London, 1732).

Franklin, Benjamin, 'Causes of the American discontent before 1768' in *London Chronicle for 1768*, reprinted 1774.
– 'An edict by the king of Prussia' and 'Rules by which a great empire may be reduced to a smaller', in *Philadelphian Public Advertiser* for 1773.
Free-born Englishman, *Paine's Political and Moral Maxims, Selected from the Fifth Edition of Rights of Man*, Parts I and II (London, 1792).

Gerrald, Joseph, *A Convention, the Only Means of Saving Us from Ruin* (London, 1794).
Godwin, William, *Enquiry Concerning Political Justice* (London, 1793).

Gordon/Trenchard, 'Inquiry into the Doctrine of Hereditary Right' in *Cato's Letters,* no 132 (London, 1723).

Hall, Charles, *Effects of Civilization* (London, 1805).
Hall, John, *The Grounds and Reasons of Monarchy Considered* (Edinburgh, 1650).
Harrington's Oceana and other Works, ed. John Toland (London, 1737).
Hodgskin, Thomas, *Labour Defended Against the Claims of Capital* (London, 1825).
– *The Rights of Natural and Artificial Property Contrasted* (London, 1832).
Holbach, Baron d', *Système de la Nature* (Londres, 1770).
– *La Politique Naturelle* (Londres, 1770).
– *Système Sociale* (Londres, 1773).
– *Essai sur les Préjugés* (Londres, 1773).
Hunt, Henry, *Letters to Radical Reformers* (London, 1821-2).

Lilburne, John, *Regal Tyranny Discovered* (London, 1647).
Linton, W.J., *James Watson, a Memoir* (London, 1880).
– *European Republicans: Recollections of Mazzini and his Friends* (London, 1892).
Locke, John, *Two Treatises of Government* (London, 1689).
Lorymer, James, *A National Convention: the Only Proper Remedy* (Hetherington, 1831).
Lovett, William, *Life and Struggles* (Tawney, London, 1920).

Macaulay, Catherine, *Observations on the Reflections of the Right Hon. Edmund Burke on the Revolution in France* (London, 1791).
Macerone, Francis, *Defensive Instructions for the People* (John Smith, alias Richard Carlile, 1832).
– *Defensive Instructions for the People* (Richard Carlile Junior, 1834).
Mackintosh, James, *Vindiciae Gallicae* (London, 1791).
Milton, John, *Tenure of Kings and Magistrates* (London, 1649).
– *Defence of the People of England* (London, 1692).
Mirabeau, Comte de, *Considerations on the Order of Cincinnatus* (London, 1785).

O'Brien, Bronterre, *Buonarroti's History of Babeuf's Conspiracy of Equality* (London, 1836).
– *A Brief Enquiry into the Natural Rights of Man* (Watson, 1852).
– *The Rise, Progress and Phases of Human Slavery* (Reeves, 1885).

Paine, Thomas, *Address to the French People on the Abolition of Royalty* (Watson, 1843).
Paine, Thomas, *The Age of Reason* (1794-6, Conway ed. 1896).
- *Agrarian Justice* (Paris, 1797).
- *The American Crisis* (1776-83, Carlile, 1819).
- *Common Sense* (1776, Kramnick ed., Penguin Classics, 1986).
- *Common Sense* (J.S. Jordan, 1791).
- *Dissertations on Government, the Affairs of the Bank and Paper Money* (1787, Carlile, 1819).
- *Dissertation on First Principles of Government* (1795, Carlile, 1819).
- *Letter Addressed to the Addressers on the Late Proclamation* (1792, Carlile, 1819).
- *Letter Addressed to the Abbé Raynal on the Affairs of North America* (1782).
- *Letter Addressed to George Washington on the Subject of the late Treaty* (Symonds, 1796).
- *Reply to the Bishop of Llandaff's Apology for the Bible* (Carlile, 1818).
- *Rights of Man* (London, J.S. Jordan, 1791-2, Collins ed. Pelican Classics, 1969).
- *Rights of Man,* Parts I and II (London, Jordan's cheap edition,1792).
- *Rights of Man,* Parts I and II (Dublin, Byrne's cheap edition, 1791-2).
- *Rights of Man,* Parts I and II (London, Printed for the Booksellers, 1792: the cheap, expurgated ed. published by Paine himself).
- *Rights of Man*, Parts I and II (London, Symond's cheap, expurgated edition, 1792).
- *Rights of Man,* Parts I and II (London, Parson's cheap, expurgated edition, 1792).
- *Rights of Man for the Use and Benefit of All Mankind* (Eaton, 1795).
- *Thoughts on the Peace* (Jordan, 1791).
Price, Richard, *Discourse on the Love of Our Country* (London, 1790).
- *Observations on Civil Liberty* (London, 1776), plus *Additional Observations* (London, 1777).
- *Observations on the Importance of the American Revolution* (London, 1785).
Priestley, Joseph, *An Essay on the First Principles of Government* (London, 1768, Dodo Press Reprint).
- *Letters to the Right honourable Edmund Burke Occasioned by the Reflections on the Revolution in France* (Dublin, 1791).
- *Disquisitions Relating to Matter and Spirit* (London, 1777).

Raynal, Abbé, *Philosophical and Political History of European Settlement and Trade in the East and West Indies* (Dublin, 1784), six vols.
– *The Revolution of America* (London, 1781).
Rousseau, Jean-Jacques, *A Project for a Perpetual Peace* (London, 1761).
– *Social Compact* (London, 1764).

Sidney, *Algernon, Discourse Concerning Government* (London, 1698).
Spinoza, Baruch de, *Theological-Political Treatise* (1670, Cambridge, 2007).
Swift, Jonathan, *Gulliver's Travels* (1726, Penguin Classics, 2003).

Wollstonecraft, Mary, *A Vindication of the Rights of Men: a Letter to the Rt Hon. Edmund Burke* (London, 1790).

Editions of Paine's Works

The Works of Thomas Paine Esq (D. Jordan, 1792).
The Works of Thomas Paine (London, 1796).
The Political Works of Thomas Paine (Sherwin, 1817).
The Political and Miscellaneous Works of Thomas Paine (Carlile, 1819).
Thomas Paine, The Working Man's Political Companion (Watson, 1834).
The Political Works of Thomas Paine (Dugdale, 1844).
The Political Works of Thomas Paine with a Copy of the People's Charter (Wheeler, 1846).
The Political Works of Thomas Paine (Watson, 1851).
The Complete Works of Thomas Paine Political and Controversial (Truelove, 1775).
The Complete Writings of Thomas Paine, ed. Philip S. Foner (New York, 1969).

Source Miscellany

Carlile Papers, Huntingdon Library, California, on Microfilm.
Carlile, Richard, *Life of Thomas Paine* (London, 1820).
Catalogue of Thomas Paine Exhibition at the South Place Institute (British Library, 1895).
Cobbett Club Scrapbook (compiled by Benjamin Tilly, 1838-47).
Conway, Moncure, *The Adventures of Thomas Paine's Bones* (Thomas Paine National Historical Association, 2002).

Eaton, *Proceedings on the Trial of Daniel Isaac Eaton for Selling the Second Part of Rights of Man* (Eaton, 1793).

Hunt, *The Trial of Henry Hunt, Esq. for an Alleged Conspiracy to Overturn the Government* (T. Dolby, 1820).

London Radicalism, 1830-1849, ed. D.J. Rowe (London Record Society, 1970).

Paine, *Whole Proceedings on the Trial of an Information on Thomas Paine* (Martha Gurney, 1793).
Place Papers in British Library, Society for Constitutional Information Minutes Book, 1792.

Report from Select Committee on Cold Bath Fields Meeting (House of Commons, 1833).
Reynolds, George, *Thomas Paine's Bones and their Owners by an Old Daylighter* (Norwich, 1908).
Rickman, Thomas, *Life of Thomas Paine* (London, 1819).
Rosary Cemetery Burial Records, Norwich.

Sherwin, W.T., *Memoirs of the Life of Thomas Paine* (London, 1819).
Somerville, Alexander, *The Whistler at the Plough and Free Trade* (Manchester, 1852-3), three vols.

Tilly, Benjamin, *A Brief History of Thomas Paine's Bones* (Watson, 1847).
Truelove, Edward, correspondence: item 684 of the Paine Collection, Thetford Public Library.

Walker, Thomas, *The Original* (London, 1874), two vols.

Walker, Thomas, *A Review of Some of the Political Events which have Occurred in Manchester during the Last Five Years* (London, 1794).

Secondary Authorities Consulted

Aldridge, A. Owen, *Thomas Paine's American Ideology* (Associated University Presses, 1984).
Ayer, A.J., *Thomas Paine* (Faber and Faber, 1988).
Assis, Mariane and Jason Xidias, *An Analysis of Thomas Paine's Rights of Man* (Routledge, 2017).

Bailyn, Bernard, *The Ideological Origins of the American Revolution* (Harvard University Press, 1967).
Barrell, John, *Imagining the King's Death* (Oxford University Press, 2000).
Beames, Michael, *Peasants and Power: The Whiteboy Movements in Prefamine Ireland* (Harvester Press, 1983).
Belchem, John, *Orator Hunt* (Oxford University Press, 1985).
– *Popular Radicalism in Nineteenth-century Britain* (Palgrave Macmillan, 1996).
– 'Republicanism, popular constitutionalism and the radical platform in early nineteenth-century England', *Social History*, 6 (1981).
Bennett, Jennifer, 'The London Democratic Association' in *The Chartist Experience*, ed. James Epstein and Dorothy Thompson (Macmillan Press, 1982).
Berton, Gary, 'The distortion of Thomas Paine's philosophy of government' in *The Legacy of Thomas Paine in the Transatlantic World*, ed. Sam Edwards and Marcus Morris (Routledge, 2018).
Bevir, Mark, *The Making of British Socialism* (Princeton University Press, 2011).
– 'Republicanism, socialism and democracy: the origins of the radical left' in *Republicanism in Victorian Society*, ed. David Nash and Antony Taylor (Sutton Publishing, 2000).
Blakemore, Steven, *Crisis in Representation: Thomas Paine, Mary Wollstonecraft, Helen Marie Williams, and the Rewriting of the French Revolution* (Ass. University Presses, 1997).
Blewett, Neil, 'The franchise in the United Kingdom, 1885-1918', *Past and Present*, XXXII (1965).

Bolla, Peter de, *The Architecture of Concepts: the Historical Formation of Human Rights* (Fordham University Press, 2013).
Bressler, Leo A., 'Peter Porcupine and the bones of Thomas Paine', *Pennsylvania Magazine of History and Biography*, 82 (1958).
Bush, M.L., *The Casualties of Peterloo* (Carnegie Publishing, 2005).
– *The English Aristocracy* (Manchester University Press, 1984).
– *What is Love? Richard Carlile's Philosophy of Sex* (Verso, 1998).
– *The European Nobility*: vol. I *Noble Privilege*; vol. II *Rich Noble, Poor Noble* (Manchester University Press, 1983 and 1988).
– Michael, 'A Message from Mab: the Manchester working class and its attachment to Percy Bysshe Shelley', *North West Labour History Journal*, 29 (2004).
– Michael Laccohee, *The Friends and Following of Richard Carlile: a Study of Infidel Republicanism in Early Nineteenth-century Britain* (Twopenny Press, 2016).

Champion, Justin, *The Pillars of Priestcraft Shaken: the Church of England and its Enemies, 1660-1730* (Cambridge University Press, 1992).
Chase, Malcolm, *Chartism: a New History (Manchester University Press*, 2007).
– *The People's Farm: English Radical Agrarianism, 1775-1840* (Oxford University Press, 1988).
– *1820, Disorder and Stability in the United Kingdom* (Manchester University Press, 2015).
– 'Republicanism: movement or moment' in *Republicanism in Victorian Society*, ed. David Nash and Antony Taylor (Sutton Publishing, 2000).
Chen, David W., 'Rehabilitating Thomas Paine bit by bony bit', *New York Times* 30 March 2001.
Claeys, Gregory, *Citizens and Saints: Politics and Anti-Politics in early British Socialism* (Cambridge University Press, 1989).
– *The French Revolution Debate in Britain* (Palgrave Macmillan, 2007).
– *Thomas Paine: Social and Political Thought* (Unwin Hyman, 1989).
Clark, J.C.D., *Thomas Paine: Britain, America and France in the Age of Enlightenment and Revolution* (Oxford University Press, 2018).
Colley, Linda, *The Gun, the Ship and the Pen* (Profile Books, 2021).
Collins, Paul, *The Trouble with Tom: the Strange Afterlife and Times of Thomas Paine* (Bloomsbury, 2006).
Conway, Moncure, *The Life of Thomas Paine* (Putnam's, 1892), 2 vols.

Cotlar, Seth, 'Thomas Paine in the Atlantic historical imagination' in *Paine and Jefferson in the Age of Revolutions*, ed. Simon P. Newman and Peter S. Onaf (University of Virginia Press, 2013).
– *Tom Paine's America: the Rise and Fall of Transatlantic Radicalism in the Early Republic* (University of Virginia Press, 2011).

Davidson, Edward H. and William J. Scheick, *Paine, Scripture and Authority* (Associated University Presses, 1994).
Dickinson, H.T., *Liberty and Property: Political Ideology in Eighteenth-Century Britain* (Methuen, 1977).
– *British Radicalism and the French Revolution, 1789-1815* (Basil Blackwell, 1985).
Doyle, William, *Aristocracy and its Enemies in the Age of Revolution* (Oxford University Press, 2009).
– 'Thomas Paine and the Girondins' in his *Officers, Nobles and Revolutionaries* (Hambleton Press, 1995), ch. 12.
Dunn, John, *Setting the People Free: the Story of Democracy* (Atlantic Books, 2005).
Dyck, Ian, 'Debts and liabilities: William Cobbett and Thomas Paine' in Dyck (ed.), *Citizen of the World* (Christopher Helm, 1987).
– 'Local attachments, national identities and world citizenship in the thought of Thomas Paine', *History Workshop*, 35 (1993).

Elliott, Marianne, *Wolfe Tone* (Yale University Press, 1990).
Epstein, James, *The Lion of Freedom: Feargus O'Connor and the Chartist Movement, 1832-42* (Croom Helm, 1982; reprinted Breviary Stuff Publications, 2015).
– *Radical Expression* (Oxford University Press, 1994).

Fennessy, R.R., *Burke, Paine and the Rights of Man* (Martinus Nijhoff, The Hague, 1963).
Finn, Margot C., *After Chartism: Class and Nation in English Radical Politics, 1848-74* (Cambridge University Press, 1993).
Foner, Eric, *Tom Paine and Revolutionary America* (Oxford University Press, 1976).
Fruchtman, Jack, *Thomas Paine, Apostle of Freedom* (Four Walls, Eight Windows, New York, 1994).
– *Thomas Paine and the Religion of Nature* (The Johns Hopkins University Press, 1993).

- 'Thomas Paine's early radicalism, 1768-1783' in *Paine and Jefferson in the Age of Revolution*, ed. Simon P. Newman and Peter S. Onuf (University of Virginia Press, 1013).
- *The Political Philosophy of Thomas Paine* (Johns Hopkins University Press, 2008).

Gardner, John, 'Cobbett's return to England in 1819' in *William Cobbett, Romanticism and the Enlightenment*, ed. James Grande and John Stevenson (Routledge, 2015).

Gilmartin, Kevin, *Print Politics* (Cambridge University Press, 1996).

Goodrich, Amanda, *Debating England's Aristocracy in the 1790s: Pamphlets, Polemics and Political Ideas* (The Boydell Press, 2005).

Goodway, David, *London Chartism, 1838-48* (Cambridge University Press, 1982).

Goodwin, Albert, *The Friends of Liberty: the English Democratic Movement in the Age of the French Revolution* (Hutchinson, 1979).

Graham, Jenny, *The Nation, the Law and the King: Reform Politics in England, 1789-99* (University Press of America, 2000), two vols.

Grande, James, *William Cobbett, the Press and Rural England* (Palgrave Macmillan, 2014).

Hammersley, Rachel, *French Revolutionaries and English Republicans: the Cordeliers Club, 1790-1794* (Boydell Press, 2005).

Hampshire, Stuart, *Spinoza* (Penguin Books, 1951).

Haseler, Stephen, *The End of the House of Windsor* (I.B. Tauris and Co., 1993).

Hay, Daisy, *Dinner with Joseph Johnson* (Chatto and Windus, 2022).

Higonnet, Patrice, *Class, Ideology, and the Rights of Nobles during the French Revolution* (Oxford University Press, 1981).

Hill, Christopher, *The World Turned Upside Down* (Temple Smith, 1972).

Hodson, Jane, *Language and Revolution in Burke, Wollstonecraft, Paine and Godwin* (Routledge, 2007).

Houston, Alan, *Algernon Sidney and his Republican Heritage in England and America* (Princeton University Press, 1991).

Israel, Jonathan, *Democratic Enlightenment: Philosophy, Revolution and Human Rights, 1750-90* (Oxford University Press, 1012).
- *The Expanding Blaze: How the American Revolution Ignited the World, 1775-1848* (Princeton University Press, 2017).

- *Radical Enlightenment: Philosophy and the Making of Modernity 1650-1750* (Oxford University Press, 2001).
- *A Revolution of the Mind: Radical Enlightenment and the Intellectual Origins of Modern Democracy* (Princeton University Press, 2010).

Jacob, Margaret C., *The Radical Enlightenment: Pantheists, Freemasons and Republicans* (George Allen and Unwin, 1981).
Jones, Heather, *For King and Country: the British Monarchy and the First World War* (Cambridge University Press, 2021).

Kates, Gary, 'From liberalism to radicalism: Tom Paine's *Rights of Man*', in Frank Shuffelton (ed.), *The American Enlightenment* (University of Rochester Press, 1993), ch. 21.
Keane, John, *Tom Paine, a Political Life* (Bloomsbury, 1995).
Kee, Robert, *The Bold Fenian Men* (Quartet Books, 1976).

Lamb, Robert, *Thomas Paine and the Idea of Human Rights* (Cambridge University Press, 2015).
Larkin, Edward, *Thomas Paine and the Literature of Revolution* (Cambridge University Press, 2005).
Lewis, Donald M., *Lighten their Darkness: the Evangelical Mission to Working Class London, 1823-1860* (Greenwood Publishing Group, 1986).
LoPatin, Nancy, *Political Unions: the Popular Politics of the Great Reform Act of 1832* (Palgrave Macmillan, 1999).
Lottas, Gunther, 'Radicals, revolution and political culture: an Anglo-French comparison' in Mark Philp (ed.), *The French Revolution and British Popular Politics* (Cambridge University Press, 1991).
Loughran, Trish, *The Republic in Print* (Columbia University Press, 2007).
Lounissi, Carine, *Thomas Paine and the French Revolution* (Palgrave Macmillan, 2018).
- 'Thomas Paine's democratic linguistic radicalism' in *Radical Voices, Radical Ways*, ed L. Curelly and N. Smith (Manchester University Press, 2016).

Mack Smith, Denis, *Mazzini* (Yale University Press, 1996).
Maier, Pauline, *American Scripture* (Pimlico, 1999).
- *From Resistance to Revolution* (Norton, 1991).
Mayer, Arno, *The Persistence of the Old Regime* (Pantheon Books, 1981).
McCalman, Iain, *Radical Underworld* (Oxford University Press reprint, 1998).

Mee, Jon, *Print, Publicity and Radicalism in the 1790s* (Cambridge, University Press, 2016).
Moore, Tony, 'Citizens of the world: Paine and the political prisoners transported to Australia' in *The Legacy of Thomas Paine in the Transatlantic World*, ed. Sam Edwards and Marcus Morris (Routledge, 2018).
Morris, Marcus, 'The neglect of Paine seems particularly strange at the present political juncture': explaining British socialists' relationship to Paine, c. 1884-1914', in ibid.

Navickas, Katrina, *Loyalism and Radicalism in Lancashire, 1798-1815* (Oxford University Press, 2009).
– *Protest and the Politics of Space and Place, 1789-1848* (Manchester University Press, 2017).
Nelson, Craig, *Thomas Paine: Enlightenment, Revolution, and the Birth of Modern Nations* (Penguin, 2006).

O'Gorman, Frank, 'The Paine burnings of 1792-3', *Past and Present*, 193 (2006).

Parssinen, T.M., 'Associations, conventions and anti-parliaments in British radical politics', *English Historical Review*, 88 (1973).
Pearl, Morris L., *William Cobbett: a Bibliographical Account of his Life and Times* (Oxford University Press, 1953).
Pentland, Gordon, *Radicalism, Reform and National Identity in Scotland, 1820-1833* (Boydell Press, 2008).
Philp, Mark (ed.), *The French Revolution and British Popular Politics* (Cambridge University Press, 1991).
– *Godwin's Political Justice* (Cornell University Press, 1986).
– *Paine* (Oxford, 1989).
– *Reforming Ideas in Britain: Politics and Language in the Shadow of the French Revolution, 1789-1815* (Cambridge University Press, 2014).
Pickering, Paul, 'A grand ossification: William Cobbett and the commemoration of Tom Paine', in *Contested Sites*, ed. Pickering and Alex Tyrrell (Ashgate, 2004).
– 'The heart of millions: Chartism and popular monarchy in the 1840s', *History*, 88 (2003).
Pocock, J.G.A., *The Ancient Constitution and the Feudal Law* (Cambridge University Press, 1957).
– *The Machiavellian Moment* (Princeton University Press, 1975).

Poole, Steve, *The Politics of Regicide in England, 1760-1850* (Manchester University Press, 2000).
Prothero, I.J., *Artisans and Politics in Early Nineteenth-Century London* (Methuen, 1979).
– 'William Benbow and the concept of the general strike', *Past and Present*, 63 (1974).
Prochaska, Frank, *The Republic of Britain, 1700-2000* (The Penguin Press, 2000).

Ramon, Marta, *A Provisional Dictator: James Stephens and the Fenian Movement* (University College Dublin Press, 2007).
Rexford Davis, C., 'Cobbett's Letters in the Library', *Journal of the Rutgers University Library* (2012).
Roberts, Matthew, *Chartism, Commemoration and the Cult of the Radical Hero* (Routledge, 2020).
– *Political Movements in Urban England, 1832-1914* (Palgrave Macmillan, 2009).
– 'Posthumous Paine in the United Kingdom, 1809-1832: Jacobin or loyalist cult', in *The Legacy of Thomas Paine in the Transatlantic World*, ed. Sam Edwards and Marcus Morris (Routledge, 2018).
Robbins, Caroline, *The Eighteenth-Century Commonwealthman* (Harvard University Press, 1959, reprinted 1968).
Rosenfeld, Sophia, *Common Sense, a Political History* (Harvard University Press, 2011).
Royle, Edward, *Origins of the British Secularist Movement, 1790-1866* (Manchester University Press, 1974).
– *Radicals, Secularists and Republicans* (Manchester University Press, 1980).

St Clair, William, *The Godwins and the Shelleys* (Faber and Faber, 1989).
– *The Reading Nation in the Romantic Period* (Cambridge University Press, 2004).
Schoyen, A.R., *The Chartist Challenge: a Portrait of George Julian Harney* (Heinemann, 1958).
Skinner, Quentin, *Liberty before Liberalism* (Cambridge University Press, 1998).
Smith, Nigel, *Literature and Revolution in England, 1640-660* (Yale University Press, 1994).

Spater, George, *William Cobbett: the People's Friend* (Cambridge University Press, 1982), two vols.

Speck, W.A., 'The image of Tom', in *The Legacy of Thomas Paine in the Transatlantic World*, ed. Sam Edwards and Marcus Morris (Routledge, 2018).

Stack, David, *Nature and Artifice: the Life and Thoughts of Thomas Hodgskin* (Boydell Press, 1998).

Stedman Jones, Gareth, *Languages of Class: Studies in English Working Class History, 1832-1982* (Cambridge University Press, 1983).

Taylor, Antony, *Down with the Crown: British Anti-Monarchism and Debates about Royalty since 1790* (Reaktion Books, 1999).

– *Lords of Misrule: Hostility to Aristocracy in Late Nineteenth- and Early Twentieth-Century Britain* (Palgrave Macmillan, 2004).

Thompson, Dorothy (ed.), *The Early Chartists* (University of South Carolina Press, 1971).

Thompson, E.P., *The Making of the English Working Class* (Pelican Books, 1968).

Thurston, Gavin, *The Clerkenwell Riot: the Killing of Constable Culley* (George Allen and Unwin, 1967).

Treuherz, Nicholas, 'The diffusion and impact of Baron d'Holbach's texts in Great Britain' in *Radical Voices, Radical Ways* ed. Laurent Curelly and Nigel Smith (Manchester University Press, 2016).

Turner, Michael J., *Radicalism and Reputation: the Career of Bronterre O'Brien* (Michigan State University Press, 2017).

Vernon, James, *Politics and the People: a Study of English Popular Culture, 1815-1867* (Cambridge University Press, 1993).

Vickers, Vikki J., *'My Pen and My Soul Have Ever Gone Together', Thomas Paine and the American Revolution* (Routledge, 2006).

Vincent, John R., *The Formation of the Liberal Party, 1857-68* (Harvester, 1976).

Wagner, Gillian, *Barnardo* (Weidenfeld and Nicolson, 1979).

Whatmore, Richard, 'A gigantic manliness: Paine's republicanism in the 1790s', in *Economy, Polity and Society, British Intellectual History, 1750-1950* ed. Stephan Collini, Richard Whatmore and Brian Young (Cambridge University Press, 2000).

Wickwar, W.H., *Baron D'Holbach* (George Allen, 1935).
- *The Struggle for the Freedom of the Press, 1819-32* (George Allen and Unwin, 1928).
Wiener, Joel H., *Radicalism and Freethought in Nineteenth-century Britain: the Life of Richard Carlile* (Greenwood Press, 1983).
- *The War of the Unstamped: the Movement to Repeal the British Newspaper Tax, 1830-1836* (Cornell University Press, 1969).
Wilson, David A., *Paine and Cobbett: the Transatlantic Connection* (McGill-Queen's University Press, 1988).
Wood, Gordon S., *The American Revolution: a History* (Phoenix, 2003).
Wootton, David, 'Introduction. The republican tradition: from commonwealth to common sense' in *Republicanism, Liberty and Commercial Society 1649-1776*, ed. Wootton (Stanford University Press, 1994).
Worden, Blair, 'Republicanism, regicide and republic: the English experience' in *Republicanism, a Shared European Heritage*, ed. Martin van Gelderen and Quentin Skinner (Cambridge University Press, 2002), vol. I (*Republicanism and Constitutionalism in Early Modern Europe*).
Worrall, David, *Radical Culture, 1790-1820* (Wayne State University Press, 1992).

Young, Penny, *The Cobbett Club* (Cobbett Society, Farnham, 2015).
- *Two Cocks on the Dunghill: William Cobbett and Henry Hunt: their Friendship, Feuds and Fights* (Twopenny Press, 2009).

Ziesche, Philipp, 'Thomas Paine and Benjamin Franklin's French circle' in *Paine and Jefferson in the Age of Revolutions*, ed. Simon P. Newman and Peter S Onuf (University of Virginia Press, 2013).
Zuckert, Michael, 'The paths of revolution: Jefferson, Paine and the radicalization of Enlightenment thought' in ibid.

Reference Notes

Introduction

1 For Claey's book, see (Boston, 1989), pp. 74, 77 and 88. For Lounissi's article, see *Radical Voices, Radical Ways*, ed. L. Curelly and N. Smith (Manchester, 2016), pp. 65-73. For Philp's article, see its reprint in *Reforming Ideas in Britain* (Cambridge, 2014), ch. 4.

2 See *The Complete Writings of Thomas Paine*, ed. Philip S. Foner (New York, 1969), II, p. 1318.

3 For the Burgh convention, see Caroline Robbins, *The Eighteenth-century Commonwealthman* (Cambridge Mass., 1959), p. 362. For the Rousseauesque convention, see below, p. 58.

4 See Michael Laccohee Bush, *The Friends and Following of Richard Carlile* (Twopenny Press, 2016), chs. 6, 9, 16 and conclusion.

5 Michael J. Turner, *Radicalism and Reputation: The Career of Bronterre O'Brien* (Michigan State University Press, 2017), pp. 117-27.

6 See Philp, *Reforming Ideas in Britain*, p. 108; Bush, *Friends and Following*, p. 72; Frank Prochaska, *The Republic of Britain* (London, 2000), ch. 4. For Cobbett Club republicanism, see below, pp. 142-3.

7 See Margot C. Finn, *After Chartism: Class and Nation in English Radical Politics, 1848-1874* (Cambridge, 1993), chs. 3 and 4; Denis Mack Smith, *Mazzini* (Yale, 1994).

8 Gregory Claeys, *Citizens and Saints: Politics and Anti-Politics in early British Socialism* (Cambridge, 1989), pt. III.

9 Edward Royle, *Radicals, Secularists and Republicans* (Manchester, 1980), pp. 198-206; Finn, *After Chartism*, ch. 7.

10 Mark Bevir, *The Making of British Socialism* (Princeton, 2011), pts I and II. Also see Marcus Morris, 'Explaining British socialists' relationship to Paine, c. 1884-1914' in *The Legacy of Thomas Paine in the Transatlantic World* (London, 2018), ed. Sam Edwards and Marcus Morris, ch. 7 (especially pp. 138-47).

11 For development of Irish republicanism, see Robert Kee, *The Bold Fenian Men* (London, 1976), pt. II. For the impact of Paine, see Marianne Elliott, *Wolf Tone* (Liverpool, 2012), pp. 118, 324-5. Also see Tony Moore, 'Citizens of the world: Paine and the political prisoners transported to Australia' in Edwards and Morris (eds.), *The Legacy of Thomas Paine*, pp. 160-6.

12 Prochaska, *The Republic of Britain*, chs. 3-6.
13 See Antony Taylor, *Down with the Crown: British Anti-monarchism and Debates about Royalty since 1790* (London, 1999), chs. 2 and 3.

Chapter I Paine on Hereditary Rights

1 *Rights of Man*, II (Collins ed., Pelican Classics, 1969), p. 250.
2 *Dissertation on First Principles of Government* (Carlile, 1819), p. 5.
3 For the very few British political thinkers who, prior to Paine, dwelt critically upon this issue, see below, ch. II d. Following the publication of Paine's *Rights of Man*, there was William Godwin's *Enquiry Concerning Political Justice* (1793), with a long section (book 5), clearly written under the spell of Paine, condemning aristocracy and monarchy as naturally incompetent and fraudulent. It contains a chapter entitled 'Of Hereditary Distinction' (book 5, ch. 10).
4 Paine published a dismissive and succinct overview in June 1791 that first appeared in the *Morning Post* and then in the appendix to his *Thoughts on the Peace* (Jordan, 1791), pp. 23-32. It took the form of a letter addressed to Condorcet and others. See Philip S. Foner (ed.), *The Complete Writings of Thomas Paine* (New York, 1969), II, pp. 1315-8. A second dismissive overview was offered in his *On the Abolition of Royalty*, first made public in Oct. 1792. See below, n. 19.
5 See *Common Sense* (Kramnick ed., Penguin Classics, 1986), pp. 69, 79; *Rights of Man* (Collins), II, pp. 194, 236.
6 *Rights of Man* (Collins), II, pp. 194, 204; *Common Sense* (Kramnick), pp. 72, 76.
7 *Rights of Man* (Collins), II, p. 223. Also see ibid., I, pp. 63-4, 144-5; *Dissertation on First Principles of Government* (Carlile), pp. 10-1.
8 For Glorious Revolution, see *Rights of Man* (Collins), I, pp. 63-4, 113. For French Revolution, see *Dissertation on First Principles of Government* (Carlile), p. 11.
9 *Common Sense* (Kramnick), pp. 72-3.
10 *Rights of Man* (Collins), I, p. 162.
11 See Carlile ed. (1819), p. 6.
12 Quoted in A.O. Aldridge, *Thomas Paine's American Ideology* (Newark, 1984) p. 120.
13 Thomas Paine, *Thoughts on the Peace* (Jordan, 1791), pp. 27-8; *Rights of Man* (Collins), I, p. 148.
14 *Rights of Man* (Collins), II, p. 226; Paine, *Letter Addressed to the Addressers on the Late Proclamation* (1792, Carlile, 1819), p. 22.
15 *Common Sense* (Kramnick), p. 76; *Rights of Man* (Collins), II, p. 194.
16 *Rights of Man* (Collins), II, p. 202.

Reference Notes | Introduction & Chapter I

17 Ibid., I, pp. 139-40.
18 Ibid., II, pp. 241-2.
19 See *Address to the French People on the Abolition of Royalty* (Watson, 1843, first ed.). Reprinted under a different title in Philip S. Foner (ed.), *The Complete Writings of Thomas Paine* (New York, 1969), II, p. 542.
20 *Rights of Man* (Collins), I, p. 103; ibid., II, p. 191.
21 Ibid., I, p. 105; ibid., II, p. 246.
22 *Dissertation on First Principles of Government* (Carlile), pp. 16 and 20.
23 See Jack Fruchtman, *The Political Philosophy of Thomas Paine* (Baltimore, 2009), pp. 50-1, 54.
24 *Rights of Man* (Collins), I, pp. 102-3.
25 Ibid, II, p. 202; ibid., I, pp. 102-6.
26 Ibid., II, p. 249.
27 Ibid., pp. 249-50.
28 Ibid., I, pp. 104-5.
29 See Amanda Goodrich, *Debating England's Aristocracy in the 1790s* (Woodbridge, 2005), ch. 2.
30 *Letter Addressed to Addressers* (Carlile), p. 19; *Rights of Man* (Collins), II, p. 191.
31 *Rights of Man* (Collins), II, pp. 188, 246-7.
32 Ibid., p. 189.
33 Ibid., p. 200; Paine, Appendix to *Thoughts on the Peace* (Jordan, 1791), p. 27 (Foner, II, p. 1317).
34 *Dissertation on First Principles of Government* (Carlile), p. 11.
35 *Rights of Man* (Collins), II, p. 200.
36 Anticipating events in a wishful-thinking manner, Paine had referred to France as a republic in the first part of *Rights of Man* (Collins, pp. 165-6). But his letter 'To the Authors of the Republican' written three months later in June 1791, revealed that, in his opinion, France was still in a state of transition and had some way to go before achieving true republican status. See the Appendix to his *Thoughts on the Peace* (Jordan, 1791), pp. 28-9 (Foner, II, p. 1318). Only in his address *On the Abolition of Royalty* of Oct. 1792 did he accept that France was now, having rid itself of monarchy, a genuine republic. See Foner, II, pp. 541-7.
37 *Dissertation on First Principles of Government* (Carlile), p. 4.
38 For theory of balance, see *Rights of Man* (Collins), II, p. 222; *Common Sense* (Kramnick), p. 69. For role of corruption, see *Rights of Man* (Collins), I, pp. 162-3.
39 *Common Sense* (Kramnick), pp. 70-71; *Rights of Man* (Collins), II, pp. 224-6, 228.
40 *Common Sense* (Kramnick), p. 81; *Rights of Man* (Collins), II, p. 225.
41 *Rights of Man* (Collins), I, pp. 103-5; ibid., II, pp. 278-9.
42 Ibid., I, pp. 160-1.

43 Paine, *Thoughts on the Peace* (Jordan, 1791), p. 28.
44 A line pursued in Frank Prochaska's *The Republic of Britain, 1760-2000* (London, 2000).
45 *Rights of Man* (Collins), I, pp. 63-4.
46 *The Age of Reason* (Conway ed. 1896), Conclusion.
47 Ibid., pp. 194-5.
48 Ibid., p. 22.
49 *Common Sense* (Kramnick), p. 78. Also see Gary Berton, 'The distortion of Thomas Paine's philosophy of government' in *The Legacy of Thomas Paine in the Transatlantic World* (London, 2018), ed. Sam Edwards and Marcus Morris, pp. 80-83.
50 Ibid., pp. 72-6.
51 See Vikki J. Vickers, *My Pen and My Soul Have Ever Gone Together* (London, 2006), ch. 4.
52 *Rights of Man* (Collins), II, p. 250.
53 Ibid., I, p. 168.
54 Ibid.
55 Ibid., I, p. 166; ibid., II, p. 183. He sets out the first principles of the new order in *Rights of Man* (Collins), I, p. 166.
56 Ibid., II, pp. 182-3, 187-8; *Dissertation on First Principles of Government* (Carlile), pp. 13-4 and 21.
57 *Rights of Man* (Collins), I, p. 168.
58 E.g., *Rights of Man* (Collins), I, pp. 74-81.
59 Ibid., II, pp. 187-8; *Dissertation on First Principles of Government* (Carlile), p. 21.
60 *Rights of Man* (Collins), I, p. 165.
61 *Dissertation on First Principles of Government* (Carlile), p. 14.
62 On petitioning, see *Dissertations on Government, the Affairs of the Bank and Paper Money* (Carlile, 1819), p. 5; on uselessness of petitioning, see *Letter Addressed to Addressers* (Carlile), pp. 34-5. His contempt for petitioning was first declared in *Common Sense* (Kramnick), p. 90. On House of Commons, see *Letter Addressed* (Carlile), ibid., p. 38.
63 Ibid., pp. 34-41, 46. For rebellion justified by political exclusion, see *Dissertation on First Principles of Government* (Carlile), pp. 13-5.
64 *Rights of Man* (Collins), II, p. 186.
65 Ibid., pp. 214-5.
66 This view was not present in *Common Sense*, but first emerged in *American Crisis*, no. 7 (Nov, 1778) when he asked in a letter addressed 'To the People of England': 'Is there such a thing as the English Constitution' (Carlile), p. 103. He provided the answer in *Rights of Man*, I (Collins), pp. 93-4, 153; and again in *Letter*

Addressed to Addressers (Carlile), p. 19.
67 *Rights of Man* (Collins), II, p. 218; *Letter Addressed to Addressers*, p. 17.
68 *Rights of Man* (Collins), II, p. 218.
69 Ibid., pp. 220, 223.
70 See J.G.A. Pocock, *The Ancient Constitution and the Feudal Law* (Cambridge, 1957), pp. 235-8.
71 *Rights of Man* (Collins), I, p. 166; *Dissertation on First Principles of Government* (Carlile), p. 17.
72 *Dissertation on First Principles of Government* (Carlile), p. 18. In this respect, this study would dispute J.C.D. Clark's belief that Paine's credentials as a democrat are suspect since 'he never quite embraced' the 'new doctrine of universal suffrage'. See his *Thomas Paine* (Oxford, 2018), p. 10.
73 Clark, *Thomas Paine*, p. 75.
74 *Rights of Man* (Collins), I, p. 166 where Paine calls for a 'renovation of the natural order of things'.
75 See p. ix.
76 *Rights of Man* (Collins), II, pp. 214-15.
77 See *The Whole Proceedings on the Trial of Thomas Paine* (Gurney, 1793), p. 5. The same libel was also evident, but not prosecuted, in part I, see Collins ed., pp. 113, 163-4.
78 See Ian Dyck, 'Local attachments, national identities and world citizenship in the thought of Thomas Paine', *History Workshop*, 35 (1993), pp. 117-35; *Rights of Man* (Collins), II, p. 250.
79 *Rights of Man* (Collins), I, pp. 141-3, 147-9.
80 *Dissertation on First Principles of Government* (Carlile), p. 16.
81 *Rights of Man* (Collins), II, pp. 253-4.
82 See below, Appendix, pp. 165-6.
83 *Letter Addressed to Addressers* (Carlile), pp. 20-1. This is how things had worked out by the close of 1792. When first published in America, *Common Sense* had been published anonymously. *Rights of Man* had always appeared under his own name. But the earliest editions were published at the very high price of three shillings for each part. Nonetheless, by mid 1792 the sixpenny edition had appeared first by Jordan in unexpurgated form and then by Symonds and Parsons with the passages removed from part II that had been cited as libellous in the action brought against Paine that year. See below, ch. III (d and e).
84 E.g. *Rights of Man* (Collins), II, pp. 241-2.
85 Ibid., I, pp. 164-7.
86 Moncure Conway, *Republican Superstitions* (London, 1872), pp. v-vi, 79-87.
87 *Rights of Man* (Collins), I, p. 166.

88 Ibid., II, p. 182-3.
89 Ibid., p. 205.
90 Ibid., I, p. 147; ibid., II, p. 206.
91 Regarded as author of African Slavery in America, which appeared, anonymously, in the *Pennsylvania Journal* for 8 March 1776, it was once thought that Paine was strongly opposed to black slavery. But nowadays, his authorship of this piece is considered highly unlikely. See Aldridge,*Thomas Paine's American Ideology*, pp. 289-91; Clark, *Thomas Paine*, pp. 93-7, 420.
92 *Dissertation on First Principles of Government* (Carlile), pp. 16-7.
93 Ibid., p. 15.
94 *Rights of Man* (Collins), I, pp. 104-5.
95 See Ibid., II, p. 166.
96 Its full self-explanatory title was *Agrarian Justice, Opposed to Agrarian Law and to Agrarian Monopoly, being a Plan for Meliorating the Condition of Man by Creating in Every Nation a National Fund*. For Paine's view of property's relationship with the economic rights of man, see Michael Zuckert's 'Two paths for Revolution: Jefferson, Paine and the radicalization of Enlightenment thought' in *Paine and Jefferson in the Age of Revolution*, ed. Simon P. Newman and Peter S. Onuf (Virginia, 2013), pp. 259-66; Robert Lamb, *Thomas Paine and the Idea of Human Rights* (Cambridge, 2015), ch. 4.
97 *Agrarian Justice* (Paris, 1797), pp. 8-9.
98 Ibid., p. 6.
99 *Dissertation on First Principles of Government* (Carlile), p.16.
100 *Agrarian Justice*, p. 8.
101 Ibid.
102 Ibid., pp. 8-9.
103 For Spence and his followers, see Malcolm Chase, *The People's Farm: English Radical Agrarianism, 1775-1840* (Oxford, 1988), chs. 4-6. For removal of customary rights from the system of tenancy, see M.L. Bush, *The English Aristocracy* (Manchester, 1984), ch. 10.
104 For O'Brien, see below, pp. 111-2. For Hyndman, see Mark Bevir, 'Republicanism, socialism and democracy; the origins of the radical left', in *Republicanism in Victorian Society*, ed. David Nash and Antony Taylor (Thrupp, 2000), pp. 76-80. For Wallace, see Edward Royle, *Radicals, Secularists and Republicans* (Manchester, 1980), pp. 196-7; Mark Bevir, *The Making of British Socialism* (Princeton, 2011), p. 156.

Reference Notes | Chapters I & II

Chapter II The Provenance of Paine's Political Ideology

1. *Rights of Man* (Collins, Pelican Classics, 1976), I, p. 162.
2. See *Thoughts on the Peace* (Jordan, 1791), pp. 25-6. Paine used 'aristocracy and 'nobility' as equivalent terms. See *Rights of Man* (Collins), I, pp. 104, 128. In referring to the English aristocracy, he usually had the peerage in mind.
3. See *Rights of Man* (Collins), II, pp. 200-1.
4. See *Thoughts on the Peace* (Jordan), pp. 27-9. Thus, in July 1791, Paine was deliberately correcting a statement made in *Rights of Man* (Collins), I (pp. 165-6) which had referred to a republican system already established not only in America but also in France.
5. See his *The Republic of Britain, 1760-2000* (London, 2000), p. 8. The quotation is taken from *Rights of Man* (Collins), II, p. 200. Here Paine lists the 'only forms of government as the democratic, the aristocratic, the monarchical and the representative'. He makes the point that a republic is naturally opposed to 'the monarchical form' and most naturally associated with 'the representative form'.
6. Philp, *Reforming Ideas in Britain* (Cambridge, 2014), p. 108. For Paine and Burke, see ibid., pp. 112-3, 115-6. Carine Lounissi identifies a range of scholars sharing this view, notably John Pocock, its possible founder. See her *Thomas Paine and the French Revolution* (London, 2018), pp. 52-3.
7. Ibid., pp. 114-5.
8. John Keane, *Tom Paine, a Political Life* (London,1995), p. 284.
9. *Rights of Man*, (Collins), I, p. 128; Keane, *Tom Paine*, p. 285.
10. For Paine's concern that peace should prevail, see *Rights of Man* (Collins), I, p. 168. For his view of the changed nature of monarchy, see ibid., pp. 164-9.
11. See Keane, *Tom Paine*, p. 313.
12. These remarks were made in two letters, first published in the *Morning Post* in July 1791. They were occasioned by Louis XVI's flight to Varennes, in consequence of which Paine composed a manifesto calling upon the French to abolish their monarchy which he had pasted to walls and doors throughout Paris. See Keane, *Tom Paine*, pp. 317-8. The two letters were reprinted in an *Appendix to Paine's Thoughts on the Peace* (Jordan), the first addressed to a group of Frenchmen, engaged in founding a Republican Club and a journal entitled *Le Républicain*. The second letter was addressed to Abbé Sieyès who wanted a republic but with an elected monarchy. Both letters advocated a republic without monarchy of any sort. For Paine's announcement that he was a good republican, see *Thoughts on the Peace*, p. 28. For Paine's declaration of war against monarchy, see ibid., p. 32. A similar outburst of ecstatic republican sentiment issued from Paine in October 1792 to celebrate the actual abolition

of the French monarchy. It took the form of an address made to the National Convention at its meeting on 20 Oct. and was published as a special supplement to *Le Patriote Français* on 27 Oct. Overlooked by Sherwin and Carlile, it was first published in English by James Watson in the 1840s. See *Thomas Paine, Address to the People of France on the Abolition of Royalty* (Watson, 1848). The story of Paine's hostility to hereditary monarchy in France is told in Lounissi, *Thomas Paine and the French Revolution*, chs. 2.2 and 4.

13 Quoted in Craig Nelson, *Thomas Paine* (London, 2007), p. 107.
14 For 'Plain Truth', see Keane, *Tom Paine*, p. 107. For references to 'common sense', see *Common Sense* (Kramnick, Penguin Classics, 1976), pp. 81 and 103. For references to 'reason' or 'nature', see ibid., see pp. 68, 76, 89-90, 91, 117.
15 *Common Sense* (Kramnick), p. 69.
16 *Rights of Man* (Collins), II, p. 241. For some elaboration, see Jack Fruchtman, *The Political Philosophy of Thomas Paine* (Baltimore, 2009), pp. 63-5.
17 *Common Sense* (Kramnick), p. 69.
18 See *Common Sense* (Kramnick), pp. 81-2 and 95; *Rights of Man* (Collins), I, pp. 166-7; ibid., II, p. 183.
19 *Common Sense* (Kramnick), pp. 96-7. For Paine's emphasis on 'the continent' in his *Common Sense* and its fantastic or visionary (rather than common-sensical) implications, see Trish Loughran, *The Republic in Print* (New York, 2007), pp. 72-3.
20 *Rights of Man* (Collins), I, pp. 165-6.
21 *Common Sense* (Kramnick), p. 98.
22 Ibid., p. 108.
23 Ibid.; *Rights of Man* (Collins), I, pp. 94, 148.
24 *Common Sense* (Kramnick), p. 109.
25 *Rights of Man* (Collins), I, p. 168.
26 Ibid., II, pp. 178, 183.
27 See ibid., pp. 290, 292.
28 Ibid., pp. 183-4.
29 For continuity between *Common Sense* and *Rights of Man*, see David A Wilson, *Paine and Cobbett, the Transatlantic Connection* (Montreal, 1988), pp. 67-75, 89-95.
30 *Rights of Man* (Collins), I, p. 166; ibid., II, p. 234. Paine, unlike Godwin, never kept a diary and his book collection suffered two fires. Given his fame, his surviving correspondence is scanty with no more than 230 letters written by himself.
31 See Keane, *Tom Paine*, p. 28; Foner, I, p. 123. Also see J.C.D. Clark, *Thomas Paine* (Oxford, 2018), pp. 66, 141, 422.

Reference Notes | Chapter II

32 See Quentin Skinner, *Liberty Before Liberalism* (Cambridge, 1998), ch. 1.
33 See *Rights of Man* (Collins), II, pp. 199-200, 202-3.
34 Ibid., ch. 3, especially pp. 204-5.
35 Paine, *American Crisis* (Carlile,1819), Letter III, p. 33. He implies having held this view long before he wrote about it: as if it had come to him naturally, like his hatred 'for cruel men and cruel measures'.
36 See below, p. 35-6.
37 See Vikki J. Vickers, *My Pen and My Soul Have Ever Gone Together* (London, 2006), pp. 79-80. For Paine's criticism of Quakerism, see his *The Age of Reason* (Conway ed.), pp. 65-6.
38 *Common Sense* (Kramnick), pp. 124-5.
39 See Vickers, *My Pen and My Soul*, pp. 82-5.
40 See Barclay, *An Apology* (London, 1736), propositions II and III (for the Bible); pp. 80, 87 and 105 (for original sin); p. 325 (for laity/clergy); proposition XI (for worship).
41 Ibid., pp. 516-22.
42 See *Common Sense* (Kramnick), pp. 124-5. For a vivid portrayal of Quaker ways and the Quaker presence in Pennsylvania, see Abbé Raynal's, *Philosophical and Political History of European Settlement and Trade in the East and West Indies* (Dublin, 1784), vol. VI, pp. 6-31.
43 Within Quaker literature was a pamphlet written by the Ebionite Edward Elwall entitled *A Declaration against All the Kings and Temporal Powers under Heaven*. See Margaret C. Jacob, *The Radical Enlightenment* (London, 1981), p. 175. It was first published in 1726 and republished in the 1730s. But there is no evidence that Paine ever read it.
44 See Moncure Conway's edition of *The Age of Reason* (New York,1896), p. 63.
45 *Common Sense* (Kramnick), p. 92; Keane, *Tom Paine*, pp. 101-2.
46 Ibid., p. 101.
47 See Foner, II, pp. 33-4.
48 See Linda Colley, *The Gun, the Ship and the Pen* (London, 2021), p. 96.
49 *Rights of Man* (Collins), II, pp. 242-6.
50 Ibid., pp. 214-15.
51 See *Rights of Man* (Collins), I, pp. 94 and 153; and ibid., II, pp. 217-18.
52 See Vickers, *My Pen and My Soul*, pp. 86-7. For the impact of his aunt, see Keane, *Tom Paine*, pp. 17-18, 25-6.
53 *Rights of Man* (Collins), II, p. 241.
54 Keane, *Tom Paine*, pp. 42-3.
55 See Dodo Press imprint, pp. 18-19 (for ideal). For impracticality, see ibid., pp. 8-9. For Priestley, see below, pp. 44-5.

56 Keane, *Tom Paine*, pp. 60-1.
57 Burke's work was not a statement of his actual beliefs. Written in a spirit of irony, it was an attempt to spoof Lord Bolingbroke and make him look ridiculous. Yet it was easily taken otherwise.
58 Also attracting Paine to the works of Swift was his belief that, although a cleric, Swift was a Deist: made evident in his having been 'a great associate with the free-thinkers of those days, such as Bolingbroke, Pope and others who did not believe in the Scriptures'. See Foner, I, p. 869.
59 See Clark, *Thomas Paine*, p. 297.
60 See Paine, *Rights of Man*, II (Collins), p. 225.
61 See *Enquiry Concerning Political Justice* (Dublin, 1793), p. viii. Suggesting the reference was to Swift's Gulliver's Travels, see Mark Philp, *Godwin's Political Justice* (New York, 1986), p. 3.
62 See *Common Sense* (Kramnick), pp. 68-9, 79-81.
63 See Keane, *Tom Paine*, pp. 73-5.
64 See below, p. 43.
65 For his time in Lewes, see Keane, *Tom Paine*, pp. 62-72; Fruchtman, *The Political Philosophy of Thomas Paine*, pp. 17-8.
66 For his journey to America, see Keane, *Tom Paine*, p. 84. For early days in Philadelphia, see ibid., pp. 91-2, Edward Larkin, *Thomas Paine and the Literature of Revolution* (Cambridge, 2005), pp. 34-47 and Rosenfield, *Common Sense*, ch. 4.
67 Jonathan Israel, *The Expanding Blaze* (Princeton, 2017), pp. 31, 60-1. For Young's association with Paine, see A. Owen Aldridge, *Thomas Paine's American Ideology* (Newark, 1984), pp. 169, 188, 198. For Spinoza's influence upon Young, see below, p. 77.
68 See Jonathan Israel, *A Revolution of the Mind* (Princeton, 2010), pp. 42-3; Keane, *Tom Paine*, pp. 106-7; Caroline Robbins, *The Eighteenth-century Commonwealthman* (Cambridge Mass, 1959), p. 350.
69 See Craig Nelson, *Thomas Paine* (London, 2006), pp. 49-50.
70 See Foner II, p. 547; and *Common Sense* (Kramnick), p. 81.
71 For Franklin/Paine, see Philipp Ziesche, 'Thomas Paine and Benjamin's Franklin's French circle', in Newman and Onuf's ed. of *Paine and Jefferson in the Age of Revolution*, p. 129. Fruchtman, *Political Philosophy of Thomas Paine*, pp. 49-52. For Paine, see above, p. 13.
72 For Franklin, see Fruchtman, *Political Philosophy of Thomas Paine*, 49-50; Keane, *Tom Paine*, p. 79; William Doyle, *Aristocracy and its Enemies in the Age of Revolution* (Oxford, 2009), pp. 86-7, 112. Franklin read *Common Sense* prior to its publication and suggested changes. See Keane, op. cit., p. 107. For Paine's account, see his *American Crisis* (Carlile, 1819), Letter IV, pp. 48-9. For Cartwright, see Keane, *Tom Paine*, p. 100. For Priestley, see Israel, *Expanding*

Blaze, p. 54; and David Wootton, 'The republican tradition: from commonwealth to *common sense*', in Wootton (ed.), *Republicanism, Liberty and Commercial Society, 1649-1776* (Stanford, 1994), pp. 34-5.
73   See Dodo Press reprint, pp. 4, 8.
74   For Sidney's importance in the American Revolution, see Alan Houston, *Algernon Sidney and his Republican Heritage in England and America* (Princeton, 1991), ch. 6. For similarities between Paine and Sidney, see Sidney's *Discourses Concerning Government*, ch. I, sections 5, 18-20. For differences, see ibid., ch. II, sections 16, 21, 28.
75   *Common Sense* (Kramnick), p. 90.
76   Clark, *Thomas Paine*, 161-2.
77   For nature of American politics, see Gordon S. Wood, *The American Revolution* (London, 2003), pp. 46-51. For nature of American Christianity, see ibid., 127-9. For an indigenous republicanism evident prior to Independence, see Pauline Maier, *From Resistance to Revolution* (New York, 1991), pp. 288-96 and Bernard Bailyn, *The Ideological Origins of the American Revolution* (Cambridge Mass, 1967), pp. 19-20 and ch. VI (3). For Paine's keen interest in newspapers, see Seth Cotlar, *Tom Paine's America* (Charlottesville, 2011), p. 29.
78   See Barclay, *Apology* (1736), p. 195.
79   For the Paine quotation, see Aldridge, *Thomas Paine's American Ideology*, p. 101.
80   Ibid., pp. 98-100.
81   Ibid., pp. 98-9.
82   In 1700, 1737, 1747, 1771. See Wootton, 'The republican tradition' in Wootton (ed.), *Republicanism, Liberty and Commercial Society*, pp. 30-1 which makes the point that Hall's tract, when republished in the eighteenth century, had been substantially revised by Toland. For a consideration of Hall's tract, see Skinner, *Liberty Before Liberalism*, pp. 55-7.
83   Aldridge, *Thomas Paine's American Legacy*, p. 101.
84   See 'The Grounds and Reasons of Monarchy Considered' in Toland's *Works of Harrington* (London, 1737), p. 3. Also see Wilson, *Paine and Cobbett*, pp. 45-7.
85   For Hall, see ibid., p. 3. For Paine, see *Rights of Man* (Collins), II, p. 197. Also see Skinner, *Liberty Before Liberalism*, p. 57.
86   See his *Dissertation on First Principles of Government* (Carlile, 1819), p. 6.
87   See Nelson, *Thomas Paine*, pp. 239-43.
88   Jack Fruchtman, *Thomas Paine, Apostle of Freedom* (New York/London, 1994), p. 199; Keane, *Tom Paine*, p. 285; Richard Whatmore, 'A gigantic manliness: Paine's republicanism in the 1790s' in *Economy, Polity and Society* (Cambridge, 2000), ed. by Stefan Collini, p. 155. Also see Lounissi, *Thomas Paine and the French Revolution*, ch. 4.

89 Keane, *Tom Paine*, pp. 317-19; Rachel Hammersley, *French Revolutionaries and English Republicans* (London, 2005), pp 32-55; and see above, n. 12.
90 See Whatmore, 'A gigantic manliness', pp. 136-8; 155-6.
91 The passage is quoted in Aldridge, *Thomas Paine's American Ideology*, pp. 119-20.
92 See Paine, *Common Sense* (Kramnick), p. 76. See John Locke, *Two Treatises of Government* (London, 1689), Bk II, ch. 8, point 116.
93 *Rights of Man* (Collins), I, pp. 63-4, 144-5; ibid., II, p. 194; *Dissertation on First Principles of Government* (Carlile), p. 9.
94 See Aldridge, *Thomas Paine's American Ideology*, pp. 119-20.
95 Locke, *Two Treatises of Government*, bk II, ch. 8, point 114.
96 See Dodo Press Edition, pp. 6-7.
97 For Paine's debt to Priestley, see Wilson, *Paine and Cobbett*, pp. 43-5.
98 See Dodo Press Edition, p. 12. For the significance of Locke's preference for principles over precedent, from which Priestley may have drawn inspiration, see J.G.A. Pocock, *The Ancient Constitution and the Feudal Law* (1957), pp. 235-8. For Paine's dismissal of the importance of precedent, see his *Common Sense* (Kramnick), p. 83; and his *Rights of Man* (Collins), II, pp. 218-9. In doing so he was also subscribing to what Swift had suggested in Gulliver's fourth voyage. See *Gulliver's Travels*, p. 230.
99 See Priestley, *An Essay on the First Principles of Government* (Dodo Press), pp. 18-9. In accepting a system of egalitarian republicanism, they differed slightly in that Priestley regarded it as an ideal that was probably beyond realisation (ibid., p. 6), whereas for Paine it was a perfectly practical proposition.
100 *Common Sense* (Kramnick), p. 65.
101 *Rights of Man* (Collins), II, pp. 232 and 220.
102 E.g. see *Rights of Man* (Collins), I, p. 167; *Common Sense* (Kramnick), pp. 67 and 97-100.
103 Priestley, *An Essay on the First Principles of Government* (Dodo Press), pp. 2-3 and 6.
104 See Wootton, 'The republican tradition' in Wootton (ed.), *Republicanism, Liberty and Commercial Society*, pp. 35-6.
105 See *Common Sense* (Kramnick), pp. 97-8; *A Letter Addressed* (Carlile, 1819), pp. 24-5.
106 For a consideration of Dragonetti's influence on *Common Sense*, see Wootton, 'The republican tradition' in (Wootton ed.), *Republicanism, Liberty and Commercial Society*, pp. 36-9. However, Wootton presents him as against monarchy (see p. 37) whereas Dragonetti's tract suggests a preference for enlightened despotism: see *Treatise on Virtues and Rewards* (Dodo Press), pp. 145-51. Israel falls into the same trap: see his *Democratic Enlightenment* (Oxford, 2012), pp. 452-3.

107 See *Common Sense* (Kramnick), p. 65.
108 Dragonetti, *Virtues and Rewards* (Dodo Press), p. 125.
109 Ibid., chapters 2-5.
110 Ibid., pp. 35, 41.
111 *Common Sense* (Kramnick), pp. 97-8. He is referring to pp. 153-5 in *Virtues and Rewards*.
112 *Common Sense* (Kramnick), pp. 110-1.
113 For the progression of Paine's belief in universal suffrage, see below, pp. 61-2.
114 See Burgh, *Political Disquisitions*, III, p. 270.
115 Ibid., pp. 428-9.
116 Apart from Burke, citations were limited to Burgh, Barclay, Bunyan, Dragonetti, Franklin, Dr Johnson, Junius, Locke, Sir William Meredith, Milton, Montesquieu, Price, Quesnay, Raynal, Rousseau, Adam Smith, Spinoza, Swift, Turgot and Voltaire.
117 See *The Age of Reason* (Conway ed., 1896), p. 64.
118 The story is told in Robbins, *The Eighteenth-century Commonwealthman,* passim, and in Bailyn, *The Ideological Origins of the American Revolution*, ch. 2.
119 See Nelson, *Thomas Paine*, p. 177.
120 *Rights of Man* (Collins), I, pp. 63-4, 113.
121 Ibid., II, p. 223.
122 For attitude to individual kings, see *Thoughts on the Peace* (Jordan, 1791), p. 32.
123 *Rights of Man* (Collins), II, pp. 214-5.
124 For Paine's remarks on constitution and precedent, see *Rights of Man* (Collins), II, pp. 216-18.
125 See Albert Goodwin, *The Friends of Liberty* (London, 1979), chs. 4-7.
126 See ibid., pp. 174-6 and 177-8.
127 See *Rights of Man* (Collins), I, pp. 61-2.
128 Price's' political works comprised his *Observations on Civil Liberty* (1776), his *Additional Observations on Civil Liberty* (1777), his *Observations on the Importance of the American Revolution* (1785) and a printed sermon *Discourse on the Love of Our Country* (1790). All post-dated *Common Sense*, but signs of Paine's dependency on Price can be found in *Rights of Man*: such as the point that despotic monarchy debased human beings by treating them like cattle; a translation of the French National Assembly's 'Declaration of Rights of Man and of Citizens' (*Rights of Man* (Collins), I, pp. 132-4) which follows virtually word for word the version appended to *Discourse on the Love of Our Country*; and the resort to statistics in *Rights of Man* II, although the figures used appear to come from Sir John Somerville's *History of the Revenue* (see *Rights of Man* (Collins), II, pp. 252, 257).

129 For Hall, see above, pp. 41-2. For Cato's Letters, see Carinne Lounissi, 'Thomas Paine's democratic linguistic radicalism' in *Radical Voices, Radical Ways* (Manchester, 2016), pp. 64, 67.
130 See Price, *Additional Observations*, p.6; Priestley, *An Essay on the First Principles of Government* (Dodo Press), p. 9.
131 See Caroline Robbins, The *Eighteenth-century Commonwealthman* (Harvard, reprint of 1968 edition), p. 117.
132 See above, pp. 28-9.
133 For Paine's egalitarianism, see *Rights of Man* (Collins), I, p. 166. Following Paine, there appeared William Godwin's *Enquiry Concerning Political Justice* (London,1793), with a long section (bk V), clearly written under Paine's spell, that condemned aristocracy and monarchy as naturally incompetent and fraudulent. It contains a chapter entitled 'Of Hereditary Distinction'. See bk. 5, ch. 10.
134 See Paine's *Letter Addressed to the Addressers on the Late Proclamation* (Carlile, 1819), p. 41; and his *Dissertation on First Principles of Government* (Carlile, 1819), pp. 15-6. Also see Burgh, *Political Disquisitions*, I, p. 51. This requirement was absent from the first edition of Cartwright's *Take your Choice* (1776), but it had been added to the second edition of 1777.
135 See Priestley, *Essay on the First Principles of Government* (Dodo Press), p. 9. Where they differed was Priestley's preference for hereditary over elective monarchy, and Paine's refusal to accept either.
136 *Rights of Man* (Collins), pp. 195-7. Also see the Appendix to Thomas Paine's *Thoughts on the Peace* (Jordan, 1791), pp. 25-32; and Keane, *Tom Paine*, pp. 318-19.
137 See Jonathan Israel, *Radical Enlightenment* (Oxford, 2001), ch. 33 and Israel, *Revolution of the Mind*, pp. 2, 19-21, 48, 56, 92-3, 102, 138, 143, 152-3, 157, 192, 239. Also see Whatmore, 'A gigantic manliness', pp. 154-5, and Margaret C. Jacob, *The Radical Enlightenment* (London, 1981), pp. 48-52.
138 On the evidence of his friend Mrs de Bonneville, it appears that eventually (by 1797), and after living for five years in France, he could read French newspapers but still had difficulty in speaking in French. See Nelson, *Thomas Paine*, pp. 295-6. This would suggest that, when composing his main political works, *Common Sense* and *Rights of Man*, reading learned tracts in French would have been beyond him.
139 The only work ever to be translated into English was *Système de la Nature*, but not before 1797. See Appendix C in W.H. Wickwar, *Baron d'Holbach* (London, 1935), p. 244. Also see Nick Treuherz, 'The diffusion and impact of Baron d'Holbach's texts in Great Britain, 1765-1800' in *Radical Voices, Radical Ways*, ch. 5.

140 Its English title was *The Origin and Progress of Despotism in the Orient and other Empires of Africa, Europe and America.*
141 For Paine, see *Rights of Man* (Collins), I, pp. 91-2; ibid. II, p. 182. For Boulanger, see *Origin and Progress*, sections XXI (against republicanism), XXII (in favour of monarchy).
142 See Israel, *A Revolution of the Mind*, pp. 44-5, 93, 99, 102, 125, 144-5, 222, 227-8. For an extensive account of the *Histoire*, see Israel's *Democratic Enlightenment*, ch. 15.
143 See Israel, *A Revolution of the Mind*, pp. 95-9, 124-5, 144-5, 149-51.
144 For Paine, see above, p. 12. For Raynal, see *Philosophical and Political History of the Settlements and Trade of the Europeans in the East and West Indies* (Dublin, 1784), vol. VI, pp. 275-6.
145 See ibid., pp. 295 and 368-9.
146 For Raynal's approval, see ibid., vol. VI, pp. 298-9, 302-4. For Paine's condemnation, see above, ch. I (a).
147 For Raynal on the Glorious Revolution, see his *Philosophical and Political History*, vol. VI, p. 148. For Paine's view, see *Rights of Man* (Collins), I, pp. 63-4, 113.
148 See Raynal's *Philosophical and Political History*, vol. VI, p. 163; and Paine's *Rights of Man* (Collins), I, p. 166.
149 See Israel, *Democratic Enlightenment*, p. 436.
150 See Aldridge, *Thomas Paine's American Ideology*, p. 270; Craig Nelson, *Thomas Paine* (London, 2006), p. 161.
151 See Paine, *A Letter Addressed to the Abbé Raynal...in which the Mistakes in the Abbé's Account in the Revolution of America are Cleared Up* (1782); Fruchtman, *Political Philosophy of Thomas Paine*, pp. 71-2.
152 *Rights of Man*, I (Collins), p. 116.
153 Ibid.
154 See *Considerations on the Order of Cincinnatus* (Pennsylvania, 1786), pp. 5, 7-8. The issue was first raised by a South Carolina lawyer Aedanus Burke in a tract entitled *Considerations on the Society or Order of Cincinnati lately Instituted... Proving that it Creates a Race of Hereditary Patricians or Nobility* (1783). It was also taken up by Richard Price in his *Observations on the Importance of the American Revolution* (1785), pp. 40-1. Benjamin Franklin was likewise involved in making objection to it. See Israel, *Expanding Blaze*, pp. 76-9. For the debate on nobility in the USA, see Bailyn, *Ideological Origins of the American Revolution*, pp. 278-81; and Doyle, *Aristocracy*, ch. 4.
155 Keane, *Tom Paine*, p. 284; Doyle, *Aristocracy*, pp. 123, 137, 156.
156 *Rights of Man* (Collins), II, p. 241, footnote.
157 *Common Sense* (Kramnick), pp. 68-9.

158 *Rights of Man* (Collins), I, pp. 104-6, 162-3.
159 See ibid., p. 128; and below, ch. III.
160 *Rights of Man* (Collins), I, p. 128.
161 Ibid., pp. 102-6, 128, 131. Also see Whatmore, 'A gigantic manliness', p. 156. For the Franklin connection, see Ziesche, 'Thomas Paine and Benjamin Franklin's French Circle' in Newman and Onuf (eds) *Paine and Jefferson*, pp. 126-130.
162 *Rights of Man* (Collins), II, pp. 178, 246-51.
163 For the connection, see Edward H. Davidson and William J. Scheik, *Paine, Scripture and Authority* (London, 1994), pp. 58-60; Jack Fruchtman, *Thomas Paine and the Religion of Nature* (Baltimore, 1993), pp. 58-61.
164 See above, p. 51.
165 *The Age of Reason*, Part II (Conway, 1896), pp. 123-4; and Paine's *Reply to the Bishop of Llandaff's Apology for the Bible* (Carlile, 1818), pp. 8 and 13. The latter was written in response to Llandaff's *Reply to the Second Part of Age of Reason* (London, 1796) and published posthumously in 1810. Also see Fruchtman, *Thomas Paine and the Religion of Nature*, pp. 58-61.
166 For Paine's theology, see his *The Age of Reason* (Conway), pp. 21, 83 and 188; and Michael Laccohee Bush, *The Friends and Following of Richard Carlile* (Twopenny Press, 2016), ch. 3. For Spinoza's monism, see Jonathan I. Israel, *Radical Enlightenment* (Oxford, 2001), ch. 13; Stuart Hampshire, *Spinoza* (Penguin, 1951), ch. 2.
167 See 'introduction' to Jonathan Israel's edition of Spinoza's *Theological-Political Treatise* (Cambridge, 2007), pp. xxvii-xxxi. For Spinoza's appreciation of republicanism, see ibid., p. 202; and R.H.M. Elwes' translation of 'Tractatus Politicus' (1895, Lubbock's Hundred Books, no. 91). Paine and Spinoza were also connected by a faith in the truth of mathematics, notably the geometry of Euclid. This was revealed in Paine's remark: 'There is not a problem in Euclid more mathematically true than that hereditary government has not a right to exist' (*Dissertation on First Principles of Government* (Carlile), p. 5). Spinoza, in seeking to be as objective as Euclid, composed his Ethics as a succession of logically related propositions rather than as a series of beguiling arguments. See Hampshire, *Spinoza*, pp. 24-5. Paine, however, was simply making the point that for him the falsity of the hereditary principle was a certainty. He was not seeking to adopt a Euclidian approach. Rather he was pursuing an argument, the effectiveness of which depended upon his remarkable skill as a writer. And there is nothing to suggest that he was aware of Spinoza's *Ethics*.
168 For Young and Blount, see Israel, *Expanding Blaze*, p. 61. For Priestley and Spinoza, see Priestley's *An Essay*, sections I-III. The two were also closely aligned by their shared materialistic outlook, with Spinoza's monism elaborated upon in Priestley's *Disquisitions relating to Matter and Spirit* (London, 1777).

169 See *An Essay* (Dodo Press), p. 6.
170 See *Theological-political Treatise* (Israel), p. 202.
171 For Priestley, see *An Essay* (Dodo Press), pp. 12-3. For Spinoza, see *Theological-political Treatise*, p. 195. For Paine, see *Rights of Man* (Collins), I, p. 166; ibid, II, pp. 220, 223.
172 For his interest in Priestley in 1757, see Keane, *Tom Paine*, pp. 42-3. For his interest in Priestley in 1775, see ibid., p. 92.
173 See Israel, *Expanding Blaze*, p. 54.
174 See above, p. 15.
175 The point is made by Aldridge in *Thomas Paine's American Ideology*, pp. 143-4.
176 For Paine, see Nelson, *Thomas Paine*, p. 296; and *Rights of Man* (Collins), II, p. 295.
177 *Rights of Man* (Collins), I, p. 116.
178 See Aldridge, *Thomas Paine's American Ideology*, pp. 119-20.
179 See Jack Fruchtman, *Thomas Paine, Apostle of Liberty* (New York, 1994), p. 282.
180 *Rights of Man* (Collins), I, p. 95 and II, pp. 287, 294.
181 *A Letter Addressed to the Addressers on the Late Proclamation* (see Carlile ed., 1819), pp. 33-4 and 39-40.
182 See his *Treatise on the Social Compact*, bk II, chs. 1-3.
183 *Rights of Man* (Collins), II, pp. 189 and 210.
184 See Keane, *Tom Paine*, pp. 116-7.
185 See *Common Sense* (Kramnick), pp. 65 and 97.
186 Ibid., p. 65.
187 It was cited in a newspaper article written by Paine in May 1776, four months after the publication of *Common Sense*. See Aldridge, *Thomas Paine's American Ideology*, p. 137.
188 See *Common Sense* (Kramnick), pp. 95-7; *Rights of Man* (Collins), II, pp. 183-4, 207-10, 290-1. A similar idea, taken from Henry IV's Grand Design, appears in *Rights of Man* (Collins), I (see pp. 166-7). Also see Keane, *Tom Paine*, pp. 133, 298.
189 For non-plain nature of Paine's style, see Jane Hodson, *Language and Revolution in Burke, Wollstonecraft, Paine and Godwin* (London, 2007), ch. 5.
190 See Keane, *Tom Paine*, p. 285; Fruchtman, *Thomas Paine*, pp. 199-201; Nelson, *Thomas Paine*, pp. 248-9.
191 For his non-classical education, see Keane, *Tom Paine*, p. 28.
192 Reprinted in Frank Shuffelton (ed), *The American Enlightenment* (New York, 1993), ch. 21.
193 Roberts, *Chartism*, pp. 116-17.
194 Ibid. p. 117.
195 *Rights of Man* (Collins), II, pp. 183-4.

196 See above, ch. 1(a).
197 See *Common Sense* (Kramnick), p. 111; Burgh, *Political Disquisitions*, I, bk. II.
198 *Dissertations on Government* (Carlile, 1819), p. 5.
199 Ibid., p. 6.
200 *Rights of Man* (Collins), II, p. 286.
201 *Letter Addressed to Addressers* (Carlile,1819), p. 40.
202 *Dissertation on First Principles of Government* (Carlile), p.11. Paine's interpretation of universal suffrage was adult male suffrage. By holding it, he was contradicting his view of the equality of rights in the representative system. This could have been the unintentional consequence of his use of the term of 'rights of man'. On the other hand, by saying that each man had the right to one vote 'and no more' he was implying that if women were allowed the vote it would confer on their fathers and husbands more than one vote.
203 See *Common Sense* (Kramnick), pp. 97-8 , 108-9.
204 *Rights of Man* (Collins), II, pp. 262-70. He calculated that one fifth of the population would qualify. They would be husbandmen (i.e. small farmers), labourers, journeymen (i.e. waged artisans) and their wives, sailors, ex-soldiers, elderly servants and poor widows. The idea of the government assuming a moral obligation to make provision out of its tax revenues for 'old age, helpless infancy and poverty' was first made public in August 1791 in Paine's 'Address and Declaration of the Friends of Universal Peace and Liberty', written for the benefit of Horne Tooke's Society for Constitutional Information. The text is to be found in Paine's *Miscellaneous Letters and Essays* (Carlile, 1819), pp. 58-61). For a consideration of this aspect, see Michael Zuckert, 'Two paths to Revolution' in Newman and Onuf (eds), *Paine and Jefferson*, pp. 256-7, and Lamb, Thomas Paine, pp. 136-7, 143-7.
205 Paine, *Agrarian Justice*, pp. 8-9, 13-4. It was a right in compensation for the process of appropriation that had taken away man's natural right to the land.
206 See his *Dissertation on First Principles of Government* (Carlile), p. 17.
207 For Hobbes and Locke: both are cited as opponents of divine right in Nelson, *Thomas Paine*, pp. 68-9. For Deism, see Justin Champion, *The Pillars of Priestcraft Shaken* (London, 1992), passim. Defoe's *Jure Divino* was published in 1706, eventually undergoing revision by William Hone in Hone's *Popular Political Tracts* (London, 1822). For Paine's Deism, see Vickers, *Thomas Paine and the American Revolution*, pp. 97-9.
208 See his *The Original and Institution of Civil Government Discussed* (London, 1710).
209 *Common Sense* (Kramnick), pp. 72-6.
210 Davidson and Scheick, *Paine, Scripture and Authority*, p. 48.
211 See above, pp. 61-2.

Chapter III Rights of Man: Sale and Suppression

1. This study repudiates Gary Kates' claim that *Rights of Man* part I favoured hereditary monarchy whereas part II advocated its rejection since both parts shared the same republican faith. See his 'From liberalism to radicalism: Tom Paine's *Rights of Man*, reprinted from Frank Shuffelton (ed.), *The American Enlightenment* (New York, 1993) p. 320.
2. See John Keane, *Tom Paine: a Political Life* (London, 1996), p. 285; J.C.D Clark, *Thomas Paine* (Oxford, 2018), p. 242.
3. *Rights of Man*, ed. Henry Collins (Pelican Classics, 1976), pp. 74-86 (passage A) and 115-31 (passage B). Passage B, running to 6,000 words, was based on information picked up by Paine on three visits he made to Paris when the Revolution was unfolding: the first from April to August 1787, the second from Dec. 1787 to June 1788, the third from November 1789 to March 1790. J.C.D. Clark regards it as the work of someone else, probably Lafayette: see his *Thomas Paine*, pp. 423-4, 240-2. Yet it was clearly the piece Paine was working on in January 1790, as revealed by Lafayette in a letter to Washington. See Keane, *Tom Paine*, p. 285. Passage A extends the narrative from July to Oct. 1789. Running to 5,000 words, it contains several references to Burke's *Reflections*, but they could have been added as Paine was composing *Rights of Man* between Nov. 1790 and Jan. 1791. For further light on the brochure, see Carine Lounissi, *Thomas Paine and the French Revolution* (London, 2018), p. 13.
4. R.R. Fennessy, *Burke, Paine and the Rights of Man* (The Hague, 1963), pp. 266-8.
5. Rather than study the work's publishing history, the tendency of Paineite scholars is to speculate upon the total number of copies circulated, an approach that is bound, because of the inadequacy of the evidence, to end in uncertainty. See E.P. Thompson, *The Making of the English Working Class* (Pelican Books, 1968), p. 117; Keane, *Tom Paine*, pp. 305, 307, 333; Mark Philp (ed.), *The French Revolution and British Popular Politics* (Cambridge, 1991), p. 5; Clark, *Thomas Paine* pp. 230 (n. 56) and 250-1; Gregory Claeys, *The French Revolution Debate in Britain* (Basingstoke, 2007), p. 47. A notable exception to this approach is Peter De Bolla's *The Architecture of Concepts* (New York, 2013), ch. 4.
6. *The Complete Writings of Thomas Paine*, ed. Philip S. Foner (New York, 1969), II, pp. 1318-20.
7. Ibid., p. 1319.
8. The publication dates of the various editions can be found noticed in the *London Chronicle* or the *Morning Chronicle* for 1791-2.
9. Foner, II, p. 1318.
10. Ibid., p. 1322.

11 Ibid., p. 1318.
12 Ibid., pp. 1321-2.
13 Ibid., p. 1322.
14 *Rights of Man* (Collins), II, p. 177.
15 For Burke's sale, see William St Clair, *The Reading Nation in the Romantic Period* (Cambridge, 2004), p. 583. Also see ibid. Appendix 9 for an attempt to compile a statistical account of best-selling works in the late eighteenth and early nineteenth centuries.
16 Foner, II, p. 1322.
17 Thompson, *Making of the English Working Class*, pp. 121-3.
18 See below, ch. III (e).
19 For print-run of each edition, see Keane, *Tom Paine*, p. 327.
20 See ibid., p. 340.
21 See below, pp. 78-9.
22 Albert Goodwin, *The Friends of Liberty* (London, 1979), p. 177.
23 Ibid., pp. 174-5.
24 Jenny Graham, *The Nation, the Law and the King, Reform Politics in England, 1789-1799* (Oxford, 2000), p. 257.
25 For Paine's relations with the Society, see Foner, II, p. 1324. For Paine's donations to it, see Graham, *The Nation, the Law*, p. 218 (n. 45).
26 See below, pp. 72, 74 (for provincial printings); and pp. 71-2 (for abridgement). For abridgements made, see below, p. 73 and p. 79.
27 For the incident, see Fennessy, *Burke, Paine and the Rights of Man*, p. 229; Graham, *The Nation, the Law*, pp. 219-20. For Cooper's republicanism, see his *A Reply to Mr Burke's Invective against Mr Cooper and Mr Watt in the House of Commons* (Manchester, 1792), pp. 20-8.
28 Keane, *Tom Paine*, p. 305, 308; Clark, *Thomas Paine*, p. 233.
29 See Graham, *The Nation, the Law*, p. 218.
30 See *Rights of Man* (Collins), II, Appendix (p. 299).
31 W.T. Sherwin, *Memoirs of the Life of Thomas Paine* (London, 1819), p. 112.
32 Foner, II, p. 910.
33 Ibid., p. 1319.
34 Paine to chairman of the SCI, 4 July 1792, recorded in the SCI Minutes Book for 6 July 1792 (Place Papers, British Library). Holcroft and Hollis took care of final arrangements for the original publication as Paine left for France to promote its publication there. See Fennessy, *Burke, Paine and the Rights of Man*, pp. 225-6; Keane *Tom Paine*, pp. 305.
35 Foner, II, p. 1319.

Reference Notes | Chapter III

36 Ibid., p. 1322; *A Letter Addressed to the Addressers on the Late Proclamation* (1792, Carlile reprint, 1819), p. 20.
37 Foner, II, p. 1322.
38 *Letter Addressed to the Addressers* (Carlile), p. 20; Foner, II, p. 1322.
39 Foner, II, p. 1322; *Letter Addressed to the Addressers*, p. 22.
40 See Keane, *Tom Paine*, pp. 304-5 (for Johnson) and p. 327 (for Chapman). The first part had been in danger of some excisions ('castrations' according to Thomas Holcroft), presumably at the hands of Johnson, but this was avoided when J.S. Jordan agreed to publish the full text with the addition of a short preface. See William St Clair, *The Godwins and the Shelleys* (London, 1989), p. 48; Fennessy, *Burke, Paine and the Rights of Man*, pp. 225-6.
41 *The Whole Proceedings on the Trial of an Information on Thomas Paine* (Martha Gurney, 1793, 2nd ed.), pp. 47 and 120.
42 Keane, *Tom Paine*, p. 340; Daisy Hay, *Dinner with Joseph Johnson* (London, 2022), p. 257.
43 *Letter Addressed to Addressers* (Carlile), p. 20.
44 Ibid., p. 21. The letter to Walker is printed in Thomas Walker, *The Original* (London, 1874), I, p. 41.
45 For consideration of this work by Peter De Bolla, see his *The Architecture of Concepts*, pp. 229-32. Very few digests of *Rights of Man* were published. Besides this one there was only one other cheap version: an abridgement of both parts in 23 pages published by John Thomson of Edinburgh in 1792. Finally, there was the expensive merger of parts I and II published by Eaton in 1795, the work of Paine himself and therefore unobjectionable.
46 *Letter Addressed to Addressers* (Carlile), p. 21.
47 In researching these cheap editions, De Bolla makes the mistake of overlooking the cheap Jordan edition and of failing to realise that the edition printed for the London booksellers is the edition Paine claimed to have published himself. See his *Architecture of Concepts*, p. 222.
48 *Letter Addressed to Addressers* (Carlile), pp. 20-1.
49 See Graham, *The Nation, the Law*, p. 264.
50 *Letter Addressed to Addressers* (Carlile), p. 21.
51 See Graham, *The Nation, the Law*, p. 333; Keane, *Tom Paine*, p. 342.
52 Especially pp. 20-1 (Carlile, 1819).
53 Foner, II, pp. 1324-5.
54 *See Letter Addressed to Addressers* (Carlile), pp. 22-3.
55 The proclamation is given in full in Thomas Walker's *A Review of Some of the Political Events in Manchester* (London, 1794), pp. 30-2.

56 See Fennessy, *Burke, Paine and the Rights of Man*, p. 243; Hay, *Dinner with Joseph Johnson*, p. 257.
57 See *Whole Proceedings on the Trial of Thomas Paine*, pp. 98-104.
58 See SCI Minute Book (B.L.) for 6 July 1792.
59 See *Letter Addressed to Addressers* (Carlile), p. 15.
60 Keane, *Tom Paine*, p. 342.
61 SCI Minute Book (B.L.), for 6 July 1792.
62 See *Letter Addressed to Addressers* (Carlile), pp. 15-6 and 23. In contrast, the earlier editions of the second part, all by Jordan and in both cheap and expensive versions, had been published in full.
63 See *Rights of Man, Part the Second* (Paine's cheap edition, 1792), pp. 43 and 78-9.
64 *The Proceedings on the Trial of Daniel Isaac Eaton for Selling the Second Part of Rights of Man* (Eaton, 1793, 2nd ed.), pp. 32-3.
65 For the passages specified as libellous, see *Whole Proceedings on Trial of Thomas Paine* (Gurney), pp. 6-43 and 98-104.
66 *Rights of Man, Part the Second* (Paine's cheap ed. 1792), pp. 21, 39-40, 43, 45, 50, 78-9, 84-5, 111.
67 Ibid., pp. 43, 78-9, 84-5.
68 See *Proceedings on the Trial of Daniel Isaac Eaton for Selling the Second Part of the Rights of Man*. The edition on trial was specified as published by Symonds and therefore expurgated (p. 2). But the Court proceeded by selecting other passages critical of the monarchy and the constitution.
69 For the poor sale of this edition, see below, p. 77.
70 Parson's work was peculiar in using the title 'Rights of Men' and in spelling the author's name as 'Pain'. For his normal publishing activities, see Jon Mee, *Print, Publicity and Radicalism in the 1790s* (Cambridge, 2016), p. 218, n. 60. Symonds had published the abridgement of *Rights of Man* by 'True-born Englishman' in early 1792 and went on to publish Paine's *Letter Addressed to the Addressers*, coincidentally with publishing his sixpenny edition of *Rights of Man*. For his pains, he suffered a long imprisonment. See Mee, op. cit., p. 138.
71 Foner, II, p. 1322.
72 See *Letter Addressed to Addressers* (Carlile), p. 15. Paine may well have been exaggerating sales to ridicule the government's attempt to stem the sale by means of the May proclamation. The proclamation had called upon subjects to profess support for the constitution which came to be expressed in the publication of addresses to the king. Paine's point was that the number of subjects who had signed these addresses was less than the number of copies his work had sold in the same period, thus demonstrating that the effect of the proclamation was to encourage rather than to discourage sales.

Reference Notes | Chapter III

73 The database of 526 copies (all published in the UK in 1791-2) is drawn from the Richard Gimbel collection in the Library of the American Philosophical Society; the Ambrose Barker collection in Thetford Public Library; the collection in the private possession of Michael Bush; and the online service for a large number of British and Irish libraries, including the British Library: Jisc Library Hub Discover (formerly Copac).

74 For this society and its connection with Paine, see Mee, *Print, Publicity and Radicalism in the 1790s*, pp. 73-90.

75 For the Association, see Graham, *The Nation, the Law*, pp. 407-8. For the effigy burning, see F. O'Gorman, 'The Paine Burnings of 1792-1793', *Past and Present*, 193 (2006), pp. 111-55. For the attack on Priestley, see Fennessy, *Burke, Paine and the Rights of Man*, p. 234.

76 See St Clair, *The Reading Nation in the Romantic Period*, Appendix 9.

77 *Letter Addressed to Addressers* (Carlile), p. 20; Graham, *The Nation, the Law*, pp. 264 and 266.

78 See above, p. 73.

79 See above, pp. 73-4.

80 *Rights of Man* (Collins), II, p. 177.

81 See *Letter Addressed to Addressers* (Carlile), p. 20.

82 See his letters to Washington (21 July 1791) and to Hall (25 Nov 1791) in Foner, II, pp. 1318-9 and 1322.

83 See Keane, *Tom Paine*, p. 333; Graham, *The Nation, the Law*, p. 219 (n. 47), Clark, *Thomas Paine*, p. 233; De Bolla, *Architecture of Concepts*, p. 232 (n. 53).

84 15 copies for the Eaton merger; 13 copies for the 1796 *Works*.

85 See Claeys, *The French Revolution Debate in Britain*, ch. 5.

86 Graham, *The Nation, the Law*, p. 335.

87 Goodwin, *Friends of Liberty*, pp. 272-3; Sherwin, *Memoirs of the Life of Thomas Paine*, pp. 137-8; Mee, *Print, Publicity and Radicalism in the 1790s*, p. 138. Eaton and Spence were acquitted on a technicality. For a full listing of indictments, see the *New Annual Register* for 1793.

88 For national convention, see *Rights of Man* (Collins), I, p. 96; ibid. II, pp. 287, 294; *Letter Addressed*, pp. 33-4, 39-40; and Goodwin, *Friends of Liberty*, ch. 8. For transportation, see ibid., p. 488. For action taken against London Corresponding Society and SCI, see ibid., ch. 9. For action against Walker, see Graham, *The Nation, the Law*, p. 602. For fresh legislation against seditious publications, see St Clair, *The Reading Nation in the Romantic Period*, p. 311. For the LCS connection with holding a Paineite convention, see Mee, *Print, Publicity and Radicalism*, pp. 88-109.

89 See Goodwin, *Friends of Liberty*, pp. 174-8 and 369-71; Clark, *Thomas Paine*, pp. 290-1; Gunther Lottes, 'Radicalism, revolution and political culture: an Anglo-French comparison' in Mark Philp (ed.), *The French Revolution and British Popular Politics*, pp. 83-5.
90 See Michael Laccohee Bush, *The Friends and Following of Richard Carlile* (Twopenny Press, 2016), ch. 6.
91 See his *The Life of Thomas Paine* (M.A. Carlile, 1820), p. xvii.
92 Bush, *Friends and Following*, pp. 86-7.
93 For *Rights of Man*, see Foner II, p. 910. For *Common Sense*, see Trish Loughran, *The Republic in Print* (New York, 2007), pp. 41-2.
94 For *Common Sense*, see Loughran, op. cit., pp. 56-8. For *Rights of Man*, see St Clair, *The Reading Nation in the Romantic Period*, pp. 256-7.
95 Foner, II, p. 1322.

Chapter IV Paine and the Tradition of Radical Reform

1 See Michael Laccohee Bush, *The Friends and Following of Richard Carlile* (Twopenny Press, 2016), pt. II.
2 See below, Appendix (b).
3 Bush, *Friends and Following*, ch. 6.
4 Ibid., ch. 18.
5 Ibid., chs. 19 and 20.
6 *Gauntlet*, p. 530.
7 See Bush, *Friends and Following*, Table A (pp. 165-70).
8 See Tilly's *A Brief History of Thomas Paine's Bones* (Watson, 1847), p. 3; *Cobbett's Register*, XXXV, col. 383.
9 See, for example, Penny Young, *Two Cocks on the Dunghill* (Twopenny Press, 2009), p. 58.
10 Paul Pickering, 'A grand ossification', in *Contested Sites*, ed. Pickering and Alex Tyrrell (Aldershot, 2003), pp. 67-8.
11 *The Trial of Henry Hunt* (Dolby, 1820), p. 156.
12 Bush, *Friends and Following*, pp. 117-19.
13 For text, see Richard Carlile, *An Effort to Set at Rest Some Little Disputes and Misunderstandings Between the Reformers at Leeds* (London, 1821), pp. 18-9. For the meeting in Stockport of delegates from these four counties to approve of the Declaration, See Bush, *Friends and Following*, p. 120.
14 Hunt, *Letter to Radical Reformers*, 11 April 1821, pp. 1-5; ibid., 9 Oct. 1821, pp. 2-5.
15 See above, p. 18.
16 *Effort to Set at Rest*, pp. 3-4; Carlile, *To the Reformers of Great Britain*, no. 5, p. 22.

17 For monarchy, see *Cobbett's Register*, XXXV, col. 384; George Spater, *William Cobbett* (Cambridge, 1982), p. 484. For church, see *Cobbett's Register*, XXXV, cols. 725 and 779; Spater, op. cit., p. 548.
18 See *Cobbett's Register*, XXXV, cols. 709-10, 781-2.
19 Bush, *Friends and Following*, p. 116.
20 Ibid., pp. 87-9.
21 That this was probably not true: see *Lion*, I, p. 27.
22 To Carver, see *Republican*, VIII, pp. 131-2.
23 See below, p. 164.
24 For this division, see Bush, *Friends and Following*, ch. 8.
25 Ibid., pp. 99-100, 129-30.
26 *Republican*, VII, p. 47.
27 Bush, *Friends and Following*, p. 129.
28 For Hunt, see the passage from one of his letters quoted in *Republican*, V, pp. 261-2. For the charge of cowardice, see Bush, *Friends and Following*, pp. 129-30.
29 *Prompter*, p. 23.
30 See his letter quoted in *Republican*, XI, p. 170.
31 *Republican*, XIII, pp. 482-7. For the context to this remark, see M.L. Bush, *What is Love?* (London, 1998), passim.
32 *Republican*, XIII, p. 493.
33 Ibid., X, pp. 755-62.
34 Ibid., XII, pp. 381-2.
35 Ibid., XI, pp. 282-3; ibid., XIII, pp. 193 and 776; *Lion*, II, p. 100.
36 Thomas Wooler was responsible for the revised edition, which he also serialised in his weekly paper the *Black Dwarf*. Several years earlier, in 1809, Bentham had asked Cobbett to be its publisher but he, at that point, was yet to approve of universal suffrage and so turned it down.
37 For antiquity of the constitution, see Cartwright, *Take Your Choice* (London,1776), p. 15; his *An Appeal Civil and Military on the Subject of the English Constitution* (London, 1797), pp. 219-26; his *The English Constitution Produced and Illustrated* (London, 1823), pp. 85, 115, 197-200. For the check on despotism, see his *Take Your Choice*, pp. 52-3.
38 See Spater, *William Cobbett*, pp. 344-5.
39 See his *English Constitution Produced*, p. 217.
40 Ibid., p. 186.
41 For the Lords, see ibid., pp. 182-3, 185. For the monarch, see ibid., pp. 146-7, 149-51. For Paine's use of this image, see above, p. 13.
42 See Young, *Two Cocks*, p. 276; John Belchem, *Orator Hunt* (Oxford, 1985), pp. 194-5; Spater, *William Cobbett*, pp. 489-90.

43 *Poor Man's Guardian* (Merlin Press), II, p. 448.
44 See *Cosmopolite*, no 27 (8 September 1832).
45 See Young, *Two Cocks*, p. 362. She is quoting from *Cobbett's Weekly Register* for 21 March 1835.
46 Ibid.
47 See Joel H. Wiener, *The War of the Unstamped* (Cornell, 1969), pp. 154-5, 166-7, 214-8.
48 *Life and Struggles of William Lovett*, ed. R.H. Tawney (London, 1920), pp. 74-5.
49 *Poor Man's Guardian* (Merlin Press), I, p. 38.
50 I.J. Prothero, *Artisans and Politics* (London,1979), p. 292. The Hetherington (1832) and Richard Carlile junior (1834) editions had frontispieces depicting a military struggle between civilians and professional troops, in which the former were getting the upper hand, whereas the 'John Smith' edition showed soldiers fighting soldiers. The Hetherington edition, followed by that of Carlile's son, focused the message down by indicating on the title page that their aim was to provide instructions on 'street and house fighting' rather than, in the manner of the 'John Smith' edition, to instruct on 'street and house fighting and field fortification'.
51 Bush, *Friends and Following*, pp. 398 and 406-7.
52 Watson was cheered when he advocated the abolition of the new police on the grounds that they were 'an incipient military force established for putting [the people] down if dared to cry for freedom'. See *Poor Man's Guardian*, II, p. 522.
53 See ibid., pp. 489-90.
54 See Prothero, *Artisans and Politics*, p. 285.
55 See Bush, *Friends and Following*, pp. 51-2.
56 For his involvement with mercury, see ibid., pp. 46-7.
57 Hibbert to Carlile 9 Aug 1833. See Microfilm of Carlile Papers, reel III.
58 See the account of Francis Place, in D.J. Rowe (ed), *London Radicalism, 1830-1849* (London Record Society, 1970), pp. 140-1.
59 Prothero, *Artisans and Politics*, pp. 281-5.
60 Wiener, *The War of the Unstamped*, pp. 215-6.
61 For banning Radical Reformers, see Prothero, *Artisans and Politics*, p. 281. For admitting the NUWC, see ibid., p. 284.
62 See Bush, *Friends and Following*, pp. 83, 86-7.
63 See his *Grand National Holiday and Congress of the Productive Classes* (London, 1832), pp. 4, 6-8; I.J. Prothero, 'William Benbow and the Concept of the General Strike', *Past and Present*, 63 (1974), pp. 132-71.
64 *Poor Man's Guardian*, II, pp. 472 and 474.
65 For its organisation, see *Poor Man's Guardian*, I, pp. 140-1, 279; ibid., II p. 621.

Reference Notes | Chapter IV

In the period 1831-33 (as recorded in the *Poor Man's Guardian*, vols. I and II), provincial branches were found operating in the North at Manchester, Salford, Blackburn, Rochdale, Hyde, Bolton, Leeds, Macclesfield, Congleton, Chorley, Middleton, Wheelton, Padiham and Heywood; in the Midlands at Birmingham, Radford near Nottingham, Northampton, Leicester and Kenilworth; in the South-east, extensively in the London area, Norwich, Chatham, Brighton, Horsham; in the South-West at Bristol, Somerton and Winchester. In London, the Union had groups of supporters in Finsbury, Wandsworth, Southwark, Tower Hamlets, Hammersmith and Camberwell. A problem of identification is set by the fact that, at the time, as well as the National Union of the Working Classes there was the National Political Union which was distinctly different in that its membership was middle as well as working class and its political reform programme allowed it to accept the 1832 Reform Act and the property franchise integral to it. What is listed above are only unions explicitly affiliated to the NUWC.

66 Belchem, *Orator Hunt*, pp. 250-5; Prothero, *Artisans in Politics*, p. 285.
67 For first meeting, see above, p. 94. For second meeting, see *Poor Man's Guardian*, II, p. 470.
68 Prothero bizarrely omits to mention the second (see *Artisans and Politics*, pp. 284, 287-8), while Lovett bizarrely omits to mention the first (see *Life and Struggles*, pp. 73-5).
69 It was printed as part of a much longer document entitled 'Rules of the National Union of the Working Classes'. See Rowe (ed.), *London Radicalism*, pp. 29-32.
70 See above, p. 11.
71 See above, pp. 17-8.
72 *Prompter*, p. 485 (for his criticism) and p. 490 (for his approval).
73 See Rowe (ed.), *London Radicalism*, pp. 29 and 141.
74 Ibid., pp. 37-8.
75 Ibid., pp. 51-2.
76 The text is to be found in the *Poor Man's Guardian*, I, pp. 140-1. It was also included in Lovett's *Life and Struggles* (pp. 74-5) and in Linton's biography of Watson. See W.J. Linton, *James Watson, a Memoir* (London, 1880), pp. 40-2. Lovett's text, like the one included in the *Poor Man's Guardian*, has an additional preamble and conclusion. It was printed as a handbill calling upon the 'Useful Classes of London' to attend a meeting to support the declaration on 7 November in front of White Conduit House and pressing the working classes throughout the country to gather in public meetings on the same day 'to re-echo these principles'. See Rowe(ed.), *London Radicalism*, p. 52.
77 See above, p. 23.

78 See Linton, *James Watson, a Memoir*, pp. 21-2.
79 Ibid., p. 41.
80 For the nature of this work, see Michael Bush, 'A message from Mab', *North West Labour History Journal*, 29 (2004), pp. 19-25. The Watson edition, although undated, must have appeared around 1840.
81 See below, p. 171.
82 Malcolm Chase, *Chartism* (Manchester, 2007), pp. 7-9.
83 Lovett, *Life and Struggles*, p. 82. When Hibbert died in 1834, Lovett described him as 'our estimable friend'. See ibid., pp. 90-1.
84 See *Working Man's Friend*, p. 106.
85 Lovett, *Life and Struggles*, pp. 73 and 77.
86 The text is to be found in the Place Papers, see Rowe (ed.), *Radical London*, pp. 122-4.
87 See David Goodway, *London Chartism, 1838-48* (Cambridge,1982), pp. 21-2.
88 Malcolm Chase, *The People's Farm* (Oxford,1988), pp. 160-2.
89 Rowe (ed.), *London Radicalism*, pp. 29 and 31.
90 Ibid., p. 52.
91 Quoted by Belchem in *Orator Hunt*, pp. 263-4.
92 *Poor Man's Guardian*, II, p. 638.
93 Ibid., p. 663.
94 Ibid., (no. 83), p. 18.
95 Lovett, *Life and Struggles*, p. 75; Linton, *James Watson*, p. 42.
96 *Poor Man's Guardian*, I, pp. 27-9.
97 Ibid., I, pp. 13-14.
98 See above, p. 18. For the history of national conventions and their association with Paine, see T.M. Parssinen, 'Association, convention and anti-parliament in British radical politics', *English Historical Review*, 88 (1973), pp. 507-32, esp. pp. 511-2.
99 *Common Sense* (Kramnick), pp. 97-9.
100 Ibid., p. 97.
101 *Rights of Man* (Collins), I, pp. 94-5.
102 Ibid., II, p. 294.
103 *Letter Addressed to Addressers* (Carlile, 1819), pp. 19, 39-40.
104 See ibid., pp. 43-4.
105 Ibid., pp. 34-5.
106 See ibid., pp. 42-3.
107 For Gerrald's proposed convention, see Albert Goodwin, *The Friends of Liberty* (London, 1979), ch. 9. For Carlile's proposed convention, see the *Republican*, IV, pp. 469-78; and, for the attempted convention in 1821, see Bush, *Friends and*

Following, pp. 120-3. For Hetherington's proposed convention, see below, pp. 106-7.

108 It is described in the conclusion to John Cartwright's *Take Your Choice* (London, 1776).
109 *Letter Addressed to Addressers* (Carlile), pp. 34-5.
110 For 1793-4, see Goodwin, *Friends of Liberty*, chs. 8 and 9; John Barrell, *Imagining the King's Death* (Oxford, 2000), chs. 3, 4, 6. For 1831-3, see below, ch. IV(f). For Chartist conventions, see Parssinen, 'Association, convention', *English Historical Review*, 88 (1973), pp. 521ff.
111 The full text is provided by a parliamentary report of an incident occurring on 13 May 1833. See Report from *Select Committee on Cold Bath Fields Meeting* (dated 23 August 1833), pp. 20-21. The point made was that this circular was first published 'when the House of Lords rejected the Reform Bill (i.e., in October 1831), as well as being republished in May 1833.
112 Lovett, *Life and Struggles*, p. 78. Suggestive of an affiliation to Bentham was the use of the phrase 'the greatest happiness of the greatest number' in the first version of the second declaration.
113 Lovett, op. cit., p. 78.
114 Ibid.
115 See below, ch. IV (f) and (g).
116 See Nancy LoPatin, *Political Unions: Popular Politics of the Great Reform Act of 1832* (Palgrave, 1999), passim.
117 See above, p. 106.
118 See Prothero, *Artisans and Politics*, ch. 15.
119 See above, pp. 199-100 (the declarations); p. 104 (Hetherington).
120 *Poor Man's Guardian*, I, p. 27. The letter resonates the very wealthy Julian Hibbert.
121 Michael J. Turner, *Radicalism and Reputation: The Career of Bronterre O'Brien* (Michigan, 2017), p. 120.
122 See *Effects of Civilization* (London, 1805), pp. 3-4, 47-9.
123 Ibid., pp. 49-50.
124 Ibid., pp. 74-5.
125 Ibid., p. 128.
126 David Stack, *Nature and Artifice: The Life and Thoughts of Thomas Hodgskin* (Boydell, 1998), ch. 5.
127 Locke, *Two Treatises of Government*, chs. V and IX; H.T. Dickinson, *Liberty and Property* (London, 1977), pp. 68-9.
128 See the remarks made by the Spencean Richard Moore of Manchester in 1822, recorded in *Drakard's Stamford News*, 13 Dec. 1822 (Radical Records, no. 10).
129 Turner, *Radicalism and Reputation*, pp. 166-7. Also see O'Brien's translation of

Buonorotti's History of Babeuf's Conspiracy for Equality (London, 1836), especially his 'To the Reader'.

130 *Buonarroti's History of Babeuf's Conspiracy*, pp. 158, 270.
131 Ibid., pp. 314-5.
132 Turner, *Radicalism and Reputation*, pp. ix-x. It appeared again ten years later in his *Propositions of the National Reform League for the Peaceful Regeneration of Society* (London, 1850).
133 Turner, *Radicalism and Reputation*, pp. 162-3.
134 Ibid., p. 46.
135 Paine's welfare schemes appear in *Rights of Man* (Collins), II, pp. 262-70; and in his *Agrarian Justice* (Paris, 1797), pp. 57-8. O'Brien's welfare plans appear in *A Brief Inquiry into the Natural Rights of Man* (1852), pp. 57-8.
136 For O'Brien, see Turner, *Radicalism and Reputation*, pp. 48-9. For Paine, see *Agrarian Justice*, preface. Watson made his point in a sermon entitled 'The Wisdom and Goodness of God Having Made both Rich and Poor'.
137 For Paine, see above, p. 14. For O'Brien, see Turner, *Radicalism and Reputation*, p. 46.
138 For Paine, see above, p. 19. For O'Brien, see Turner, *Radicalism and Reputation*, p. 58.
139 See ibid., p. 87 and below.
140 See *Poor Man's Guardian*, III, p. 397; ibid., p. 422. Leaders offering advice to the trades' unions appeared in issues 131-6.
141 Turner, *Radicalism and Reputation*, pp. 177-8.
142 Ibid., p. 150.
143 Ibid., pp. 96-8; *Poor Man's Guardian*, II, p. 130.
144 Turner, *Radicalism and Reputation*, p. 146.
145 Ibid., p. 126.
146 Ibid., pp. 124-5.
147 *Poor Man's Guardian*, II, pp. 617-8.
148 Ibid., pp. 649-51
149 *Destructive*, pp. 352-3.
150 *Poor Man's Guardian*, II, pp. 617-8.
151 Ibid., p. 638.
152 Ibid., p. 646; ibid., p. 655; *Poor Man's Guardian*, II (no. 83), pp. 6-7.
153 Ibid. II, pp. 645-6.
154 Ibid., p. 637. O'Brien's rejection of Paine is touched upon in Matthew Roberts, 'Posthumous Paine in the United Kingdom, 1809-1832', *The Legacy of Thomas Paine in the Transatlantic World* (London, 2018), ed. Sam Edwards and Marcus Morris, pp. 125-6.

155 Ibid., pp. 99-100.
156 For Hetherington, see above, p. 104. For the declarations, see above, pp. 99-100.
157 See a series of leaders on the nature of property, all by O'Brien in the *Poor Man's Guardian* from 6 Dec 1832 to 20 April 1833. For citations of Hodgskin, see ibid., II, pp. 33, 56 and 125.
158 See above, pp. 104, 107.
159 See *Poor Man's Guardian*, I, pp. 400 and 407.
160 Ibid., I, p. 400.
161 Ibid.
162 Ibid., pp. 400 and 407.
163 Ibid., II, pp. 60 and 133.
164 Ibid., I, pp. 418-19. Also see Prothero, *Artisans and Politics*, p. 360 (n. 35).
165 *Poor Man's Guardian*, II, p. 60.
166 Ibid., p. 124.
167 Ibid., p. 133.
168 Ibid., p. 140.
169 See Chase, *The People's Farm*, pp. 146-7.
170 *Poor Man's Guardian*, II, p. 140.
171 Ibid., pp. 140-1.
172 Ibid., pp. 147-8.
173 *Working Man's Friend*, pp. 17, 33, 41 and 65.
174 To include him, the full title of the party was National Union of the Working Classes and Others.
175 *Destructive*, p. 103.
176 Ibid.
177 For 'Letter from a Poor Man', see above, pp. 103-4, 109.
178 *Poor Man's Guardian*, II, p. 144.
179 For the 1831 proclamation, see above, p. 104. When questioned about the 1833 proclamation by a select committee of parliament, Melbourne claimed that it was 'hardly a proclamation' (i.e. a royal proclamation). See *Report from Select Committee on Cold Bath Fields Meeting* (House of Commons, 1833), pp. 190-1. Essentially, it was a notice of illegality, authorised 'by order of the secretary of state'. Since it was not signed, it was thought to lack validity: see ibid., p. 32 (Stallwood), Watson's *Working Man's Friend*, p. 173 (taken from the *True Sun*) and comments by John Gast in *Poor Man's Guardian*, II, p. 165. The Union committee also questioned its genuineness, claiming that it might have been a loyalist 'lark': ibid., p. 79 (Carpenter). Melbourne claimed that it was a well-tried and tested emergency device but admitted that it had been used only once before: in response to the Fast Day Procession, also organised by the Union,

held on 21 March 1832. See ibid. pp. 190-1. He failed to recall the occasion of its use in 1831. In resting not on the law or on the royal prerogative, but upon his own personal interpretation of what was legal, its soundness was arguably in question.

180 See *Poor Man's Guardian*, II, p. 157.
181 For the placard, see ibid. The original placard is depicted in Hannah Awcock's online article 'On this Day: the Cold Bath Fields Riots, 13 May 1833'. It reproduced word for word much of the announcement made by Russell in the *Poor Man's Guardian*. See *Poor Man's Guardian*, II, pp. 144 and 154.
182 *Poor Man's Guardian*, II, p. 154.
183 Ibid., p. 157.
184 See *Poor Man's Guardian*, which provides the Union's account of what happened with reprints of pieces that had appeared in the *Times* and the *True Sun* (vol. II, pp. 155-60) ; the *Gauntlet* which printed another piece from the *Times*, plus a piece called 'Another account' and 'Testimony of an Eye-witness' (who was probably Julian Hibbert) (see pp. 232-6), as well as reports on the examination of prisoners at Bow Street Police Station (pp. 234-5) and relating to the Coroner's Inquest on Culley (pp. 246-53); and *Report from Select Committee*, passim. A study of the incident by Gavin Thurston, entitled *The Clerkenwell Riot* (1967), honestly admits which side he is on not only in the book's title but also in its dedication to 'My Friends in the Metropolitan Police'. Although an apology for the police, it usefully provides a plan of Cold Bath Fields based on one prepared for the Commons' Select Committee, and facsimiles of the proclamation ordered by the Home Secretary to declare the meeting illegal and of the circular/placard produced by the NUWC to announce the meeting.
185 *Poor Man's Guardian*, II, p. 158.
186 *Gauntlet*, p. 232. Taken from the *Times*.
187 For one o'clock, see *Poor Man's Guardian*, II, p. 158. Taken from the *New Sun*. For two o'clock, see ibid.
188 See *Report from Select Committee*, p. 70 (Carpenter).
189 Taken from the Francis Place Papers located in the British Library, all three declarations appear in Rowe (ed.), *London Radicalism*. For first declaration, see pp. 29-33. For second declaration, see p. 52; For third declaration, see pp. 122-4.
190 *Report from Select Committee*, pp. 78-9 (Carpenter).
191 Ibid. For the lack of hustings, see *Times* report reprinted in *Gauntlet*, p. 233.
192 For the military, see *Gauntlet*, p. 233 (from *Times*); and *Report from Select Committee*, pp. 115 (De Roos), 127 (Bulkeley).
193 Ibid.
194 *Gauntlet*, p. 233 ('Another Account').

Reference Notes | Chapter IV

195 *Report from Select Committee*, pp. 18-9 (Rowan and Mayne).
196 The figure 3,000-4,000 was given in a *Times* report, reprinted in *Gauntlet*, p. 233.
197 *Poor Man's Guardian*, II, p. 158.
198 For the eye-witness account, see *Gauntlet*, p. 235. The *Poor Man's Guardian* (p. 158) suggests that police commissioners along with 1,800 policemen had been there 'early on the ground', so before noon.
199 See the report in *Poor Man's Guardian*, II, pp. 91-3.
200 Implied by Lord Melbourne: see *Report from Select Committee*, pp. 191-2.
201 *Poor Man's Guardian*, II, p. 158; *Gauntlet*, p. 235 ('Testimony of an Eye-witness'). The committee members present were identified by Place. See Rowe (ed.), *Radical London*, p. 125. They were Lee, Mee, Yearly, Preston and probably Russell. Two had resigned on 10 May (Petrie and Bayley). There is no evidence to suggest that former leaders of the Union, such as Lovett, Watson, Hetherington and Cleave, were present. And Petrie's reason for resigning – the result of faction-fighting within the leadership – might have applied to them. See ibid., p. 125.
202 *Poor Man's Guardian*, II, p. 158. For Mee on the railing, see *Gauntlet*, p. 248 (De Roos). For Lee on the railing, see ibid., p. 246 (Stallwood). There are several versions of the speech, the result of witnesses thinking Mee had addressed the crowd as 'important'(*Poor Man's Guardian*, II, p. 158); or 'respectable' (*Report from Select Committee*, pp. 70, (Carpenter), 194 (Beasley)) or 'gentlemen' (*Gauntlet*, p. 246 (Stallwood)).
203 See *Report of Select Committee*, p. 79.
204 *Poor Man's Guardian*, II, p. 158.
205 See above, p. 117.
206 See *Report from Select Committee*, pp. 19-20 (Rowan and Mayne).
207 *Poor Man's Guardian*, II, p. 158; *Gauntlet*, pp. 233 ('Another Account'), 235 ('Testimony of an Eye-witness'). For Irish appearance, see *Working Man's Friend*, p. 170 (quoting from the *Globe*).
208 That they were from south of the river, on the evidence of their flags, see *Poor Man's Guardian*, II, p. 27. For a Camberwell connection, see *Gauntlet*, p. 235 ('Testimony of an Eye-witness'). For the route taken, see the evidence of Joseph Dell, who encountered them in Holborn and accompanied them to the meeting (*Gauntlet*, p. 235).
209 Ibid., p. 249.
210 *Report from the Select Committee*, pp. 124 (Bulkeley), 129-30 (May), 210 (Jeffery).
211 See the eye-witness account of the cabinet maker, John Jeffery (*Report from Select Committee*, p. 210).
212 *Gauntlet*, p. 233 ('Another Account'); *Report from Select Committee*, p. 210. (Jeffery).

213 See ibid., p. 79 (Carpenter).
214 For the man in the white hat, see *Gauntlet*, p. 233 ('Another Account'). For the circular in favour of national conventions, see *Report from Select Committee*, p. 8 (police commissioners' report) and 20-21 (Rowan and Mayne). The Union's placard giving notice of the meeting also received little notice. The tendency of the eyewitnesses was to confuse it with the government's proclamation declaring the proposed meeting as illegal. William Carpenter's mention of it (see *Report of the Select Committee*, p. 70) was most unusual. It was more common for people to be drawn to the meeting by the government proclamation banning it. As the journalist James Grant put it: 'I did not see the proclamation (i.e., placard) which was issued by (i.e., for) the National Convention, and I should not have known that the meeting was to be held if I had not seen the government proclamation'. See *Gauntlet*, p. 248. For the number of copies printed see Rowe, *London Radicalism*, p. 122. That no mention was made of a national convention by Mee at the meeting was pointed out by William Carpenter who stood close by and within hearing. See *Report from Select Committee*, p. 79.
215 For previous declarations of intent to hold such a meeting, see above, pp. 103-7, 147-8 and ch. IV (f).
216 See an anonymous loyalist account printed in the *Gauntlet*, p. 233 ('Another Account'). Several of these colours, confiscated by the police, were exhibited before the Commons' Select Committee. See *Report from Select Committee*, pp. 146 (Clipson), 152 (Swindlehurst), 155 (Tyrrell), 180 (Redwood).
217 It takes up the whole issue for 11 April 1832 (II, no. 44). Also see the *Working Man's Friend*, p. 144.
218 Ibid., pp. 155-6.
219 *Poor Man's Guardian*, II, p. 158.
220 *Report from Select Committee*, p. 10 (Rowan and Mayne).
221 *Report from Select Committee*, p. 210 (Jeffrey). For Gough Street unit, see *Gauntlet*, pp. 233 ('Another Account'), 248 (De Roos).
222 *Poor Man's Guardian*, II, pp. 158-9; *Report from Select Committee*, pp. 182-4 (Hunter); *Gauntlet*, pp. 233 (from the *Times*), 246 (Stallwood), 247-8 (Courtenay), 235-6 ('Testimony of an Eye-witness'). Police and military accounts claim that no injuries were inflicted on the crowd, whereas civilian accounts predominately claim a carnage committed by the police.
223 For aim to seize the flags, see *Report from Select Committee*, p. 129 (May).
224 *Gauntlet*, p. 247 (Everard); *Report from Select Committee*, pp. 36 (Stallwood), 100 (Robertson), 164 (Courtenay).

225 Ibid., pp. 156 (Baker), 171-2 (Abbott), 180 (Redwood); *Gauntlet* (from the *Times*), p. 233.
226 *Poor Man's Guardian*, II, p. 158.
227 *Report from Select Committee*, pp. 106-7 (Browning).
228 Ibid., pp. 43 (Hudson), 57 (Newton), 83 (Bowyer).
229 *Report from Select Committee*, pp. 57 (Newton), 107 (Browning).
230 Ibid., pp. 171-2 (Abbott). For drunkenness, see *Gauntlet*, p. 250 (Robinson); *Report from Select Committee*, pp. 36-7 (Stallwood), 44 (Hudson).
231 *Gauntlet*, p. 245 (papers relating to coroner's inquest on Culley).
232 Ibid., pp. 235-6.
233 For the select committee's opinion, see *Report from Select Committee*, pp. 3-4. It was based on an examination of over 60 witnesses (p. 5). For the Coroner's Inquest, the verdict of the jury found fault with the police for failing to read the Riot Act and the proclamation declaring the meeting illegal, for failing to prevent the meeting from taking place, and for their 'ferocious, brutal and unprovoked' conduct, see *Gauntlet*, p. 252. For convictions for stone-throwing, see *Report from Select Committee*, pp. 207-8.
234 See *Poor Man's Guardian*, I, pp. 320–2 (for procession), p. 333 (for view of police).
235 For police noting what had been said by the Union leaders prior to the meeting, see *Report from Select Committee*, pp. 18-20 (Rowan and Mayne).
236 *Poor Man's Guardian*, II, pp. 163-4.
237 Ibid., pp. 169-70.
238 See *Working Man's Friend*, p. 258.
239 See below, p. 165-6.
240 See *Gauntlet*, pp. 265-6.
241 See Bush, *Friends and Following*, ch. 20.
242 Ibid., pp. 412-3.
243 Ibid., pp. 413-6.
244 Ibid., pp. 400-401; *Prompter*, p. 35.
245 See Bush, *Friends and Following*, pp. 422-3. He was no longer proprietor of the Rotunda, having allowed his lease to lapse in March 1832. See ibid., p. 403.
246 Ibid., pp. 423-6.
247 For Carlile's damaged reputation, see M.L. Bush, *What is Love? Richard Carlile's Philosophy of Sex* (London,1998), pp. 120-31. For his drug habit, see ibid., pp. 4-5.
248 Bush, *Friends and Following*, pp. 453-4.
249 See ibid., conclusion.
250 See ibid., pp. 457-62. For his 'true Christianity', see ibid, pp. 35-7.
251 *Poor Man's Guardian*, II, p. 238; ibid., p. 244.

252 Ibid., III, p. 440; ibid., IV, p. 429. Lovett made a similar point, see his *Life and Struggles*, I, pp. 88-9. So did Watson, see Linton, *James Watson*, pp. 43-4.
253 *Poor Man's Guardian*, III, pp. 357-8. For a series of O'Brien leaders on trades' unions, see Ibid., pp. 18 (Feb. 1834), 25-6, 50, 58, 65-7, 74-5, 81, 84, 123, 129-30, 222, 294, ibid IV, pp. 428, 545, 630 and 711.
254 Made evident in *Poor Man's Guardian*, vols. III and IV.
255 Ibid., IV, pp. 761-2, 785-6.
256 See above, ch. IV (e).
257 See Paine, *Rights of Man* (Collins), II, p. 188.
258 See above, pp. 93-4.
259 *Poor Man's Guardian*, II, p. 619.
260 Ibid., p. 621.
261 See above, pp. 17-8.
262 *Poor Man's Guardian*, II, p. 100 (1833).
263 Ibid., III, p. 440.
264 Ibid., III, p. 22.
265 For 1831, see *Poor Man's Guardian*, I, pp. 39-40. For 1832, see ibid., II, pp. 480 and 482-3. For 1833, see ibid., pp. 236 and 247-9. For 1834, see ibid., III, p. 200. On this occasion there was no report, only an advertisement of the forthcoming event.
266 See above, pp. 113-5.
267 *Poor Man's Guardian*, III, p. 33.
268 Ibid., pp. 81-2.
269 Ibid., p. 82.
270 *Poor Man's Guardian*, III, p. 114.
271 Ibid., p. 291.
272 Ibid., p. 305.
273 Ibid., p. 307.
274 Ibid., p. 362.
275 Ibid.
276 Ibid., p. 342.
277 Ibid., p. 374.
278 E.g. ibid., III, pp. 155 and 163; ibid., IV, pp. 663, 729, 730.
279 For O'Brien's land nationalisation scheme of the mid-1830s, see ibid., III, pp. 140, 154, 330, 370-l. For his faith in universal suffrage, see above, p. 113.
280 James Epstein, *The Lion of Freedom: Feargus O'Connor and the Chartist Movement, 1832-42* (London, 1982), pp. 77-8.
281 See Paul Pickering, 'The heart of millions: Chartism and popular monarchy in the 1840s', *History*, 88 (2003), p. 243.

Reference Notes | Chapter IV

282 See ibid., p. 235. As leader of the London Working Men's Association, Lovett was involved in presenting a memorial to Queen Victoria. Following its rejection, he sent an address to the USA telling its citizens that they had shown the world that a monarchy was not a necessary prerequisite of a nation's greatness, whereas a Paineite republican would have made the point that a nation's greatness must wholly depend upon its being a republic.

283 See Linton, *James Watson*, pp. 45-7.

284 Chase, *Chartism*, pp. 7-9; Linton, *James Watson*, pp. 46-7.

285 See A.R. Schoyen, *The Chartist Challenge: a Portrait of George Julian Harney* (London, 1958), pp. 12-4.

286 See Dorothy Thompson (ed.), *The Early Chartists* (London, 1971), doc. 3.

287 See Jennifer Bennett, 'The London Democratic Association', *The Chartist Experience*, ed. by James Epstein and Dorothy Thompson (London,1982), p. 90.

288 Ibid., pp. 90-94.

289 Quoted by Schoyen in *The Chartist Challenge*, pp. 28-9. For a member of the NUWC uttering the same remark, see above, p. 117.

290 Bennett, 'The London Democratic Association', p. 94.

291 Ibid., pp. 102-3.

292 For an emphatic treatment of this point, see Matthew Roberts, *Chartism, Commemoration and the Cult of the Radical Hero* (London, 2020), ch. 5.

293 See Chase, *Chartism*, ch. 3. Another account in Epstein, *Lion of Freedom*, ch. 4 is over-emphatic about its revolutionary purpose. For the term, see Linton, *James Watson*, pp. 47-8; Lovett, *Life and Struggle*s, I, p. 205.

294 Linton, *James Watson*, p. 47.

295 See above, ch. IV(d).

296 See Pickering, 'The heart of millions', *History*, 88 (2003), p. 243.

297 See below, Appendix (b).

298 They all appear in a scrapbook, kept by Tilly and now in the possession of this book's author.

299 *A Political Tract by the Cobbett Club of London*, no I, pp. 40, 54-5.

300 See preface, pp. 1-2.

301 Roberts, *Chartism, Commemoration and the Cult of the Radical Hero*, p. 119.

302 Pickering, 'The heart of millions', *History*, 88, pp. 243-6.

303 Bush, *Friends and Following*, pp. 51-2.

304 For radical expectations of Queen Caroline, see, e.g., Spater, *William Cobbett*, pp. 401-8; and Carlile's *Republican*, IV, pp. 505-6, 517-8.

305 See Matthew Roberts, *Political Movements in Urban England*, 1832-1914 (Basingstoke, 2009), pp. 31-2.

306 See Gregory Claeys, *Citizens and Saints* (Cambridge, 1989), ch. 6.

307 For the distinction between Paine and Cartwright, see Caroline Robbins, *The Eighteenth-Century Commonwealthman* (Harvard, 1959 but reprinted from the 1968 ed.), pp. 361-2.

308 See above, pp. 16-7.

309 For Carlile's campaign to give the vote to women, see Bush, *Friends and Following*, pp. 20-1.

Chapter V General Conclusion

1 Robert Kee, *The Bold Fenian Men* (London, 1976), pp. 17-19; Marta Ramon, *A Provisional Dictator: James Stephens and the Fenian Movement* (Dublin, 2007), pp. 112-23.

2 *Rights of Man* (Collins, Pelican Classics, 1976), I, pp. 94-5; II, p. 294

3 See the Carlile (1819) edition, pp. 19, 39-40.

4 *Rights of Man* (Collins), II, pp. 262-4; *Agrarian Justice* (London, 1797), pp. 8-9.

5 See *Rights of Man* (Collins), II, p. 250.

Appendix: the Tale of Tom Paine's Bones

1 This work of detection is indebted to H.E. Howard, schoolmaster and crime writer, who showed the way in his teaching of history and in the novels he published under the nom-de-plume R. Philmore. I am grateful to the Thetford Branch Library for allowing me access to the Thomas Paine Collection, and the Rosary Cemetery in Norwich for letting me study its burial records.

2 Leo A. Bressler, 'Peter Porcupine and the bones of Thomas Paine', *Pennsylvania Magazine of History and Biography*, 82 (1958), p. 185.

3 Paul A. Pickering, 'A grand ossification: William Cobbett and the commemoration of Tom Paine', in *Contested Sites*, ed. by Pickering and Alex Tyrrell (Farnham, 2004), pp. 57, 71, 72.

4 See his *William Cobbett, the Press and Rural England* (Basingstoke, 2014), pp. 2 and 111. A similar account is given by Trish Loughran in *The Republic in Print* (New York, 2007), p. 14.

5 Paul Collins, *The Trouble with Tom: the Strange Afterlife and Times of Thomas Paine* (London, 2006), p. 233.

6 Ibid., p. 78.

7 For Mary Tilly, see ibid., p. 81. For Benjamin Tilly, see ibid., pp. 194-5. For the true dates of death, see their death certificates at GRO.

8 Collins, *Trouble with Tom*, p. 81.

9 Ibid., p. 249.

10 Ibid., pp. 176 and 185. For Tilly's reacquisition of the bones, see below, p. 175.
11 See *Catalogue of Thomas Paine Exhibition at South Place Institute* (London, 1895), exhibit 68 [hereafter, *Catalogue of Paine Exhibition*].
12 Collins, *Trouble with Tom*, pp. 186-7.
13 Paine Collection, Thetford Public Library, item 684.
14 Collins, *Trouble with Tom*, pp. 185-6.
15 See below, p. 177.
16 See below, p. 172.
17 For Mrs Ball, see below, p. 176. For Edward Smith, see below, p. 168 (his information on Chennell). For lock of hair, see below, p. 167.
18 Hereafter, see Conway's *Adventures*. There are two versions: one with this title and published by the Thomas Paine National Historical Association. It did not appear in full until 2002, although completed a century earlier. The other version was published in the *New York Sun* for 25 May 1902 and headed 'Where are Thomas Paine's Bones?' The 'Adventures' version is used here simply because it allows a more specific reference to be made to the content. However, the *New York Sun* version makes some revisions to the manuscript upon which the 'Adventures' version was based. For example, it dismisses as 'mythical' the point made in the 'Adventures' version (p. 2) that a little finger was removed before the remains were brought to England. It also rephrases the account of Alexander Gordon's connection with the remains, clarifying what happened.
19 Hereafter, Reynolds' *Thomas Paine's Bones*, p. 4. For his remarks on Mrs Ball, see ibid., p. 8. The catalogue of the 1895 Paine exhibition is in the British Library. 'Old Daylighter' was a reference to someone connected with a Norwich newspaper called *Daylight* that ran from 1878 to 1909.
20 *Poor Man's Guardian*, III, p. 364.
21 Located in the Place Newspaper Collection, set 51, of the British Library.
22 *Cobbett's Political Register*, XXXV, col. 383.
23 See *The Book of Wonders*, part the first (London, 1821), pp. 30-1. Also see *A Brief History of the Remains of Thomas Paine* (London, 1847), p. 5 [hereafter, Tilly's *Brief History*]. Also see Marguerite de Bonneville's account of the burial: printed in Craig Nelson, *Thomas Paine* (London, 2006), p. 323.
24 *Cobbett's Political Register*, XXXV, cols. 382-4.
25 Ibid., cols. 383-4 and 636.
26 For spectacular funeral, see ibid., col. 783. For monument, see ibid., cols. 783-4. For public exhibition of remains, see ibid., col. 636. For celebration of birth, see ibid., cols. 709-10, 781-2. For statue, *Black Dwarf*, III, col. 803. For Paine Clubs, see *Cobbett's Political Register*, XXXV, col. 709.

27 For his self-defensiveness, see, for example, his speech to the Radical Reformers at a dinner held in the first week of December 1819 to welcome him back to England (*Black Dwarf*, III, cols 802-3); and his letter of 6 Jan. 1820 to Earl Grosvenor (*Cobbett's Political Register*, XXXV, cols. 633-9).
28 *Cobbett's Political Register*, XXXV, cols. 383-4.
29 For example, see ibid., col. 384 and cols. 776-7. Also see Ian Dyck, 'Debts and liabilities: William Cobbett and Thomas Paine' in Dyck (ed.) *Citizen of the World* (Bromley, 1987), pp. 98-9.
30 These beliefs were elaborated upon in *Common Sense* and *Rights of Man* and simply summarised in his *Dissertation on First Principles of Government* (London, 1795). The role of corruption in a mixed system is stated in the conclusion of *Rights of Man* (Collins, Pelican Classics, 1969), I, p. 162.
31 See *Cobbett's Political Register*, XXXV, cols 384, 635-6 and 725; *Black Dwarf*, III, col. 802.
32 *Cobbett's Political Register*, XXXV, cols 387-9.
33 Ibid., XL, col. 546.
34 See *Agitator*, no. 1, p. 4 and II, p. 12. The named associates were a Mr Hulme of Lancaster, a Mr Clarke, a coach-limner of New York, a Mr Scott, formerly of Stamford, England, and Mr Morton, executor of Paine's will.
35 See Pickering, 'A grand ossification', p. 63; George Spater, *William Cobbett: the Poor Man's Friend* (Cambridge,1982), pp. 377-8.
36 *Cobbett's Political Register*, XXXV, col. 382.
37 Ibid., col. 777.
38 For acclaim, see Spater, *William Cobbett*, pp. 384-6; *Cobbett's Political Register*, XXXV, nos. 14-16. Some of these addresses may have had references to Paine removed prior to publication. For the outrage provoked, see, for example, *Book of Wonders*, cols. 31-4. Cobbett reckoned that three hundred newspapers made adverse comment. See *Cobbett's Political Register*, XXXV, col. 777.
39 Ibid., col. 382.
40 Ibid., col. 384. He brought with him Cobbett's report on Paine's remains, for publication in the Register.
41 See *Book of Wonders*, col. 30.
42 *Cobbett's Political Register*, XXXV, col. 777.
43 See *Book of Wonders*, col. 30.
44 See Spater, *William Cobbett*, pp. 384-6. His communications with the people at this time are reported in no. 13 of his *Register*: see his letters to the 'Reformers in and near Manchester' (cols. 387-9), to the people of Liverpool (col. 389), to the boroughreeves and constables of Manchester and Salford (cols. 392-5) and to the inhabitants of the County Palatine of Lancaster (cols. 401-4); and his account of

a roadside meeting near Coventry (cols. 403-8).
45 *Black Dwarf*, III, cols. 802-3.
46 Ibid., col. 803.
47 *Cobbett's Political Register*, XXXV, cols. 635-6.
48 Ibid., cols. 723-5, 737-8, 741-2.
49 Pickering, 'A grand ossification', p. 62.
50 See *Cobbett's Political Register*, XXXV, col. 776.
51 Ibid., col. 709.
52 Ibid., col. 783.
53 Pickering, op. cit., pp. 64-7.
54 Michael Laccohee Bush, *Friends and Following of Richard Carlile* (Twopenny Press, 2016), table A (pp. 165-70).
55 Ibid., XI, p. 171.
56 Ibid., VII, pp. 177-8.
57 See John Gardner, 'Cobbett's return to England in 1819', in *William Cobbett, Romanticism and the Enlightenment*, ed. James Grande and John Stevenson (London, 2015), p. 64.
58 Spater, *William Cobbett*, p. 392.
59 See Malcolm Chase, *1820* (Manchester, 2013), pp. 17 and 44.
60 For action taken against the supporters of Carlile, see ibid., p. 71; Bush, *Friends and Following*, pp. 90-1. For action taken against the principal leaders of parliamentary reform, see ibid., pp. 208-9. For Cobbett and the Cato Street Conspiracy, see Gardner, 'Cobbett's return to England in 1819', p. 67.
61 *Cobbett's Political Register*, XXXV, col. 538. Also see Spater, *William Cobbett*, p. 397.
62 Ibid., pp. 65ff.
63 See John Keane, *Tom Paine, a Political Life* (London, 1995), pp. 440-41.
64 All appeared in his *Miscellaneous Letters and Essays on Various Subjects by Thomas Paine*: 'To the Council of Five Hundred' (Jan., 1798), p. 123; 'To the English People on the Invasion of England' (New York, May 1804), pp. 146-54; 'Of Gun-boats'(New York, March 1807), pp. 215-20); and 'Of the Comparative Powers and Experience of Ships of War, Gun-boats and Fortifications' (New York, July, 1807), pp. 221-5. See Bush, *Friends and Following*, pp. 80-1.
65 See Tilly's *Brief History*, p. 5; Conway's *Adventures*, p. 7. King's family seat was at Ockham in Surrey, raising the possibility that the remains were removed to Surrey, not Hampshire.
66 See Spater, *William Cobbett*, p. 398.
67 For biographical details on Tilly, see Penny Young, *The Cobbett Club* (Farnham, 2015, published by the Cobbett Society), pp. 1-3. Also see Reynolds, *Thomas*

Paine's Bones, pp. 6-7, 25-6; C. Rexford Davis, 'Cobbett letters in the library', *Journal of the Rutgers University Library* (2012), p. 52; Spater, *William Cobbett*, p. 523.
68   See Tilly's *Brief History*, p. 5. For Tilly's admission, see Reynolds' *Thomas Paine's Bones*, p. 14.
69   Tilly's *Brief History*, p. 5.
70   See 'Surrey notes and queries' in *West Surrey Times* for 19 Jan. 1889. The plate came to be placed inside the chest containing the bones. See Tilly's *Brief History*, p. 5. It remained there until the 1860s and then mysteriously disappeared. See Reynolds' *Thomas Paine's Bones*, p. 22.
71   Tilly's *Brief History*, pp. 5-6; Reynolds' *Thomas Paine's Bones*, p. 16. Both are ambiguous as to whether the name inscribed was 'Paine' or 'Cobbett'. According to Conway, it was 'Cobbett'. See *Conway's Adventures*, p. 12.
72   Tilly's *Brief History*, p. 6; Reynolds' *Thomas Paine's Bones*, p. 16; Conway's *Adventures*, p. 6-7.
73   For Chennell's ownership of the coffin, see Edward Smith's contribution to *Notes and Queries*, series iv (1), p. 84. That Chennell had bought the coffin at the Normandy Farm auction of Jan. 1836, see 'Surrey notes and queries' in *West Surrey Times* for 19 Jan. 1889. That there was a pot of Paine's bones in the coffin, see a letter of George Williams, printed in the *Observer*, 14 February 1937. A contrary account was provided by George Reynolds, claiming that Chennell acquired the bones in 1833 as a payment for conveying Paine's remains from London to Normandy Farm (see Reynolds, *Thomas Paine's Bones*, p. 20). This supposition overlooks the fact that, at the time and until Cobbett's death, the remains were in a sealed chest.
74   Conway's *Adventures*, p. 12; Reynolds' *Thomas Paine's Bones*, pp. 26-7.
75   See *Notes and Queries* for 1887, series vii (3), p. 336. That the tradesman mentioned by Smith as the source of his information was Chennell's son, see Conway, *Adventures*, p. 11.
76   *Notes and Queries*, series iv (1), p. 24; *West Surrey Times*, 19 Jan. 1889.
77   See the *Observer*, 14 Feb. 1937 (letter to editor from George Williamson).
78   For the sum paid, see Conway's *Adventures*, p. 11. Conway suggested that Chennell bought the bones from the Wests, but it was the Wests who bought them from Chennell. See George Williamson's letter in the *Observer*, 14 February 1937.
79   Tilly's *Brief History*, p. 6; Conway's *Adventures*, p. 7.
80   Tilly's *Brief History*, p. 6
81   Ibid., pp. 6-7; Conway's *Adventures*, pp. 7 and 9; Reynold's *Thomas Paine's Bones*, p. 16. A contrary account was provided by Alexander Somerville who in October

1844 visited Ash in search of the bones and claimed he was told by 'Mr Weston' (West?) that six months earlier 'a gentleman' from London took the bones to London for burial. This appears less plausible than the Tilly account, especially because of what we know about Tilly's possession of the skeleton from 1844 until 1869.

82 See Tilly's *Brief History*, p. 5. There is a photograph of the house in Young's *The Cobbett Club*, inside of back cover. For the other addresses, see below, pp. 175-6.
83 Reynolds' *Thomas Paine's Bones*, p. 23; quoting from *Cobbett's Political Register*.
84 Tilly's *Brief History*, pp. 7-8.
85 Tilly's view of the constitution is set out in *A Political Tract by the Cobbett Club of London* (London, 1839), pp. 54-5 and also in a number of petitions to parliament to which he subscribed and probably drafted: one presented to the Commons on 12 August 1839, clauses 4, 5 and 11; another presented to the Lords on 8 June 1841, clauses 2, 7 and 8. For the objectional innovations, see the petition presented to the Commons on 1 September 1841, clauses 5-7, and the petition to the Commons of 6 August 1838, clause 6. These petitions are to be found in a Cobbett Club scrapbook kept by Tilly and summarised in Young's *The Cobbett Club*, pp. 7-8, 14-5.
86 For the former meaning of republicanism, see Cobbett Club scrapbook, the petition presented to the Lords on 8 June 1841, clause 7. For its latter meaning, see *A Political Tract by the Cobbett Club*, p. 54.
87 Cartwright was the main advocate of a House of Commons elected by universal male suffrage in accordance with the ancient constitution of the Anglo-Saxons. His advocacy began in 1776 (the same year that Paine proposed just the opposite in *Common Sense*) in *Take Your Choice*, culminating in *The English Constitution Produced and Illustrated* (London,1823), his definitive repudiation of Paine's provocative remark, as cited on the title page: 'No such thing as a constitution exists in England.'
88 See *A Political Tract by the Cobbett Club of London*, pp. 49ff.
89 See ibid., p. 54.
90 See a long essay entitled 'Grinding the Poor' by Benjamin Tilly which is partly printed and partly in manuscript. It appears in the Cobbett Club scrapbook, p.11.
91 See Tilly's *Brief History*, pp. 2-3. For the André incident, see Keane, *Tom Paine*, pp. 202-3. André's bones were finally reburied in Westminster Abbey, with a monument, in 1821. See Pickering, 'A grand ossification', p. 62 and n. 42 (p. 75). For the importance attached by Benbow to the André incident in the repatriation of Paine, see the *Agitator*, I, p. 4. For Benbow's prominence in commemorating Paine at this time, see Pickering, 'A grand ossification', p. 70.

92 Bressler, op. cit., *Pennsylvania Magazine of History and Biography*, 82 (1958), p. 185; Morris L. Pearl, *William Cobbett: a Bibliographical Account of his Life and Times* (Oxford, 1953), p. 205, n. 1.
93 Reynolds' *Thomas Paine's Bones*, p. 20. For Cowen's background, see the entry in *Oxford History of National Biography*, vol. 13.
94 See Bush, *Friends and Following*, pp. 200-3.
95 For this episode in his life, see W.J. Linton, *James Watson, a Memoir* (Manchester, 1880), pp. 22-3.
96 For the text, see *Life and Struggles of William Lovett* (ed. R.H. Tawney, 1920), pp. 74-5 and in Linton's biography of Watson, pp. 40-2. Lovett's version has an additional preamble and conclusion.
97 In spite of attempting to publish all Paine's works, Carlile, in a catalogue of Paine's works published in 1820, had to admit that this item was 'not seen'. For Watson's edition of it, see Linton, *James Watson*, p. 25 (footnote). It was included in Paine's complete works as published by William Dugdale (1844) and by Edward Truelove (1875).
98 See Margot Finn, *After Chartism* (Cambridge, 1993), p. 176. His commitment remained strong in 1870, evident in his enthusiasm for the Third French Republic (ibid., p. 276), but became passive to the point of denial after his election as MP for Newcastle in 1874. See Antony Taylor, *Down with the Crown* (London, 1999), pp. 98-9.
99 Reynolds' *Thomas Paine's Bones*, p. 20; Conway's *Adventures*, pp. 8-9. For Tilly's City address, see *London Trade Directory* for 1852.
100 Reynolds' *Thomas Paine's Bones*, pp. 8 and 20; Conway's *Adventures*, p. 10. These facts came to light as a result of a correspondence between Cowen and Conway. See Conway's *Adventures*, pp. 8-9.
101 Complicating the story, as told by Conway, is the response Ainslie's daughter Margaretta gave to Conway when in 1877 he enquired about the skull. She claimed that she saw it as a child (b. 1833) but thought it got lost in a house move, thus suggesting that it was acquired long before the auction of 1853 (Conway's *Adventures*, p. 9). This, however, was contradicted by her brother Oliver who claimed it was bought at the auction in 1853 and passed on to him on his father's death (ibid., p. 10).
102 See William E. Paul, *English Language Bible Translators* (Jefferson NC, 2003), pp. 8-9.
103 This information is provided by Conway. See his *Adventures*, pp. 9 and 11.
104 See Donald M. Lewis, *Lighten Their Darkness: the Evangelical Mission to Working-Class London, 1828-1860* (New York, 1985), ch. 3, especially pp. 72 and 75.

105 See Appendix to Ainslie's *An Examination of Socialism* (London,1840), p. 62. Truelove recalled the occasion thirty-six years later. See Conway's *Adventures*, p. 9.

106 See the correspondence between Conway and Truelove in the Paine Collection, Thetford Public Library, item 684. I am very grateful to Penny Young who transcribed this correspondence for my own personal use. Especially important is the letter Conway wrote to Truelove in May 1896, citing a letter from Truelove to Conway of Dec. 1876. See document no 4. In the same file is also an important letter from Truelove to Ainslie written in 1863 or 1864 (see document no. 7) which Truelove must have passed on to Conway.

107 See Conway's *Adventures*, p. 11.

108 For this second meeting, see Conway's *Adventures*, p. 9 and Thetford Paine Collection, item 684, document 4. Truelove's move to High Holborn is evident in his publication of George Drysdale's *Elements of Social Science* (London,1867) with Truelove's address given as 256 Holborn to which is added 'Removed from Temple Bar' (i.e. from '240 Strand, Three Doors from Temple Bar' where he had a shop since 1852).

109 For the extent of his conversion compare two of his funeral sermons: *Devotement to the Well-being of Mankind the Highest Form of Glorifying God* (London,1856); and *Discourse on the Death of William Hervey* (Brighton,1863).

110 See Conway's *Adventures*, p. 11. For Conway learning of Ainslie's ownership of the skull, see ibid., p. 9.

111 See Truelove's letter to Ainslie of 1863-4, Thetford Paine Collection, item 684, document no. 7.

112 For Holyoake and Conway, see Conway's *Adventures*, p. 11.

113 In 1852 he gave Mornington Road as his address in his pamphlet *The Defence of the Innocent* (1852), p. 29. He retained it as a residence until his death in 1876, the bones in situ. See Conway's *Adventures*, p. 11. He gave Trowmer Lodge as his address in 1852. See Conway's *Adventures*, pp. 9-10. It was also his address in 1852. See his pamphlet, *The Defence of the Innocent* (1853), p. 8. He was still renting the place in 1868. See Collins, *Trouble with Tom*, p. 182.

114 Conway's *Adventures*, pp. 10-11.

115 Ibid., pp. 9 and 11.

116 Ibid., p. 11.

117 See David W. Chen, 'Rehabilitating Thomas Paine, Bit by Bony Bit', *New York Times*, 30 March 2001. Also see Pickering, 'A grand ossification', p. 57. One snag would be the lack of heirs, Paine having been an only child and childless himself. Another would lie in the unavailability of other physical remains. See below.

118 Conway's *Adventures*, p. 11. For the contents, see below, p. 179.

119 Conway's *Adventures*, p. 11. This would suggest he had been shown the contents of the chest earlier, probably on that occasion when he paid Tilly a visit and found him sitting on the trunk to do his tailoring work.
120 See *London Trade Directories* for 1852, 1853, 1854, 1858, 1859 and 1860. He moved from 41 Gresham Street in 1851 (see Census Return for 1851) to 40A Gresham Street by 1852 and to 38 Gresham Street by 1853, remaining at that address until 1860.
121 For Mary's death in June 1860, see GRO. For Swain's membership of the Cobbett Club, see the Cobbett Club scrapbook: he chaired a meeting that produced a petition to the House of Commons, dated 6 July 1842. For Swain as Tilly's employer, see Reynolds' *Thomas Paine's Bones*, p. 6 .The rest of the evidence lies in the London Trade Directories. In the directory for 1859 Swain ceased to be listed as a clothier; in the directory for 1860 he was listed as a publican. Also see Census Return for 1861.
122 I am grateful to Penny Young for suggesting this not-implausible explanation.
123 The connection was made in Reynolds' *Thomas Paine's Bones* (p. 8), which declares that 'after Swain's death Tilly's business on his own account had failed'. As it stands this is incorrect since Swain did not die until 1880: that is, a decade after Tilly's death. However, if 'the death of Swain's tailoring business' is substituted, Reynolds' account begins to make sense, even more so as Reynolds' associated Tilly's business failure with his wife's death (see ibid.), which did occur in 1860.
124 For residence with niece, see Reynolds' *Thomas Paine's Bones*, p. 21 and Census Return for 1861 (under Pelley). For residence with the Balls, see Reynolds' *Thomas Paine's Bones*, p. 7. Harrow-on-the-Hill was the birthplace of Tilly's wife, making it likely that Mrs Ball was connected to Tilly through friendship or kinship with his wife. For residence with the Ginns, see ibid., pp. 5 and 7; Conway's *Adventures*, p. 8; and Tilly's death certificate (GRO).
125 For scrapbook, see Penny Young, *The Cobbett Club* (Cobbett Society, 2015), pp. 1-3. For interview with Mrs Ball, see Reynolds' *Thomas Paine's Bones*, p. 8.
126 For 1850s, see Reynolds' *Thomas Paine's Bones*, pp. 6 and 8. For 1860s, see ibid., p. 8.
127 Ibid., pp. 5 and 7.
128 For gift of bones, see ibid., p. 5. For date and details of Tilly's death, see his death certificate at GRO. For his composition on the new poor law, see Young, *The Cobbett Club*, pp. 8-12.
129 See Reynolds' *Thomas Paine's Bones*, pp. 7-8.
130 Conway's *Adventures*, p. 8.
131 For the payment, see Reynolds' *Thomas Paine's Bones*, p. 5. For discovery of the bones' disappearance, see ibid., pp. 5-6; Conway's *Adventures*, p. 8. The papers

included manuscripts of 'The Monster Register' and 'The Poor Man's Bible', both dictated to Tilly by Cobbett, Tilly's own composition 'The Westminster Rebellion, or the Fight for the Honey Pot', and 'The Life of Cobbett', mostly written by Cobbett but completed by Tilly. There was also a letter from Daniel O'Connor to Cobbett and papers concerning the case of John Wright v. William Cobbett. See Reynolds' *Thomas Paine's Bones*, pp. 6-7, 25-7. For disappearance of burial plate, see ibid., p. 22. For brain and hair, and the explanatory note from Tilly, see ibid., p. 14.

132 Ibid., pp. 4-6; Conway's *Adventures*, p. 8.
133 Reynolds provided a very misleading account of what Conway had discovered, claiming that Gordon had seen the bones in Manchester in 1873 and that Conway had heard of them in 1876 (Reynolds' *Thomas Paine's Bones*, p. 21), whereas Conway had simply stated that Gordon had seen them in 1873 (without indicating where) and that Gordon, not himself, had heard of them in 1876 (Conway's *Adventures*, p. 12).
134 Conway's *Adventures*, p. 12.
135 Ibid.
136 See under Alexander Gordon (1842-1933), in *Oxford Dictionary of National Biography*, vol. 22.
137 Such as Alexander Somerville in 1844. See his *Whistler at the Plough* (Manchester, 1852), pp. 305-7. Or Edward Smith of Walthamstow in 1876. See *Notes and Queries* for 1887, series vii (3), p. 336.
138 For the disappearance of the two at the same time, see Reynold's *Thomas Paine's Bones*, p. 22. The separation of the plate from the coffin was the work of Cobbett when he decided, between 1833 and 1836, to turn it into a grain bin. Thereafter, the plate remained in the chest with the bones until, on Tilly's death, it passed to the Ginns. See above, p. 177.
139 For hair acquired by Conway, see his *Adventures*, p. 12. For the relics acquired by Tilly in 1833 and passed to Reynolds in 1878, see Reynold's *Thomas Paine's Bones*, p. 26 and Conway's *Adventures*, p. 8.
140 See Reynold's *Thomas Paine's Bones*, p. 27. For the quarrel with Barnardo, see Gillian Wagner, *Barnardo* (London, 1979), pp. 67, 87-9 and the *Oxford Dictionary of National Biography* under John Barnardo.
141 See Reynolds' *Thomas Paine's Bones*, p. 27; *Catalogue of Paine Exhibition*, note attached to exhibit 94; Conway's *Adventures*, p. 13; Collins, *Trouble with Tom*, pp. 202-3. For the glass cover, see *Catalogue of Paine Exhibition*, exhibit 93; Conway's *Adventures*, p. 12 and Reynolds' *Thomas Paine's Bones*, p. 29.
142 The catalogue survives in the British Library, entitled 'Catalogue of Objects of Historical Interest Connected with Thomas Paine, his Friends and Adversaries

and with Incidents of the Struggle Caused by his Writing'. For Breeze's contribution, see exhibits 93 and 94. For the Smith/Conway contribution, see exhibit 274.
143 Ibid., see exhibit 108 for his snuff box, owned by Clair Grece of Redhill, Surrey; exhibit 68 for his table, owned by Truelove and certificated by Paine's close friend Thomas Rickman; and exhibit 485 for the piece of timber, owned by Louis Breeze. For the death masks, see exhibits 218-9, owned by the artist Ambrose Vago.
144 See Reynolds' *Thomas Paine's Bones*, p. 29.
145 Ibid., p. 28.
146 See Conway in the *New York Sun* for 25 May 1902.
147 See Conway's *Adventures*, p. 12.
148 See Collins, *Trouble with Tom*, pp. 225, 229 and 232; *New York Sun*, 25 May 1902; *New York Times*, 15 Oct. 1905.

Index

Aberdeen, 88
Absolute monarchy, see royal absolutism
Adams,
 – John, 40
 – W.E., 6
Adventures of Thomas Paine's Bones (Conway, 1902), 157
The Age of Reason (Paine), 4-5, 7-8, 16, 33, 37, 47, 55, 64, 81-3, 87, 151, 163, 175
Agitator (Benbow), 157-8
Agrarian Justice (Paine), 23, 152
Agrarian Law, 23
Agrarian Monopoly, see Land nationalisation
Ainslie,
 – Oliver, 157, 174-5
 – Rev. Robert, 172-4
Aitken, Robert, 38
Aldridge, A.O., 40-1, 43
Alfred, King, 142, 144, 170
American
 – Republic (USA), 3, 13-5, 27, 61, 93-4, 136-7
 – Revolution (USA), 17, 31, 35, 53-4, 113, 135-6, 143
American Crisis Papers, 29
Anglican Church (Church of England), 35, 63, 149, 172
Anglo-Saxon constitution, 19-20, 30-1, 52-3, 92-3, 142, 144, 146, 165, 170
Ash, Surrey, 167-9

Ashton-under-Lyne, 88
Australia, transportation to –, 82, 129

Babeuf, 111, 113
Ball, Mrs, 156-7, 176
Barclay, Robert, 33, 41
Barnardo, Dr, 178-9
Baxter, John, 20
Benbow, William, 83, 97-8, 117, 134, 157-8, 161
Bentham, Jeremy, 45, 92
Berthold's Political Handkerchief, 95, 116-7
Bill of Rights (1689), 11-12, 18-20, 35, 47-8, 76, 151, 165, 170
Birmingham, 61, 69, 71, 74, 81, 88, 98, 103, 132
Blackstone, Sir William, 92
Blount, Charles, 51, 55
Bolingbroke, Lord Henry, 36, 144
Bolton, 88, 132
Boulanger, Nicolas-Antoine, 51
Bradford, 132
Bradlaugh, Charles, 7, 83, 147, 152
Brayshaw, Joseph, 89-90
Breeze, Louis, 179-80
Bressler, Leo, 155
A Brief History of the Remains of Thomas Paine (Tilly, 1847), 157
Brissot, Jacques-Pierre, 42
Bristol, 132

British Association for Promoting Cooperative Knowledge, 102
Brooks, John, 83
Brutus, see Hibbert
Buchanan, George, 40-1
Buonarroti's History of Babeuf's Conspiracy for Equality (1836), 111, 134
Burgh, James, 4, 46-7, 50, 92, 105, 138
Burke, Edmund, 12, 28, 35-7, 49, 65, 69, 105
Byrne, Patrick (publisher), 77, 80

Capitalism, 22, 108, 110, 112, 145
Captain Swing Riots, 95
Carlile,
– Jane, 82, 132
– Richard, 5-6, 82-3, 87-91, 95-101, 104, 131-3, 144, 147, 161, 164-6
Caroline, Queen –, 144, 165
Carpenter, William (journalist), 123-4
Carver, William (New York), 90
Chapman, Thomas (printer), 70, 72
Charles I, 40, 48
Chartist
– Association, 4-5, 60, 101, 105, 113, 129, 138-45
– Conventions, 106, 129-30, 141-2, 151
Cheetham, James, 43
Chennell, John, 156, 167-9
Chester, 74
Christianity, 16-17, 21, 55, 88-9, 91, 113, 132-3, 139, 147, 149, 151, 160, 174
Civil War (English), 20
Claeys, Gregory, 3
Classical republicanism, 32, 36
Claviere, Etienne, 42
Cleave, John, 95, 97, 176
Clitheroe, 96

Cobbett,
– William, 6, 83, 87-95, 108, 124, 149-50, 158-61, 163-7
– Club, 6, 142
Cocke, Mistress, 35
Coercion Act (1833), 124
Cold Bath Fields
– incident, 121-31
– prison, 120
– reform meeting, 124
Collins,
– Anthony, 51
– Paul, 153
Common Sense (Paine), 3, 11-12, 16, 29-31, 33-4, 36-7, 39-47, 51-2, 54-5, 57-60, 64, 70-1, 84, 104
Commonwealth, Cromwellian, 4, 28, 41, 48
Condorcet, M. de, 3, 42-3, 59
Constitutional monarchy, 3, 50-2, 69
Constitution, written, 34-5, 48, 76, 81-2, 90, 93, 103-5, 119-20, 150
Conway, Moncure, 21-22, 156-7, 175, 177-80
Coombes, J.C., 140-1
Cooper, Thomas (Manchester), 70
Counter insurgency legislation, 82; also see Six Acts
Cousins, B.D. (publisher), 83
Coventry, 81, 132
Cowen, Joseph, 156, 171, 175
Crome, J. (Sheffield), 74
Culley, Police Constable, 122, 127-8

De Jure Regni Apud Scotos (Buchanan, 1579), 40-1
Declaration of Rights, see Bill of Rights
Defence of the People of England (Milton, 1692), 39-40

Defensive Instructions for the People (Macerone, 1832-3), 96, 126-7
Defoe, Daniel, 49, 63
Deism, 17, 33, 65, 151, 163
Democracy, 8-9, 16, 31-2, 39, 44, 53, 55-6, 64, 145-7. Also see Universal Suffrage and Representative System
Dewsbury, 88
Dialogue on the Law of Kingship Among the Scots (Buchanan, 1680), 40-1
Diderot, Denis, 51-2
Discourses Concerning Government (Sidney, 1698), 39, 50
Dissenters, 63, 69
Dissertation on First Principles of Government (Paine, 1795), 11-2, 39, 43, 144
Dissertations on Government, the Affairs of the Bank and Paper Money (Paine, 1786), 61
Divine Right, 12, 21, 40, 63-4, 150
Dragonetti, Giacinto, 45-6
Dublin, 67, 71, 77, 80
Dugdale, William (publisher), 143

East London Democratic Association, 139-40
Eaton, Daniel, 5, 80-1
Edinburgh, 79, 88
Egalitarian republicanism, 36, 44, 47, 50, 55-6
Elective monarchy, 50-1, 60, 93, 97
Elitist republicanism, 50
The English Constitution Produced and Illustrated (Cartwright, 1823), 93
Equality of Rights, 15, 19, 44, 63, 112

Essay on the First Principles of Government (Priestley, 1768), 36, 39, 44, 55-6
Euclid, 11
Excise, officers of –, 37

Fabian Society, 7
Failsworth, 88
Ferguson, James, 36
Filmer, Robert, 43
Fitzgerald, Lord Edward, 59
Foskett, George, 97, 100
Fox,
 – Charles James, 59
 – George, 33
Franklin, Benjamin, 36, 38-9, 54
French
 – Constitutional Assembly (1789), 12
 – Invasion of England (Paine plan), 165-6
 – Republic, 3, 7, 13, 15, 27, 115
 – Revolutions, 17, 28, 35, 48, 54, 65, 69, 88, 92 (1830), 95 (1830), 111, 113, 134-5, 136 (1830), 143

Garrisons, establishment of – (1792), 81
Gauntlet (Carlile), 87, 130, 133
General will, 58, 105
Genoa, Republic of –, 15
George
 – III, 33-4
 – IV, 165
George, John, 116-18
Gerrald, Joseph, 82
Ginns, Mr and Mrs, 157, 176-7
Glasgow, 88
Glorious Revolution, 4, 20, 28, 46-9, 52, 69, 75-6, 130, 170
Godwin, William, 37, 71

Gordon,
- Alexander, Rev., 156, 177
- Thomas, 47, 50
Gore, William, of Worcester, 125, 128
Grand National Holiday (Benbow, 1832), 97-8
Grande, James, 155
Grant, Ulysses, 22
Great Yarmouth, 88, 132
Greenock, Scotland, 88
The Grounds and Reasons of Monarchy Considered (Hall, 1650), 41-2, 49
Guildford, 168
Gulliver's Travels (Swift, 1726), 37

Habeas Corpus Act, suspension of (1794), 82
Hall,
- Charles, 109-10
- John (engineer), 67, 78
- John, 41-2, 49
Happiness, General –, 44-6, 55, 58, 115
Harding, C.G., 6
Harney, Julian, 139-41
Harrington, James, 22, 41, 49
Harrison, Frederick, 6
Hazlitt, William, 155
Headstrong Club (Lewes), 38-9
Hereditary
- monarchy, 3, 6, 11-12, 15-16, 20-1, 29-30, 41-3, 46, 49-50, 56-8, 60, 63, 76, 83, 94, 100, 102, 117, 119, 132
- nobility, 3, 6, 12-16, 21, 29-30, 43, 46, 48-9, 53-4, 56-8, 60, 100, 102, 119, 132, 138
- rights of men, 31, 60, 83
Hetherington, Henry, 5, 82, 95-7, 99-100, 104, 106, 109, 115, 126, 138

Hibbert, Julian (classicist), 95, 97, 100-1, 103, 109, 119, 125, 128, 130, 133
Higham, Charles (bookseller), 138
Hoadly, Benjamin, bishop, 47, 63,
Hobbes, Thomas, 18, 57, 63
Hodgskin, Thomas, 102, 110, 115
Holbach, Baron de, 51-2
Holcroft, Thomas, 71
Holland, republic of –, 15, 57
Hollins, 132
Hollis, Thomas Brand, 71
Holt, Daniel (bookseller), 81
Holyoake, George Jacob, 173
House of Commons, 5, 15-6, 18, 30, 39, 46, 50, 61, 76, 92, 139, 141, 146, 165
House of Lords, 5, 8, 13-4, 16, 28, 54, 61, 63, 76, 92-3, 104, 107, 118, 139
Huddersfield, 88, 132
Hulme, Obadiah, 92, 105
Hume, David, 63
Hunt, Henry, 5, 89-95, 99, 103, 105, 108, 129-30, 138-9, 162-3
Hyndman, H.M., 24

An Illustration of the Rights of Man (1792), 74
Independent Labour Party, 24
Innovation, Paine and –, 19
Institution of the Working Classes, (8 Theobald's Road), 98, 133, 134
Ireland, 79-80
Irish
- Coercion Bill; see Coercion Act
- republicanism, 8
- Republican Brotherhood, 149

Jacobins, 88
James II, 47-8
John Reeves' Association, 78
Johnson, Joseph (publisher), 71-2

Jones, John Gale, 164
Jordan,
 – D. (publisher), 77-8
 – J.S. (publisher), 65, 72-4, 77-9, 81, 84
Jure Divino (Defoe, 1706), 49

Kates, Gary, 60

Labour, value of –, 102-3, 108-10, 140, 145
Labour Party, National –, 5
Labour Defended Against the Claims of Capital (Hodgskin,1825), 110
Lafayette, Marquis de, 42, 59
Land Nationalisation, 7, 24, 111, 113, 138
 – Society, 24
Lee,
 – Richard Egan, 95, 117, 124, 126
 – William, 38
Leeds, 88-9
Leicester, 74, 81, 131
Letter Addressed to the Addressers on the Late Proclamation (Paine,1792), 45, 58, 62, 74, 77, 81, 105, 150-1
Lewes, Sussex, 38
Lexington Green, 34
Lilburne, John, 49
Linton, W.J., 6, 141, 151, 172
Liverpool, 160-2
Locke, John, 19, 23, 41, 43-4, 47, 49-50, 58, 63, 110
London, 36, 66, 68-70, 72-4, 79, 87-8
 – Association of the Working Classes, 139
 – City Mission, 172
 – Constitutional Society, see Society for Constitutional Information
 – Corresponding Society, 4, 20, 65, 78, 82
 – Democratic Association, 140-1
 – Revolution Society, 48-9

Londonderry, 80
Lorymer, James Baden, 95, 106, 126
Louis XVI, 12, 28-9, 42, 50
Lounissi, Carine, 3
Lovett, William, 97, 100-1, 107, 139

Macaulay, Catherine, 66
Macerone,
 – Colonel, 96, 126-7
 – lances, 126
Machiavelli, Niccolo, 32
Mackintosh, James, 66
Magna Carta (1215), 18, 35, 48, 124, 165
Malcolm II of Scotland, 41
Malthus, Thomas, 110, 112
Manchester, 61, 69-70, 73, 81, 88, 98-9, 132, 162
 – Massacre (i.e. Peterloo), 87, 91, 96, 99, 161
Maréchal, Silvain, 111
Margarot, Maurice, 82
Marshall, Prof. John, 174-5
Martin, Benjamin, 36
Masque of Anarchy (Shelley,1832), 96
Mazzini, Joseph, 6-7, 63, 131, 151-2
McGowan and Muir of Glasgow (publishers), 83
McManus, Terence, 149
Mee, James, 117, 124-7
Melbourne, Lord, 101, 107, 123
Meredith, Sir William, 30
Middle classes, 135, 137-8
Mill, James, 110
Milton, John, 39-40, 47
Mirabeau, Comte de, 42, 53
Molesworth, Robert, 47
Montesquieu, Baron de, 51
Muir, Thomas, 82

251

Nation, 18, 22, 30, 39, 49, 53
National
– Convention (Chartist), see Chartist Conventions
– Convention/Congress (Paine's), 4, 18, 47, 58, 81, 90, 97-8, 103-6, 116-9, 126, 130-2, 150-1
– Political Union, 96-7, 108
– Republican League, 7
– Union of the Working Classes and Others, 5, 24, 82-3, 94, 96-102, 108, 111-3, 115-8, 124-5, 129, 133-4, 136, 139, 171; and also see Cold Bath Fields incident
Neville, Henry, 32
New Rochelle, New York State, 179-80
Newark, 81
Nobility, see Hereditary nobility
Noble, Daniel (bookseller), 36
Norman Conquest, 18, 30, 52, 92, 142
Normandy Farm, Surrey, 167-8
Norwich, 69, 81, 88, 132
Nottingham, 81, 88, 132

O'Brien, Bronterre, 5-7, 24, 109, 111-15, 129, 134-5, 137, 140, 145, 152
O'Connor, Feargus, 5, 60, 124, 139, 141
Octagon Chapel, Norwich, 177
Oldfield, Jesse, 167
Oldham, 88, 132
Ollive, Samuel, 38
Owen, Robert, 7, 102, 108, 114-15, 138, 152, 172-3
Oxford University, 41

Padiham, 103

Paine, Thomas,
– in America, 29-31, 34, 38-40, 54, 64
– in England, 4-5, 15-16, 18, 21, 24, 27, 32-8, 41, 44-51, 55-6, 59-62, 68-9, 72, 75-6, 78-9, 80-2, 84-5
– in France, 42, 51-9
Paine
– clubs, 159, 163
– dinners, 90, 163-4
– Exhibition (1895), 157, 179
Paine's
– bones, 87-90, 97, 142, 149-50; and see Appendix
– burial (1809), 158
– edition of *Rights of Man*, 72-6, 78-9
– exhumation (1819), 158-9
– funeral, plans for, 159, 163-4
– monument, 159, 163, 170-1
– *Political and Moral Maxims*, 73
– republic, 160
– trial (Dec 1792), 72, 75-6, 78, 81
Paisley, 88
Palafox Junior, see Hibbert
Palmer, Thomas Fyshe, 82
Paris, 42
Parsons, Joseph (publisher), 72, 77-8
Patriotism, 20
Pendleton, 94
Penn, William, 33
People's Charter, 101, 111, 139, 141
Peterloo, see Manchester Massacre
Petitioning, 18, 91, 99, 105, 142
Petrie, George, 117-8
Philadelphia, 33, 38
– Chapel, Finsbury Square, 98
– Magazine, 38
Phillips, Richard, 81
Philp, Mark, 3, 28-9

Index

Physical force, approval of –, 95-6, 130, 133
Pickering, Paul, 155
Plan of Parliamentary Reform (Bentham,1817), 90
Poland, 15, 51
Police, metropolitan, 96, 121-5, 127-9
Political disorder/revolt, 14, 17-8
Political Disquisitions (1774), 46, 61; and see Burgh, James
Poor Man's Guardian, 95-6, 98, 103-5, 109, 111-4, 116, 118, 123, 129-30, 134-7
Portsmouth, 88
Precedent, 18-9, 35, 44, 56, 59, 90, 170
Preston, 103
Price, Rev. Richard, 47, 49-50
Priestley, Rev. Joseph, 36, 39, 44-5, 47, 50-1, 55-6, 78
Primogeniture, 14-15, 41, 101, 119, 122
Principles, 19-20, 44, 90
Prochaska, Frank, 27-8
Proclamations, 75 (May 1792), 104 (November, 1831), 120, 125 (May, 1833)
Project for a Perpetual Peace (Rousseau,1761), 59
Prompter, 87, 100, 132
Property, 19, 23-5, 50, 78, 100, 104, 110-2, 115, 120, 122, 138, 151
Public duty, 62-3
Publica (i.e. David Edward Williams), 118-9

Quakers, 32-5, 47, 59
Queen Mab, 101; and see Shelley, Percy Bysshe

Radical Reform Association, 89-93, 96-7, 138, 141, 149, 162, 164
Raynal, Abbé, 52-3, 57
Reflections on the French Revolution, (Burke,1790), 37, 48, 65, 67, 71
Reform
– Act (1832), 92, 107-8, 116, 170
– League, 5
Regicide, 48, 112
Remonstrance, reform by –, 105
Representation system, 19, 32, 50, 61
Republican
– (Carlile), 87-105
– (Hetherington), 95, 97
Republicanism (types of), 130-31, 170; also see American republic, Egalitarian republicanism, Elitist republicanism, French republic, Irish republicanism and the Representative system
Revolution, Paine's view of, 17-8
Reynolds, Rev. George, 157, 176-80
Ricardo, David, 110
Rickman, Thomas Clio, 95
Ridgway, James (publisher), 81
Rights of Man
– (Paine), 1, 4, 8, 11-12, 17-20, 27-31, 33, 37, 39, 42-3, 45, 48-52, 54-5, 57-8, 60-1, 64, ch. III, 94, 105, 150
– *for the Use and Benefit of Mankind* (Eaton, 1795), 80-1
Robbins, Caroline, 4, 38
Roberts, Matthew, 60, 144
Robespierre, Maximilian, 6, 111, 113-5, 137
Rosary Cemetery, Norwich, 156, 177-8
Rosenfeld, Sophia, 29
Rotheram, 74
– Caleb, 36

Rotunda in Blackfriars, 88, 97-8, 132-33
Rousseau, Jean-Jacques, 4, 36, 53, 56-9
Royal absolutism, 3, 7, 20, 50-1, 60, 65, 69
Royal Tyranny Discovered (Lilburne, 1647), 49
Royton, 132
Rush, Benjamin, 34, 38

Salford, 136
Scotland, 41, 47, 73, 79
Sharp, John, of Greenock (publisher), 83
Sharples, Eliza, 133
Sheffield, 61, 69, 74, 79, 81, 132
Shelley, Percy Bysshe, 96, 101
Sherwin, William (publisher), 5-6, 70, 82-3, 150, 165
Sidney, Algernon, 32, 39, 47, 50
Sieyès, Abbé, 42, 50
Six Acts (1819), 164
Skirving, William, 82
Smith, Edward, of Walthamstow, 156, 167-8
Social Compact (Rousseau, 1764), 56-7
Social Democratic Federation, 7, 24
Socialism, 7-8, 138, 152, 172-3
Socialist League, 7
Société des Républicaines, 43
Society
 – for Constitutional Information, 48, 65, 68-70, 74-7, 82
 – of United Irishmen, 80
Spence, Thomas, and the Spenceans, 24, 81, 102, 108, 111
Spinoza, Baruch de, 4, 38, 51, 54-7
Stephens, James, 149
Stockport, 88
Swain, Job, 175-6
Swift Jonathan, 37
Switzerland (Geneva), 57

Symonds, H.D. (publisher), 72, 77-8, 81, 84
Take Your Choice (Cartwright, 1776), 19, 144
Taxation, 14, 17-18, 20, 22, 45-6, 59, 108, 111-2, 122, 135, 144-5
Taylor, Rev. Robert, 132-3
Temple of Reason (Fleet Street), 88
Tenure of Kings and Magistrates (Milton, 1649), 39-40
Thales of Miletus, 102-3
Thetford, 34-5, 61
Thomas Paine Exhibition (1895), 157, 179
Thomas Paine's Bones and their Owners (Reynolds, 1908), 157
Thomson, John (Edinburgh publisher), 79
Tilly, Benjamin, 6, 142, 150, 155, 157, 167-72, 175-7, 179-80
Toland, John, 41, 49, 51
Tooke, John Horne, 5, 37, 43
Tractatus Theologico-politicus (Spinoza, 1670), 4, 54-5
Treatise on Virtues and Rewards (Dragonetti, 1769), 45-6
Trenchard, John, 47, 50
Trial of Paine (Dec. 1792), 72, 75-6, 78, 81
Trueborn Englishman (Defoe, 1701), 49
Truelove, Edward (publisher), 156, 173-5
Two Treatises of Government (Locke, 1698), 23, 37, 43
Tyler, Wat, 20
Tyrannicide, 40

Union Public House, King's Cross Road, 122
Unitarianism, 172-3, 177

Universal suffrage, 4-5, 19, 31, 61-2, 64, 85, 92, 96, 107, 111-13, 129, 138, 143-4, 152, 159

Venice, Republic of –, 15
Verral, Henry, 38
Victoria, Queen –, 144
Vincent, Mrs Henry, 176
Vindication of Natural Society (Burke), 36-7
Voluntary enrolment project, 132-4
Voltaire, 51

Walker, Thomas (Manchester), 73, 82
Wallace, Alfred Russell, 24
Warden, Benjamin, 97, 100
Washington, George, 28, 31, 65-6, 70-1
Watson, James (publisher), 6, 83, 95, 97-8, 100-101, 130, 143, 156, 171, 175
West, George, 168-9
Whatmore, Richard, 43
Wheeler, T.M., 143
Whig
 – Club of Ireland, 80
 – tradition, 47-9, 58-9
Wighton of Kelso (publisher), 83
Wilkes, John, 47-51
William and Mary, 12, 48, 76
William IV, 87-8, 97, 144
Wisbech, 88, 132
Wollstonecraft, Mary, 66
Wooler, Thomas, 91, 163
Works of Thomas Paine Esq. (D. Jordan, 1792), 77-8
Works of Thomas Paine (1796), 80-1
Working Man's
 – *Friend* (Watson, 1833), 101, 119, 127
 – *Political Companion* (Watson, 1833), 101

Wyatt, James, 163

Young, Thomas (republican physician), 38, 55